# THROUGH ENEMY SKIES

## WITH WARTIME BOMBER COMMAND AIRCREWS

**Books by the Author**

Non-fiction
*Bomb on the Red Markers*
*Fighter! Fighter! Corkscrew Port!*
*The Fear In the Sky*
*Through Enemy Skies*
*We Kept 'Em Flying*

Peakland Air Crash Series:
*The South* (2005)
*The Central Area* (2006)
*The North* (2006)

*Derbyshire's High Peak Air Crash Sites, Northern Region*
*High Peak Air Crash Sites, Central Region*
*Derbyshire's High Peak Air Crash Sites, Southern Region*
*White Peak Air Crash Sites*

Faction
A Magnificent Diversion Series
(Acclaimed by the First World War Aviation Historical Society)
*The Infinite Reaches* 1915–16
*Contact Patrol* 1916
*Sold A Pup* 1917
*The Great Disservice* 1918

*Blind Faith: Joan Waste, Derby's Martyr*
*Joyce Lewis of Mancetter, Lichfield's Feisty Martyr*

Fiction
*In Kinder's Mists* (a Kinderscout ghost story)
*Though the Treason Pleases* (Irish Troubles)

# THROUGH ENEMY SKIES

## WITH WARTIME BOMBER COMMAND AIRCREWS

Pat Cunningham, DFM

'Pat, you've got a Distinguished Flying Medal. Just for a change, how's about showing us some distinguished effing flying?'

Me regular nav, Squadron Leader Roy Gibbard, No. 114 (Argosy) Squadron

Front cover: Trainee Air Observers Billy Stephens and Boyce Sproston, among the earliest of Bomber Command's casualties.

Rear cover: Sergeant Gerry Dane and his crew debriefing. When they were shot down on 12 May 1943, over the Ruhr, Dane remained at the controls as the crew abandoned. He did not survive.

First published 2014 by DB Publishing, an imprint of JMD Media Ltd, Nottingham, United Kingdom.

ISBN 9781780914121

Printed and bound by Copytech (UK) Limited, Peterborough.

# Contents

# Acknowledgements

To the copyright holders authorising the use of their photographs: Richard Haigh, manager, intellectual properties, Rolls-Royce; Nicola Hunt, intellectual property rights copyright unit, MOD; archives staff, Imperial War Museum; Judy Nokes, licensing adviser, HMSO (Crown Copyright/ MOD); archives staff, Royal Air Force Museum. Craving the indulgence of those for whom all contact attempts have failed.

To Malcolm Barrass, whose superlative website Air of Authority is an utterly dependable source.

To Paul Dalling, for editing the manuscript, and to Simon Hartshorne, for creating the book.

To Clive Teale, aviator and grammarian, for proof-reading and technical advice. Similarly to Ken Johnson and Ken Clare for down-to-earth criticism.

To Derby City Council's Housing Standards and Enforcement Services Department for bestirring the periodically lethargic Derwent Living.

To the oncologists of Derby Royal and Nottingham City Hospitals who, early in 2014, advised me against waiting for mainstream publishers to put this book on their list, and not to start another long one, whether as author, or reader ...

To the ever-ebullient – and consistently irreverent – staff of:

ASDA/Macdonald's, Spondon; Four Seasons Café, Park Farm, Derby; Croots Farm Shop, Duffield; The Wheatcroft's Wharf Café, Cromford; Caudwell's Mill Café, Rowsley; and in particular, Hobb's Tea Rooms, Monsal Head.

To the National Trust staff at Kedleston Hall for both irreverence and forbearance.

To the immeasurable expedition afforded by Google.

Despite such inestimable assistance, any errors remaining, and all opinions expressed are my own

Pat Cunningham, DFM

## Private publications by the Author

*'Now We Are Ninety'* (tribute to mother ...)

*'The Elephant Box, Volumes 1 # 2'* (a grandfather's tall tales)

*'By Fell and Dale, Volumes 1 # 5'* (walker's logs)

*'Frozen Tears'* (a Polish family's wartime odyssey)

*'Flotsam'* (short pieces)

*'Jetsam'* (short pieces)

Autobiographical Series:

*'Brat to Well Beloved'* (RAF Aircraft Apprentice to Air Electronics Officer)

[And, vice Gilbert and Sullivan ... ]

*'Apprentice to a Pilot'* (RAF pilot training)

*'The Kind Commander'* (RAF captaincy)

*'The Simple Captain'* (civil captaincy)

In preparation:

*'Frozen Tears'* (wartime romance)

*'The Ignorant Walker's Companion'* (a walker's reflections)

*'The Tenant'/'The CEO'* (experiences of a housing association)

*'Fifty Years Of Peace: 1945-1995'* [Celebratory Stones in Derbyshire]  (Memoirs of RAF 'peacekeeping' personnel from Malaya to the First Gulf War)

*Pat Cunningham,*
*DFM, BA, Lic Ac, cfs, RAF, 2014*

# Introduction

Between them these ten personal accounts of RAF Bomber Command aircrew chart the history of Britain's bombing campaign in the Second World War. Starting with the disastrous misemployment of the force in the opening weeks of the conflict – misemployment which led to the Command's halting essays into night-navigating over Germany with propaganda leaflets –, they progress from bombing raids with each aircraft acting independently, to strategic operations in which hundreds of heavy bombers were channelled towards accurately-marked release points. Some crew members detail their involvement with the electronic aids that made such precision marking possible. Others recall tours begun when the focus of operations had changed to tactical support of the Allied land forces, and defence against Hitler's indiscriminately-aimed 'V' weapons. Later accounts close with reminders that, even after Germany surrendered, there was still a war raging in the Far East that seemed set to drag on interminably.

Although the accounts rarely touch upon any higher-level planning conferences than the pre-operation briefing, Bomber Command was never a blinkered force. Squadron commanders would tell crews what their target was; an oil facility, an aircraft factory, or a ball-bearing works, and as the invasion neared, rail and communications centres. However, such relatively junior commanders, and their crews, could only accept that the designated targets were indeed vital to the enemy's war effort, and therefore, worth the sacrifice so many comrades had already made and that they were only too likely to be called upon to make themselves. At the same time they were well aware from training results how inaccurate their best efforts could be.

This introduction supplements the personal accounts by reviewing the policies that gave form to Bomber Command's six-year-long campaign.

On 8 July 1940, with Hitler's armies victorious after the battle of France, and poised to begin what Prime Minister Winston Churchill had expected, a month earlier, would be called the 'battle of Britain', Churchill wrote privately to the Minister for Aircraft Production, Lord Beaverbrook, urging him to hasten the availability of the promised heavy bombers. He went on, 'when I look round to see how we can win the war I see that there is only one sure path ... and that is absolutely devastating, exterminating attack by very heavy bombers from this country upon the Nazi homeland'. And as Churchill was known for his meticulous use of language, the word 'exterminating' must be given its full weight.

Other politicians who had publicly trodden similar ground remain vilified to this day. In 1932 de facto Prime Minister Stanley Baldwin, accepting as a truism Italian General Douhet's contention that the bomber will always get through, told the House that the man in the street should realise that 'there is no power on earth that can protect him from being bombed ... That the only defence is in offence, which means that you have to kill more women and children more quickly than the enemy if you want to save yourselves.' In 1938 Prime Minister Neville Chamberlain was to suffer for his seemingly complacent attitude to appeasement, and his re-use of Disraeli's 'Peace for our time' statement.

The fact that the Allies' eventually-overpowering bombing campaign proved the fundamental truth of Douhet's maxim, and that, far from being complacent, Chamberlain not only authorised a vast increase of the RAF budget to augment the expansion begun in 1934, but had the Air Council prepare a list of priority targets, reveals both politicians to be casualties of their own percipience.

The Air Council were also to be vilified. Predominantly airmen, they necessarily took advice on targets from leading industrialists and increasingly from staffers of the Ministry of Economic Warfare. They also had to assess the views of military theorists, not least the influential Lidell Hart who held that enemy bombing would cause Britain 250,000 casualties in the first week of any future conflict. The nub of the Air Council's decision was that oil had to head the RAF's target list, with the domino effect from bombing German industry bringing about the collapse of the enemy's morale and with it, his desire to further pursue the war.

In the event, wartime experience was to suggest, and post-war analysis to conclusively prove, that bombing was never to be the decisive factor either in crippling the Reich's industry or in accomplishing its military defeat. As for morale, the 1870 Siege of Paris, and the recent Spanish Civil War, had shown the resilience of populaces under bombardment.

To be fair, perhaps there were just too many misconceptions, too many half-truths, too many imponderables; so that, rather than have no policy, the planners were forced to adopt the best available. This, though, placed RAF Bomber Command in an invidious position. Directed to bomb specific targets, very conscious of how both press and BBC had inflated its capabilities to the nation, and while struggling to remedy shortcomings it was only too well aware of, it was cast into an arena beset from the outset by conjectural judgements, personal dogmatism, and political expediency.

Air Chief Marshal Ludlow-Hewitt had been appointed Air Officer Commanding-in-Chief of Bomber Command in 1937, a year after its formation, since when he had worked tirelessly to make his command efficient. Even so, in July 1939, just two months before the outbreak of hostilities, he had felt obliged to report to the Air Council that Bomber Command was 'entirely unprepared for war', and 'unable to operate except in fair weather', citing the 478 bombers which had set down, lost, in the last two years. Although Ludlow-Hewitt was effectively re-appointed sideways not long afterwards, all his successors, most notably 'Bomber' – Air Chief Marshal 'Butch' – Harris, were to declare that his professionalism had saved Bomber Command from annihilation.

This reflected the catastrophic opening phase of the much-vaunted bombing offensive and the near-decimation of unescorted RAF bombers sent out in daylight to attack shipping off the enemy coast. Ludlow-Hewitt promptly switched strategies, and set the Command to range Germany by night, dropping propaganda leaflets, but more importantly, honing its navigational skills. In the next phase night-bombers acting as independent units were dispatched to raid the Ruhr. However, with some crews dropping their bombs on nothing more accurate than the navigator's estimated time of arrival, both photo-reconnaissance and Intelligence studies soon showed how little was being achieved. Other sources strongly suggested that the same was true where denting enemy morale was concerned.

By the time the planners had confirmation of such failings, however, Bomber Command was, quite literally, finding its way. With its operation polished by hard-won experience, with the assistance of electronic aids to navigation and bombing, and with ever more aircraft and aircrews being supplied, it was becoming an extremely effective weapon. That the planners might be revising their opinions on the efficacy of the panacea targets first advocated, yet refusing to re-think the operational directives, was not the concern of the crews.

The planners, of course, were well schooled in the first principle of war: the maintenance of the selected aim. Further, for them to be seen to vacillate might have had a disastrous effect on aircrew morale, especially before a consensus was reached on how much operational flying would give the volunteer aircrews a reasonable chance of survival. Volunteers, that is, who were nightly exercising so much courage in what opponents – but not the British public! – now condemned as 'area-bombing' attacks – 'exterminating' attacks, even. This book's concern, though, remains with the aircrews who had been given the duty of taking the fight to the enemy, not with the ongoing doubts of the higher echelons.

That said, what virtually all the included accounts reflect is the sense of bewilderment felt once the war ended, not particularly over the lack of recognition afforded Bomber Command, but at the opprobrium visited upon it.

In fact, few seemed to have seen the lack of recognition as a slight at the time. However, once allied with the belittling post-war attitude to Bomber Command, resentment grew. Even then, all that was looked for was that operational-aircrew status should be acknowledged. Until 5 June 1944 the Aircrew Europe Star had given just that recognition to all those who had flown on operations for a two-month period. The award, however, had then been discontinued, after which operational aircrew had nothing to reflect their status unless they had gained Distinguished Flying Crosses or

Medals. Yet so simple, one would have thought, to reframe the conditions governing the Aircrew Europe award!

As for the national cold-shouldering of Bomber Command and its leaders, most veterans mildly-enough blame Churchill for choosing political expedience in 1945. Certainly, most view such tardy acknowledgements as the 1992 statue to 'Butch' Harris, the 2012 Bomber Command Memorial, and particularly the 2013 award of a Bomber Command Clasp – not medal – as too little, and far too late.

Yet what every contributor reflects above all, is the satisfaction that, having volunteered to fly as aircrew, he did so with full heart. Bomber Command, with its 55,573 dead, received no glowing Churchillian testimonial on a par with 'The Few', but to have had the great man avow, in July 1940, that the envisaged bomber campaign was something 'without which I do not see a way through' showed how he viewed it then. And indeed, how Britain viewed it. When, in both cases, it was needed.

*Pat Cunningham, DFM, RAF 1951–1973*

# 1. We Paved Their Way

## Sergeant William (Billy) Henry Stephens, air observer

'Hitler is up to his tricks again. In spite of this I cannot believe there will be a war … the consequences would be so terrible …

*William (Billy) Stephens with five-year-old sister, Pam, 1939*

In 1934, with the international community proving either unwilling or unable to stop Germany rearming, the government approved a massive expansion for the RAF. In 1937, however, after Air Chief Marshal Ludlow-Hewitt had been appointed to command the newly-established Bomber

Command, he was forced to tell the Air Council that, partly due to the disarray caused by the expansion, his command was 'unable to operate except in fair weather', citing in particular that 478 bombers had put down in the last two years simply because they were lost. And this, over Britain, in daylight!

On 6 February 1939, therefore, when nineteen-year-old William (Billy) Stephens of Newcastle-under-Lyme attested as a trainee air observer – the observer aircrew category changed to that of navigator in 1942 –, he was sent to one of several hurriedly set up navigational schools, in his case, to Desford, near Leicester.

A year earlier, having excelled in all respects at the prestigious Wolstanton Grammar, Billy had found no difficulty in securing a good job in insurance. The routine, though, had quickly palled. *'Life in the office,'* he had written, *'is artificial.'*

In the course of some seventy letters written home between 8 February and 26 September 1939 – retained by his sister, Pam, and much later lovingly reproduced by his niece, Janet –, Billy described his RAF training. And if the letters show him just as much schoolboy-civilian as flier, nevertheless through those letters we glimpse all the participant airmen, fliers and non-fliers, for whom Billy – and those he passed with –, paved the way.

On arrival at Desford, a civilian-run establishment recently designated No. 7 Elementary Flying Training School, Billy and his fellow aspirant observers, sixty of them, were warned that they must do six-months' work in three. It was a warning Billy took seriously. *'If we fail they can throw us out,'* he wrote, *'or make us mechanics: we're entirely in their power …'*

Lectures started at once. *'There's such a lot to learn and to be remembered, magnetic, true, and compass bearings, variation and deviation, instruments: altimeters and airspeed indicators; and morse …'*

Quite apart from the volume of work, there was the problem of settling to communal life, more especially as Billy found virtually all those around him to be *'high class, high hat, all speaking "BBC", though a cheery lot.'* Happily, Billy found instantly congenial company with another trainee, a fellow Midlander, Boyce Sproston, a year or two older than him, from Weston Coyney, near Stoke.

Discipline, together with Service uniform, was largely to be left until they moved to the RAF Depot at Uxbridge on completion of the Desford course. They had an early taste of it, however, when assembled for their first pay parade. *'The sergeant had us form fours and march up and down outside the lecture rooms, then "route march" to the main office. We clowned about, and laughed, especially when he halted us and the rear ranks hadn't heard and crashed into the front ones. Then he ordered, "Squad dismiss", which really tickled us.'*

Billy's observation, 'The sergeant had us form fours' really rolls back the years! The RAF, like the British army, had been marching four abreast since for ever. In August 1939, just a few months after Billy was writing, the British services dropped the fourth rank and marched three abreast, old soldiers and old airmen alike, long bewailing the loss of the 'missing man'.

If parading to be paid was a novelty, the amount received was wondrous. *'With the 1/6d [7.5p] a day we're paid for flying, I am paid £2/4/0 [£2.20p] with nothing to find from that. As bed and board must cost £2/2/0 [£2.10p] this means the actual weekly pay is £4/10/0 [£4.50p]. Not bad, eh! I've decided to send home 10/- [50p] a week for mother. After laundry and haircuts this leaves me with £2 to save. But I have got holes in my socks so I could do with some wool to darned well darn them with.'*

The wealth of classroom work notwithstanding, Billy was thrilled when detailed for his first flight. *'We were due to fly in a big Anson. The Engineer told us to be very careful at getting in and out. And if anyone wants to spew, don't do it over the plane, but into the nosebags provided, and throw it over the side. In the end, this "flip", as they call it here, was cancelled because the weather wasn't good enough, although we couldn't see much wrong with it'.*

***Billy and Boyce about to fly in an Avro Anson***

In fact, Britain's uncertain weather so hazarded continuity that a year later – from April 1940 – they would have trained under the Empire Air Training Scheme in the dependable weather conditions of Canada, Rhodesia, or South Africa, or even of the then-neutral United States. Billy's generation really were trail blazers!

As it was, he first flew on Saturday, 13 February 1939, recording, '*Boyce and I wore our flying suits, with the parachute harness, and having collected a parachute, went up with Pilot Officer Watson, a swell guy. We flew from Desford to Coventry and Northampton, and back, map reading from features at 1,500 feet and 120 knots. I found it both exciting and interesting, although I was a bit scared, and felt slightly sick at the end of the fifty minute or so journey. Today we were off again, this time to Kettering and Rugby, and I was neither scared nor feeling airsick. I also traced the course fairly easily. The railways are easiest to see, especially when the trains are belching smoke. The reservoirs are also very fine landmarks, the exact shape is given on the map and you can see it quite clearly from above.*'

From then on flights became more demanding. *'We fly for ten minutes on a given compass course, after which we join up the pinpoints we've marked so far to give the track. If you compare your course with the track, the difference allows you to calculate the speed and direction of the wind. We repeated this exercise three times, and are to go up again tomorrow.'*

As they did. *'We flew to Cranwell and Peterborough, the exercise being to calculate groundspeed and time of arrival. Given the track, and the speed and direction of the wind, we have to work out the course we need. We use a special instrument called the course and speed indicator which costs £17. Each of the sixty of us has one, so you can reckon where the tax payers money goes. Desford has seven Avro Anson planes which cost about £2,000 each, also about 20 Tiger Moths for the pilots.'*

*Navigational circular slide rule*

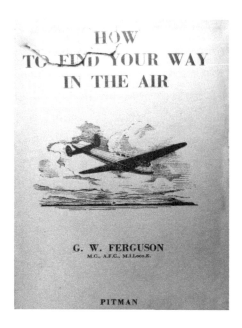

***Pitman's navigational manual, 'How To Find Your Way In The Air'***

'*I seem to be good at trigonometry, though magnetism, compasses, and deviation have me guessing. But I've bought a 3/6d [17.5p] Pitman's navigation book to help with the intricate problems. I really intend to work hard, so it won't be my fault if I fail.*'

On his next flight, '*We were given the magnetic course and had to subtract the variation to get the true course, then make pinpoints along the actual track, and so calculate the velocity and direction of the wind.*'

Clearly, navigational training required intense concentration from the trainees, but flying straight and level could bore the staff pilots to death. As Billy recorded, '*Our pilot caught up with another Anson and started a mock air battle. It was very, very thrilling, believe me, but a little dangerous. You see, we were chasing the other plane and he was diving and soaring with us at his tail. My stomach was going over and over, but I didn't feel sick at all. It was great fun ...*'

Predominantly, though, it was business. '*I'm certainly not finding the work easy, and it gets harder every day. Tomorrow we are to navigate to Duxford and if we get lost, too bad, the pilot will not correct us.*'

In the event, the flight went well. *'I was very pleased with myself as we sighted Duxford for I had estimated the time to the minute, though I'd had to have the pilot change course six degrees to the right halfway through because the wind had changed.'*

Success clearly brought a moment of reflection. *'You just can't compare life in an office, with this. Even if I fail I shall stay in and become, perhaps, a wireless operator, although I hope I pass as the money is nifty.'*

Exams, though, were looming. *'I shall be OK on the maths and dead-reckoning papers* ['dead': from deduced reckoning] *but the magnetism and meteorology papers get me down, because we have such a lot of little things to remember, and I'm not much good at this. As observers, we have to be navigators, bombers, gunners, photographers, and should be able to bring the plane down in an emergency. But enough grousing, I cannot expect to do wonders at first, and must keep on trying.'*

On 16 March Billy, clearly a little concerned, observed, *'Rumour has it that about a dozen out of the sixty are leaving.* However, on 17 March, with some results in, he brightens *'I was 31st out of 60, but then I was always a pessimist except for swimming and running … Boyce was 35th.'*

And viewing the exams in perspective, *'The school tells Air Ministry of anyone they feel doesn't come up to standard and those rejected are given the option of leaving the service or rejoining* [remustering] *to learn one of the trades* [That is, as a ground technician. And the option had to be given because all fliers are volunteers].

Freshly doubting, Billy then reported, *'The sergeant warned that half a dozen who passed the exam are to go because of their poor air performance.'* Another source of concern, then, but a day later he wrote, *'A trip on Tuesday restored my confidence. I brought the pilot right over Hornchurch, then altered course for Grimsby.'* The weather would so often intrude, however, *'We'd been on that leg for only about seven minutes when we got a weather recall: it was foul, raining, and with bad visibility.'*

Now, though, with training worries temporarily allayed, international events drew comment. *'Hitler is up to his tricks again. In spite of this I cannot believe there will be a war … the consequences would be so terrible … I hope mother doesn't worry about me, for I am better off than the young fellows who are civilians, because in the event of war, we would have a definite job, and would probably know how to do it.'*

And in early April Billy noted, *'People on holiday have been watching the planes all day, and having their teas on a piece of open ground. It makes us all feel like holidays instead of work.'*

Meanwhile more advanced flying exercises continued to extend them. *'Off at 9.00 for Okehampton. The direct track led over the Bristol Channel, but Boyce had to alter course to avoid a Danger Area. Turning towards Weston-super-Mare, however, the weather was a bit black and as we got further on we noticed snow dropping just below us and cloud forming over the mountains. The pilot said he wasn't going to chance going on, so at Taunton we changed course for Yatesbury …*

*We filled up with petrol and oil, and with me navigating, set off for Norwich. Fifty miles out, though, oil streamed from the port engine: the mechanics at Yatesbury had put nine gallons in instead of six. We made a bee line for Cranfield, a large RAF base littered with Blenheim bombers, and a crowd of RAF men soon put it right.*

*Getting airborne again we came to a balloon barrage, so I had to set course for Henlow aerodrome, then reset the course to Norwich, getting there without any trouble. Then we set off for Desford, reaching it at 16.05 hours having kept on the track all the way.*

*Much to my pleasure Mr Holland, the pilot, said it was very satisfactory. I was happy, but very tired, as flying all day seems to put a big strain on your nerves, and you have to be working all the time, no chance for a quiet gaze out the window.'*

A good trip. And a salient truth learnt: that every other crew member can take time off, but not the navigator.

Billy anticipated five days' 'holiday' for Easter, except that, 'We may have to stay on because we are behind with the flying programme owing to the bad weather. … Today we did an exercise in intercepting a train (imaginary) running from Boston to Peterborough. This is easy enough to do when you apply a kind of diagram which involves relative velocity.'

In fact, the 1941 RAF Air Navigation manual would list some eighty-five such procedures the aspirants would have had to become familiar with!

They were introduced also, to night flying. 'We were quite successful on our night flight last week, and it was thrilling but dangerous when landing and taking off. We were to fly to London and back … and it was rather difficult to follow the course because we could only see the lights of the towns, and some of these began to go out about 12 o'clock.'

'Rather difficult' would become 'infinitely more difficult' once the blackout was imposed!

In mid April an overflight of Bournemouth ushered in another facet of the observers' task, that of reconnaissance. 'We had to do a report on the aerodrome, telling how many planes were on the field, and where the hangars are situated, etc.'

But more exams lay ahead, 'I've been working from 9 until 11 each night for the last week, and still I don't know half as much as I ought to. It's very annoying when other fellows don't do as much work and still know more than I do. But then of the 34 boys at the Sywell observer training school 21 failed the exam, which is terrible. Of 59 at Perth, 24 failed, which is almost as bad. You can gather that this job is not very easy, especially for me who was born with only a few brains.'

On 27 April, though, Billy was able to write, 'I'm feeling happy tonight, as the exams are almost over. We had DR plotting and reconnaissance today, and I did very well in both. So I've made a good start. We have meteorology tomorrow and then we're finished, and off to Uxbridge … so provided everything goes well I should be on my way towards being a regular Sergeant of the RAF.'

Everything did go well. 'I came 24th out of 49 [So eleven had already fallen by the way!]; Boyce was 32nd. I had 96% for maths, but got everything right, so they must have knocked the odd four off for writing.'

All very gratifying, but again external events intruded. '*I saw the article in The People about conscription, and it looks as if it might come into force … Mother should console herself now, when she thinks I could have been in the army earning 14/- [70p] a week if I hadn't joined up here …*'

30 April 1939, RAF Depot, Uxbridge. '*I've heard some conflicting stories about Uxbridge, but it's only for a fortnight.*' A fortnight though, in which Billy was introduced to the more whimsical side of flying training. '*Today I was given the broom handles to wash. I had to dust my locker, brush and polish the floor next to my bed, then clean the windows. Also I had to scrub out my kitbox with soap and water and spend two hours cleaning all the brass on my hats, Kitbag, harness, etc.*'

Billy's 'harness' – webbing – was the 1937-pattern, load-carrying frame, made of cotton webbing, based upon a wide belt, which bore a bayonet frog, pouch, and water bottle, and shoulder straps supporting a backpack, with a separately-slung sidepack. The blue-grey webbing had to be blancoed, and the brass buckle and attachments metal-polished.

*On Saturday we were run around the camp, a good two miles, at a very fast pace to shouts of "What's the matter with you? Get off your knees." We finished this streaming with sweat, but the drill instructor then gave us light exercises so that it dried on us, the damn fool. We then got changed and went out for an hour's gruelling drill, slow marching, turning on the march, forming fours, saluting and so on. He was bawling and shouting all the time. The obvious order to have done all this, in my opinion, is drill first, then PT, then the run, then a shower and rub down. As it was, we were fagged out after the run. But mostly we've been dealing with the uniforms, so the worst is yet to come.*

*We were made to march to the tailor's shop, a mile away. Fitting me, the tailor said, "You ain't half got some timber, ain't you?" He meant a big backside. The drill instructor, though, then made us march absolutely correctly back again but with a greatcoat, two tunics and two pairs of trousers over one arm. When we got back he marched us around the square until we were all perfectly in step. I wouldn't mind if they were reasonable …*'

Naïve Billy, looking for reason in a drill instructor! yet perhaps the barrack-square bawling seeded an awareness of rank, and indeed, status, for next day he wrote, '*You will see LAC on the address. This means leading aircraftman, don't forget to put this on … I saw some of the ordinary fellows, aircraftmen class two, doing cookhouse fatigues. They are a very rough crowd in comparison with my friends who are all educated …*

And before leaving Uxbridge there was a closing whimsy. '*We stood perfectly still for two hours as Wing Commander James gave us a stiff inspection, while a warrant officer watched for anyone who moved and called them all the names under the sun.*'

On 13 May 1939 they arrived at No. 2 Armament School, at Acklington, near Newcastle upon Tyne, where they were to qualify in bombing and gunnery.

'*We've been learning to use the Vickers' K Gas-Operated Gun: it fires 950 rounds a minute, which is pretty quick when you think about it.*

*They issued all 90 of us Desford and Prestwick boys with flying kit, so it must have cost a fabulous amount. We had a flying helmet and goggles, a fur flying suit, and then another canvas suit with zip fasteners to go over the fur one, and a beautiful pair of shiny black boots which are lined with wool and come up to our knees and must cost anything up to £2 each.*

*I used my new flying suit on Tuesday, in a Hawker Hind biplane bomber. I was in the open gun turret with a camera gun and took 32 photographs of another plane flying about 100 yards away. It appears, though, I would have missed every time because I didn't properly allow for the other plane's speed.*'

Billy would not be the last newcomer to air gunnery to be surprised at how difficult if was to hit even a formating fighter.

*Yesterday we went on the 25 yards range on the sands and shot 70 rounds with the Vickers. This morning, though, we were to fire from the turrets of planes, which meant a terrific slipstream of 100 miles an hour pulling at the gun. These particular Hinds also have Browning guns in their wings which fire at the colossal speed of 1,150 rounds a minute. Next we fire off 60 rounds at a drogue: a sleeve target towed by another plane.*'

4 June 1939. *'Now we've turned to bombing a target out at sea, using a sight that costs £90. The sight is very complicated and they expect you to use it after just half an hour's instruction. On Thursday I went up three times and did eight bombing runs on each flight. The bombs cost 10/6 [52.5p] each, so that's £12/12/0 [£12.60p] and then there's petrol, pilots' wages etc. Our training must cost a tremendous sum.*

*Bombing's not very easy, as you are lying on your stomach looking through the bottom of the plane, and hot blasts of air and spots of oil are continually flying in your face from the Hind's engine. We fly at 6,000 feet, and when the target is approaching, you have to keep it running down the drift wires by directing the pilot and saying left or right or steady. At the same time you must reach out and switch on the particular bomb you want to drop, and then, just as the target gets on the sights, press a button. Then you see the bomb curling gracefully downwards and after a few seconds exploding in the sea. Most of mine were about 100 yards away, but that didn't matter provided the bomb dropped in about the same position relative to the target. Tomorrow, though, we've got to try to hit the target.'*

6 June 1939. *'Yesterday I was waiting all day but because a sea mist blotted out the target, I only dropped eight bombs. Same again today. So I'm browned off, as they say in the RAF. When I went up my pilot flew at 10,000 feet, that is, almost two miles, which is very much higher than I've been before. The temperature is only six degrees above freezing up there, and quite a change from down below.*

*I did pretty well at the bombing, and yesterday nearly hit the target, but that was from 6,000 feet. Today, the nearest was 50 yards. Of course, a great deal depends on the pilot, he must fly straight, and keep the plane absolutely level otherwise the bombs go all over the place.*

*I would say our relations with the pilots are fair, because although they are mostly quite decent, we have trouble over some "dummy runs"* [Abortive bombing passes]. *These occur when we fly over the target but the target doesn't quite come into the sights and it's therefore useless to drop the bomb, as it would be a long way off. When these occur, it means that time is wasted, and we have to turn and fly over the target again. They are, of course, inevitable, as it is very, very difficult to get a good sight.'*

In time to come the bomb-aimer's muttered, 'Going round again,' would be the most unwelcome of intercom messages, committing the crew, as it did, to dwelling for interminable minutes more as they laboriously positioned – with their volatile load! – for a second run over a searchlight-swept, bomber-crowded, flak-torn, fighter-laden target …

23 June 1939. *'Bombing exam today, and I think I've passed. If I have, I'll be leaving here as an acting sergeant on Saturday.'*

Billy had indeed passed, as had Boyce, and another friend, George Wood, all being posted to No. 144 Squadron, stationed at RAF Hemswell, in Lincolnshire, and equipped with Hampden bombers. They were now sergeants, and sewed on the highly regarded 'O' half-wing, observers' brevet. Even so, they had flown less than seventy hours, and almost all by daylight.

*Billy*

*Observer's brevet and sergeant's stripes*

Full of enthusiasm as the new-joiners were, it soon became clear that the Service's vast expansion had left the squadron ill equipped, the available resources having to be spread among the many new units. On 28 June 1939 Billy wrote: '*We have to borrow kit whenever we fly: no easy thing. This morning I was told I was to fly with the CO. I dashed about and managed to get a parachute and harness, and borrowed two maps and some instruments from the navigation officer. Then, just as I worked out the course, the flight was cancelled.*

*I am to go with him tomorrow, however. We are to fly 20 miles out to sea to a position 53° 17´ N latitude and 01° 31´ E longitude* [Essentially, off Skegness, north of Cromer]. *From there we fly to a certain place by wireless bearings, and then back home. Let's hope I can get hold of all the equipment I need by the 10 o'clock take-off time.*

*They don't seem to want to bother with us yet as we are inexperienced. One chap just couldn't get any kit and the pilot was waiting for him for a quarter of an hour and was very angry. When we get our kit and settle down, of course, we should be in clover.*'

What none of them could know, of course, was that, just halfway through their Acklington stint, and just three months before the outbreak of hostilities, Ludlow-Hewitt had warned the Air Council that Bomber Command still 'lacked the strength and efficiency to go to war within any predictable period'. His uncomfortable forthrightness drew a line under his (already illustrious) career. But as the RAF official history would put it, at that time Bomber Command was 'an investment in the future'. Sadly, it was an investment that was to include Billy.

2 August 1939. '*We went from Hemswell to Tiree Island, off the west coast of Scotland. Then to Leuchars (near Dundee) and back to Hemswell. The weather report wasn't too bad, but we met a lot of rain storms and cloud. There were two officers on board, one piloting and other navigating, but at Tiree they changed, and I took over the navigating.*'

Billy touches here upon the stratification of RAF fliers into commissioned officers and other ranks. In 1914 the Royal Flying Corps had seen no need to commission pilots. The Royal Naval Air Service had done so, however, and with recruiting falling off, the RFC – the RAF from 1918 – had been forced to follow suit. Until 1993 this stratification would even extend to the gallantry decorations awarded.

On 24 August 1939 Billy's father wrote: '*My word, Bill, the news is bad tonight. They've called up the Terriers* [Territorial Army] *and police specials are on duty here. It does not look very happy for your leave, still we cannot help it but hope something will happen that will avoid a war.*'

Billy had been at Halton, the large RAF training establishment in Buckinghamshire, representing Hemswell at water polo, one of several sports at which he excelled. On 29 August, he responded: '*We played one game, and won. Then the sports were cancelled, and everybody was recalled from leave. If war is declared, we have to go to Egypt.*

*I don't want you to worry, because personally I don't think there'll be any real trouble.*'

Like so many others, he clung to hope. '*If we have a bit of luck Hitler will have to climb down. The crisis doesn't worry us much, so don't you worry.*'

On 1 September 1939, however, hope faded. Billy wrote, '*The news is very bad today and Germany has attacked Poland, so I think it is now only a matter of time before we join in. If I were you, Dad, I should join something like the Auxiliary Fire Service, or they will probably put you in something you won't like. We are expecting to be told to get ready for Liverpool anytime now …*

*I don't know whether I shall have the opportunity of seeing you again, Mother and Dad, but in case I don't, I'll take this chance to tell you how very much I appreciate the way you brought me up, and the many sacrifices you made to send me to the grammar school. It was at Desford, though, that I realised for the first time the value of a Mother's and Father's love …*'

Saturday, 2 September 1939
'*The situation is very grim at the moment, Mother, but I don't want you to worry so much about me. You must be brave and keep smiling … like we all are here, although we may be asked to go on very dangerous missions shortly. In spite of the danger, however, nobody is worrying about it. Instead we all had a drink of beer and a sing-song and were very merry.*'

Sunday, 3 September 1939
Billy's father wrote: '*I heard the fateful news on the wireless this morning at 11.15 and I felt very depressed because I was hoping at the last moment war may have been averted, but it is not to be, for Hitler never knew the end of his wants. We have just heard the King's speech and now both France and us are at war. We can only hope it will not be a long one …*'

Billy's mother added: '*I hope Boyce and all of you are cheerful … I wish I could just see you and have a little talk …*'

Monday, 4 September 1939. Billy wrote from Hemswell:
'*The rumour about going to Liverpool, then Egypt, was only to put off the spies, so a few of the planes went to Liverpool's Speke aerodrome for a few days, but returned last night. Here, I've been standing by for the last three days, ready to take-off and raid German battleships in the North Sea. Last night we sat in the planes with the engines running, but it was washed out.*'

In fact, even as No. 144 Squadron had been sitting, engines running, at Hemswell, twenty-three bombers from other stations had actually got airborne and launched an attack. Any damage done to enemy vessels was minimal, but five Blenheims and two Wellingtons had failed to return.

In later years losses of 3.4% were normal enough, while even 8.7% on heavily defended Berlin was accepted. To lose just over 30% of the force, however, would have been unthinkable. And untenable.

Blithely unaware of any of this, Billy explained confidently, *'We fly in formation, and Boyce is in the plane next to mine, so we'll be covering each other when attacked by fighters.'*

Pal, then, supporting pal. In truth, the defensive armament in the aft-fuselage position was sadly puny, two, rearward-facing single Vickers machine guns, one above and one below the fuselage. Indeed, Ludlow-Hewitt had recently reported, *'Captains and crews have very little confidence in the ability of the gunners to defend them against destruction by enemy aircraft.'*

Tuesday, 5 September 1939. Billy's mother wrote: *'I do hope you get back safe, Billy, if you do have to fight. I cannot say all I think, then again it would not do ...'*

His father told him: *'We are all very proud of you, and if you are put to the test I know you will show that same spirit there as you did on the playing fields. Give our kind regards to Boyce ... It upsets little Pam when she sees Mother so troubled.'*

Thursday, 7 September 1939. Billy wrote from Speke (Liverpool): *'Arriving here we hit the coast at Southport. The only way we could reach the aerodrome was by going down the coast and up the river because of the terrific balloon barrage all around the town. They've sent us here because it is a safer place than Hemswell to store all the Hampdens. It is very unlikely that the German aircraft will get as far as the west coast. It's been a very peaceful war for us up to the present, because we've made no raids, and we've not seen any German aircraft.'*

Recalling this period in his 1944 book, *Enemy Coast Ahead*, Guy Gibson, who by then had found fame as the leader of the Dam Busters, wrote that on 3 September 1939, when his squadron (No. 83) left Scampton to attack German shipping, he had never flown a Hampden at night, nor taken off with a full bomb load. They had also been briefed that German capital ships had only machine guns for anti-aircraft defence. Low cloud had thwarted that particular raid but in the following weeks No. 83 squadron had been detailed for nothing but concentrated sessions of night-flying training.

Similarly, for the next fortnight or so Billy's squadron alternated between Hemswell and Speke, carrying out training at Squires Gate, Blackpool. *'After a three-day stay at Speke we had no sooner landed at Hemswell than we had to get off again and fly to Squire's Gate to shoot 200 rounds at a drogue.'*

Friday, 8 September 1939, Speke: '*No. 61 Squadron who came here with us, left this morning, so we should return to Hemswell soon.*'

It is noteworthy that none of Billy's letters was censored. And though censorship might have been in force, letters from other sources show that the regulations were not always that strictly adhered to …

Saturday, 9 September 1939:

Billy spoke of the ex-Desford lads sticking together, noting, '*Sometimes we don't get on too well with the other sergeants, but we don't mind because there are so many of us that we can do without their help.*'

The 'other sergeants' referred to are non-fliers. The problem was that from 18 January 1939 all airmen-fliers became 'instant' sergeants, a measure (albeit only creakily implemented) that caused understandable resentment among ground tradesmen who might have taken twenty years to achieve that rank. With up to four sergeant fliers to each Hampden, groundcrew senior NCOs, with long service behind them, and often somewhat set in their ways, found themselves swamped by youngsters, particularly in the mess.

Sunday, 10 September 1939

Billy's mother wrote: *'I went to see Boyce's mother on Thursday afternoon. She'd had no letter but held that no news is good news, so I felt better. It is a lovely shop they have, and very busy, which is a good thing, she told me, for she doesn't have time to think. … You will find me here to greet you whenever you come, if only you have luck to come …'*

Saturday, 16 September 1939, Hemswell

Billy writes, *'We work seven days a week practising air firing at Squire's Gate then going back to Hemswell.'*

Tuesday, 19 September 1939, Hemswell: *'It doesn't seem as if a war is on here, no mention of going on raids or fighting is made. We are merely practising bombing and gunnery the same as we would in peacetime.'*

As Billy wrote he would not have heard that, just the day before, twenty-two Wellingtons had reached the Heligoland-Wilhelmshaven area but had run into Messerschmitt Bf109 fighters. Again, minimal damage to German shipping. But fifteen bombers had failed to return.

A horrific, and utterly unsustainable 68% of the force lost!

Billy went on: *'I may be able to get a day or two off shortly. The trouble is I'm on a flying crew, and we can't get off very much. You see each aircraft has a crew of four and they always fly together in the same kite.'*

No notion, though, of this 'flying crew' being 'our crew'. In fact, Billy's crew comprised, Flying Officer John Tulloch Burrill Sadler, from Melbourne, Australia, pilot; Sergeant R.L. (Jock) Galloway, a sergeant pilot, but detailed as navigator; Aircraftman Class One James White Cummings, air gunner – and probably wireless operator; with Billy, though a qualified observer, being detailed as the other gunner.

So while Billy and Galloway were sergeants, Cummings was an airman, and Sadler an officer; little chance then, of all four gelling off duty. And not much more when airborne, for the Hampden had no effective in-flight access between crew stations. Instead, Billy's reference shows that the concept of 'aircrew' still had some way to go. Of course, as the squadron settled, the various specialities would have been re-assigned to buttress later-joining, less-experienced crews, Billy, for example, would have flown in his highest-qualified category, as navigator.

Tuesday, 26 September 1939. Billy's mother: *'It was good of you to send a telegram to let us know your pass has been cancelled. I feel the world is full of disappointments just now. Little Pam said to me, "I told you he would come", and when I said, "But he hasn't come", she looked at me …'*

On Tuesday, 26 September 1939, postmarked 27 September, Hemswell, Billy responded hearteningly, *'Sorry to have disappointed you about the leave. But cheer up, I have a little good news … All being well – don't be too certain, because you can never tell what's going to turn up – I should be able to get home on Saturday night …*

Except that on Saturday morning a telegram announced that Billy was missing on operations.

'REGRET TO INFORM YOU THAT YOUR SON SGT STEPHENS IS REPORTED MISSING FROM OPERATIONS ON 29 SEPTEMBER LETTER FOLLOWS. OC 144 SQUADRON.'

It would be over two months before hopefulness and dread were reconciled, a letter from Air Ministry advising that Billy must now be presumed dead.

The background to this tragedy was that on Friday, 29 September 1939, No. 144 Squadron carried out its first, non-abortive sortie of the war, bombing shipping in the Wilhelmshaven approaches.

As planned by No. 5 Group, twelve Hampdens proceeded in two independent sections of six with the squadron's commanding officer, Wing Commander James Cunningham, leading the first. He took off at 0640, and when one aircraft turned back, unserviceable, formed his remaining five machines – including those crewed by Billy and Boyce –, into a single vic.

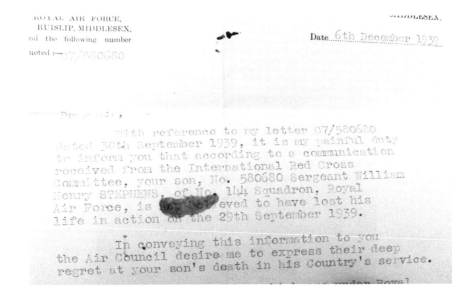

ROYAL AIR FORCE,
RUISLIP, MIDDLESEX,
nd the following number
uoted :— 07/580680

MIDDLESEX.

Date 6th December 1939

Dear Sir,

With reference to my letter 07/580680 dated 30th September 1939, it is my painful duty to inform you that according to a communication received from the International Red Cross Committee, your son, No. 580680 Sergeant William Henry STEPHENS, of No. 144 Squadron, Royal Air Force, is now believed to have lost his life in action on the 29th September 1939.

In conveying this information to you the Air Council desire me to express their deep regret at your son's death in his Country's service.

*Confirmatory letter, 6 December 1939*

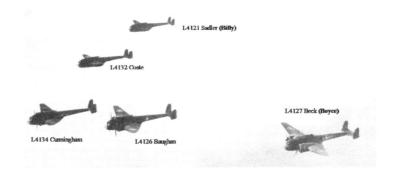

L4121 Sadler (Billy)

L4132 Coste

L4134 Cunningham

L4126 Baugham

L4127 Beck (Boyce)

*A five-strong vic of Hampdens, showing the positions of Billy's and Boyce's aircraft on 29 September 1939*

The Group-designated route took his formation some considerable way north of Heligoland before turning it south for Wilhelmshaven, the plan being that, as enemy ships returning from the North Sea were known to proceed southwards past Heligoland, the force could mount attacks on any they encountered.

***The Heligoland Bight (Bay) area,*** **Illustrated London News**

The second formation, under a flight commander, Squadron Leader Lindley, took off a little later. However, being routed more directly, it arrived off Heligoland first, and coming upon two destroyers, commenced an attack. Its leading vic scored no hits, but came under such intense anti-aircraft fire – so much for Intelligence's 'only machine-gun defences!' –, that, with a navigator wounded, Lindley broke off the engagement and returned to base. Sergeant George Wood, flying in that section, later wrote to Billy's parents, '*As we went into action Bill's group were seen approaching in the distance but after that we were all fully occupied.*'

Billy's formation avoided the now stirred-up flak from Heligoland but were confronted by some twenty Messerschmitt Bf109 fighters, scrambled in the face of the first threat and just arriving on the scene. All five Hampdens were shot down, with just four crew members surviving, one from each of four aircraft.

In the soulless statistics of air-staff evaluation, 100% of Cunningham's section, and 45% of the entire force, lost!

In 1945, after six years of prisoner-of-war incarceration, Jock Galloway, Billy's navigator, described the extraordinary example of nose-thumbing with which the engagement opened.

'*We were flying at the right rear of the vic when a fighter tucked in between our mainplane and tailplane, forwards of the arc of fire of Billy's guns and shielded from the other Hampdens. He then peeled off and rejoined his squadron. After that I saw bullets threshing the sea ahead and below us, then we hit the water and I lost consciousness.*'

Another newly-liberated POW, Pilot Officer Coste, recalled: '*The Messerschmitts attacked in vics of five, closing astern to fifty yards. My aircraft, the fourth to be attacked, was set on fire and I crashed onto the sea ...*'

In fact, the Hampden gunners – conceivably Billy or Boyce – actually downed two fighters, although both German pilots survived. Billy's Hampden, L4121, was claimed by *Oberleutnant* [flying officer] Gunther Specht; and Boyce's, L4127, by *Hauptman* [flight lieutenant] Dickors, both of *Zerstörergeschwader 26* [effectively, No. 26 Squadron, Luftwaffe]. Boyce was buried in Sage Cemetery, Oldenburg. Billy's body was never recovered.

**Oberleutnant *[flying officer] Gunther Specht, of* Zerstörergeschwader *26 [effectively, No. 26 Squadron, Luftwaffe] claimed Billy's Hampden** (*Courtesy* **Bundesarchive**, *by Harrison*)

The air staff were compelled to take notice of the unacceptable cost of these early armed-reconnaissance sorties and turn instead to honing the RAF's skills by such night operations as leaflet-dropping and minelaying. Indeed, Harris, the legendary leader of the Command, would declare that without such a change of direction, and Ludlow-Hewitt's career-sacrificing forthrightness, Bomber Command, 'would have been … beyond all hope of recovery within a few months'.

Naturally, the new strategy was not without cost, so that on the night of 5 October 1940 George Wood's Hampden failed to return from minelaying in the Elbe Estuary.

In the event, it would take a good two years to fully build upon the sacrifices made by Billy, and Boyce, and by George, and the rest of their comrades, but undoubtedly the technologically-honed bludgeon that was Harris's Bomber Command from 1943 onwards owed everything to the pinprick raids of those who had paved the way.

## 2. Well, I've Always Been Pretty Lucky

**Sergeant Eric Clarke, wireless operator/air gunner**

Arriving in Finchley just as the all-clear sounded after an air raid, I found myself clambering over rubble, and around fire engines, would-be rescue workers, and crews struggling to stem a burst water main. A dear old lady tapped my shoulder, 'Drop one on 'em for me, Lad,' she urged.

*Sergeant Eric Clarke, 1941, air gunner*

I was born on 22 April 1913 and when the war broke out in September 1939 I was twenty-six, had been married for two years to Gladys, and was working as an estate agent.

Work aside, since 1936, when RAF Finningley opened, just five miles to the south, I'd grown used to seeing aircraft around, more especially after the Handley Page Hampden bombers arrived in 1938 and 'the boys in blue', with their pilot and observer brevets, became everyday sights.

Although I was married, my call-up papers were bound to arrive. So, on 5 June 1940, having heard enough from two uncles who'd been at Passchendaele to know that a rifle and bayonet wouldn't suit me, I presented myself to the Sheffield recruiting office and asked to fly with the RAF as a navigator: even then we used that term, although we meant 'observer', meaning the one who wore the 'flying 'O' brevet', and not only did the navigation but the bomb aiming and some gunnery in addition. The board were sorry, but as I hadn't been to grammar school, they said, they couldn't accommodate me – I'd won a grammar-school place but my family couldn't afford to let me take it. Would I volunteer for wireless operator/air gunner, instead? And with rifle and bayonet in mind, I signed the smilingly proffered form and, after a period of deferred service, was duly summoned.

On 13 August 1940 I reported to No. 3 Recruiting Centre, at RAF Padgate, near Warrington, Lancs, for kitting out, and two days later was posted to Blackpool for a combination of recruit training and elementary instruction in electrical and wireless theory. The main undertaking at this stage, though, was to learn to send and receive morse to a speed of twelve words a minute: I recall we loved to create cadences with our dits and dahs, for instance, sending the rhythmic phrase, 'Beef essences', and being smutty with, 'She was only a wireless operator's daughter but she "did dit because da-da did dit".' As for getting around to the various venues, the drill corporal, having learnt that, as a member of the Church Lads' Brigade I'd once won the all-England drill competition, appointed me senior man and left me to get our fifty-strong contingent to where they had to be.

In December 1940 we moved to No. 2 Signals School at RAF Yatesbury, near Calne, in Wiltshire, where we deepened our theoretical knowledge, finally tested out on morse at twenty words a minute, and became familiar with the current wireless equipment. This included operating them in the de Havilland Dominie biplane.

During the course I was hitching home on a forty-eight hour pass and arrived at a lorry park in Finchley just as the all-clear sounded after an air raid. And so I found myself clambering over rubble, and around fire engines, would-be rescue workers, and crews struggling to stem a burst water main. Amid the turmoil I felt a tap on my shoulder, and turned to face a dear old lady. 'Drop one on 'em for me, Lad,' she urged. It was to be the first, but far from the last, time I was to have this happen.

In April 1941, now qualified as an aircrew wireless operator, with the rank of aircraftman class one, I was posted to RAF Finningley – back home! – to await a vacancy on a gunnery course, in the interim getting up a few times in Hampden bombers.

On 18 May 1941 the vacancy came up and I was sent to No. 8 Bombing and Gunnery School at RAF Evanton, on the Cromarty Firth where, after fifteen hours of practical air-firing, I was promoted to sergeant and became both wireless operator and air gunner. That is, a WOp/AG, or as we said, 'wop-aygee'.

On 14 June 1941 it was on to No. 16 Operational Training Unit (OTU) at RAF Upper Heyford, in Oxfordshire, for a three-month course during which we learnt to operate the Hampden. Bearing in mind that first-line squadrons had the pick of the available machines, those on the OTU tended to be a bit weary, indeed, what with crashes and failures to cope, our course gained the dubious distinction of having lost more trainees than any other.

In later times one crewed up at OTU, but not in our day, so on completing the course I was posted as an individual to No. 49 Squadron, reporting to RAF Scampton, near Lincoln, on Sunday, 21 September 1941. As it happened, having collected my arrival chit from station headquarters, I found myself doing the rounds with another new WOp/AG, Patrick Maloney. Pat was an Irish cockney and we became good friends.

*Eric Clarke, and Hampdens, June 1941*

'Arriving' consisted of having the chit signed at every section on the station one would have dealings with, from accounts to flying clothing, ultimately handing in our completed arrival chits at station headquarters. Having dropped off our kit at our assigned billet – formerly married quarters –, we repaired to the sergeant's mess.

The following morning, having made our way to the wireless operators' crewroom in No.2 Hangar, we discovered that the squadron's twenty or so WOp/AGs were split into 'A' and 'B' Flights. Pat and I became members of 'B', under Flight Sergeant Jack Gadsby, DFM, who had joined the squadron in 1938 and was on his second tour of operations. 'A' Flight's senior-NCO-leader was Sergeant Wally Ellis, DFM and bar, who had also been with the squadron since 1938 and had done his first operational flight as a leading aircraftman, before airmen aircrew became sergeants. Pat and I, at twenty-eight, were of an age with a few of the senior chaps, but as most of the lads were nearer twenty, we found ourselves both new boys and oldies.

Perhaps because of this, when we entered what was to be our crewroom on that first morning we were taken aback. Chaps playing at cards or dominoes were sprawled about with tunics undone – it was before the days of battledress –, the air was thick with cigarette smoke, there were unwashed mugs on every ledge, and the floor hadn't been swept for weeks. As new boys we stuck it for a while, then went in early one morning and 'blitzed' the place – as we'd begun to say –, amazing everyone as they arrived. Intrigued, Jack Gadsby agreed to having a cleaning rota and next time I had a pass I brought back lettering material and put the bulletin boards in order ...

The daily routine varied, we discovered, according to whether or not the squadron had been warned for an operational task. If there was no op planned, the days were partially occupied with training flights, lectures, and activities like parachute packing. For the most part, though, it was cards and dominoes. I did join in on occasion, but only when really pressed, and I'd never gamble.

When an op was pending we'd get word at about 0900 hours. Then, depending upon the number of aircraft serviceable, Jack Gadsby would detail us, first, to carry out a daily inspection on a particular aircraft – that is, a ground check of the equipment –, and later, to carry out a night-flying-test – NFT. This would mean getting airborne for about fifteen minutes while all the systems were tested, but as crews were not normally fixed back then, the pilot doing the test might not be the one you flew with that night.

As the hours passed we'd eye the tractors towing loaded trains of ordnance from the bomb dump, for this offered our first clue of what the night held for us. We might see bombs, which would mean the Ruhr – Happy Valley, as the old sweats knew it – ; mines would indicate a 'Gardening' operation, laying them in enemy waters.

You'd only discover who you were flying with when you saw the operations board, and even then you'd only know them if they were senior NCOs and you'd met them in the mess. If they were officers, they'd most likely be strangers. We were intensely interested in the pilots, of course, discussing their merits, and demerits, and adjudging them as 'spot-on', 'super', 'wizard', but also 'dopey' and 'crazy' and some quite unprintable things. Hardly surprising then, that although affinities were formed in the air they were tenuous at best.

The Hampden needed four men to crew it, a pilot; an observer  who both navigated and acted as bomb aimer (after 1942 'observer' was to be re-categorized as 'navigator'); and two wireless operator/air gunners (the category 'air gunner' did not exist at that time). One WOp/AG would fly at the wireless set, and also operate the upper guns, the other would occupy the lower gun position, known as 'the tin'.

*The Hampden, showing the lower gun position, 'the tin'*

Crews stabilized more after we got the Manchesters, with their seven-man crews, but even then there was little enough mixing between airmen aircrew and officers until we boarded, especially as we retained separate crew rooms

Although I'd joined the squadron on 21 September 1941, a temporary surplus of gunners meant that it was 13 October before I actually got airborne. Then, though, it was to be straight in at the deep end, on an op! Not that I'd been given any inkling that this was imminent, indeed, it was teatime before Jack Gadsby told me I'd to be at briefing at 1800 hours, just an hour or so later.

I discovered I was to be crewed with a Sergeant Pilot Robinson and a Sergeant Pilot Stuart Black – a New Zealander, flying as observer –, neither of whom I knew. Sergeant Bill Mossop, of the vintage of Jack and Wally, was to operate the wireless, while I was to occupy the tin.

At briefing the squadron commander identified the target as the synthetic rubber factory at Huls, at Krefeld, in the Ruhr, and indicated the routing designated by Group. Then the various specialists addressed us in turn, the meteorologist, the navigation officer, then signals, and Intelligence, and we were given our individual take-off times. At that stage each crew huddled about the chart its navigator had prepared. Briefing complete, we went back to our various messes for a night-flying supper.

At 2300 hours, fully kitted in tunics, jerseys, flying suits and lifejackets, we assembled in front of the hangar to await the crew wagons. There was no excitement, I remember, just quiet conversation and discussion. Then the transport arrived, cigarettes were stubbed out, and we clambered aboard. An officer from another crew got in beside the WAAF driver, while the balance of two crews piled in the back.

I particularly remember the absence of nerves, recalling only the badinage.

'I've done ten ops. How many've you done?' 'Get some in ...' I did not volunteer that it was my first.

When we spilled out beside our aircraft we waited as the pilot had a word with the groundcrew flight sergeant. Then, 'Let's get going,' he said.

Throughout the darkness engines were starting up, and there was distant shouting of clearances, 'Starting number two ...', 'Chocks away ...'

The pilot and observer disappeared into the front hatch. Bill Mossop climbed up through the lower gun position – the tin – and took his seat by the set, leaving me to follow on.

For a while then we were all busy working through our checks. For my part I stowed my 'chute, checked the safety catches on my guns – twin, gas-operated Vickers –, and plugged in the bayonet-type oxygen tube. Mentally, I worked through the drill for baling out: lift 'chute from stowage, snap it to chest, pull lever, kick hatch, and let myself fall: Bill would then drop directly from the upper station through the hole. All that done, I waited my turn for the intercom checks: good intercom was vital, and just one defective headset could jeopardize the whole operation.

'Hello Skipper, Navigator here ...' and so on around the crew.

The engines coughed their way into life, the airframe vibrating ever more violently as they were run up and checked. Then we were taxying out. And, my checks complete, I clambered up to join Bill in the wireless-operator's cockpit.

Repositioning was necessary because, with the fuselage being too narrow to offer any reasonable crash position, both WOp/AGs had to cram into the wireless station for take-off and landing, standing like nested spoons, or vertical sardines. Seventy years later, when aviation archaeologists were mystified on excavating two skeletons pressed together in a Hampden, I was able to explain that, if baling out was not an option, this was the standard crash drill.

As always, as we awaited our turn to take off, I found myself dwelling upon Gladys. Originally we'd decided against having children while the war was on, but having heard the BBC announce, 'Seventeen of our bombers are missing ...' Gladys had immediately changed her mind, so that even now we were anticipating the arrival of our first child.

There was a jolt as the brakes came off and the engines rose to full power. And then we were rumbling down the runway.

Just moments more, I realised, and I might be burning alive, or a little later, drowning in the North Sea ... It also struck home that the load we carried would hazard innocents. Though this was immediately overlain by the memory of the old lady in Finchley, and by the throb of unsynchronized engines as enemy bombers cruised the red sky roofing Sheffield. Just the same, even as our wheels left the ground and the rumbling died away, I took further refuge in the double reflections, 'Well, they started it ...' for the last, and 'Well, I've always been pretty lucky,' for the first. Though the latter would need to hold true, for that temporary surplus of gunners preceding this op had only cleared as others got the chop.

'Wheels up, Skip,' reported Black. 'Confirming course 109 degrees magnetic.'

I got the thumbs up from Bill, and began clambering down into my position in the tin. Once settled, I checked in on the intercom, and with that satisfactory, swung the guns from side to side. Regarding the word 'settled', however, please understand it to mean being committed to sitting with neck cricked, elbows cramped to ribs, and knees cranked high for up to eight hours. I'd already determined that the moment I was senior enough, I'd fly up at the set, and leave the tin to others.

We were flying level at 12,000 feet, the twin engines set to beat together as one. 'Crossing the Norfolk coast, Skip,' from Black. Then, from Bill, luxuriating at the set, 'Nothing from Group, Skip.'

On ops it was the wireless operator's job to listen out for Group's instructions, passed by morse code, on the hour-plus-fifteen-minutes. Only in rare circumstances could he break wireless silence and transmit, for a single key note might give away the aircraft's position. Even in an emergency he could only do so on instructions from the captain. And that meant the pilot, for regardless of rank, he was the captain.

No message this time, then, so no recall. We really were on our way! So, goodbye England! Hopefully, just for the time being ...

'Approaching enemy coast, Chaps. To the right's a known night-fighter zone, so keep your eyes skinned.'

I was scanning the night continuously, but there was a lot of cloud, and I could see nothing. Unfortunately, the cloud thickened, swiftly becoming ten-tenths. At Wesel, our turning point for Huls, we changed heading on Stuart Black's ETA, flying blind. Gradually, as we approached the target area Robinson took us down to 3,000 feet, where we dropped a flare, but without effect, even though the Hampden afforded the nav a good downwards view. After twenty minutes, therefore, we headed north-east for Essen, where we dwelled for another twenty-five minutes before steering a generally northerly course back through the Ruhr. Only over Holland did a brief clearance enable us to drop on an opportunely seen flarepath.

Having been airborne for 6 hours 20 minutes, we climbed wearily into the crew wagon, were sleepily debriefed – 'Everyone's back, Gentlemen' –, went in to breakfast, and then to bed.

On entering the billet I encountered Pat. He'd just got up.

'How was it?' he asked.

I'd have mumbled something vague. Indeed, I was so bemused myself that, later that day, I asked Bill Mossop to sum up the sortie: 'A fat lot of no good,' he grunted. What he'd have said on learning that we'd bombed a dummy airfield might have been worth hearing. By the time Intelligence was able to tell us this, though, he'd finished his tour, and been posted.

Of course, a set tour of operational sorties was a relatively new concept at that time, the RAF's essential aim being to formulate a commitment that gave aircrews a reasonable chance of surviving. Initially it had been left to commanders on the squadron to decide when a flier should be rested. In fact, such views still weighed, but in general a tour was now reckoned at thirty operational flights, or two hundred hours on operations, whichever came first.

Like Bill, my other companions on that first op had only just recovered from injuries sustained in September, a month earlier, after laying mines off Oslofjord, where the pocket battleship *Admiral Von Scheer* had been holing up between forays. Running out of fuel on the return, they had crashed near Banff, in Scotland. On 12 December 1941, just two months after we flew together, Sergeant Robinson would make another crash landing, this time at RAF Bircham Newton, near King's Lynn, as a result of damage sustained in a fighter attack over Bremerhaven during which Stuart Black, by then a flight sergeant, was killed.

In late 1941 there was little stability among the pool of wireless operators. Some left as they became tour-ex, as in Bill Mossop's case, then there would be new arrivals, and some were lost on ops. Indeed, in a space of time during which fifteen NCO aircrew failed to return, seven were WOp/AGs. As for new arrivals, too often we'd hardly get to know them. A Sergeant W.S. Way, arrived, let it be known that he was expecting his commission, and went down during what came to be known as the Channel Dash. He was posted missing as Pilot Officer Way, so hopefully he ended up in a POW camp.

In such a setting I was not at all surprised, therefore, to find myself once again crewed with strangers on my second op. Just the same I flew that one as wireless operator, smiling inwardly as my WOp/AG buddy stopped being cosy and clambered down to the cramped-up tin, allowing me to spread myself about my domain.

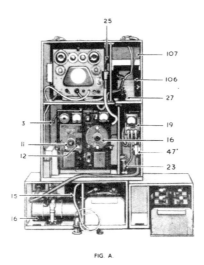

FIG. A

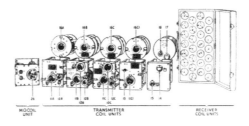

*The transmitter/receiver T1083 R1082*

Putting down my fold-up seat I could perch before the set, the Transmitter/ Receiver T1083/R1082. This five-valve receiver needed a skilled hand on the tuning knob and another on the feedback knob. And even then the combination required a different coil for each frequency. While seated I could comfortably reach the trailing-aerial reel. Equally convenient, a long headset lead allowed me to continue to monitor the receiver when I mounted footrests to take station at the twin Vickers where I spent most of any op.

With a Sergeant Pilot Bow at the controls, we took off at 1800 hours for Mannheim. The weather had been forecast as fine, but as we crossed the Belgian coast searchlights and flak forced us up to 18,000 feet where we found ourselves flying through thundery tops with lightning flashing all around. This persisted until we reached the target area when, having let down to 14,000 feet, we saw our river-junction aiming point. From then on, though, the weather became so rough that on the return we ran short of fuel and had to put in to Horsham St Faith, near Norwich, touching down in torrential rain and staying overnight. We'd been airborne for over seven and a half hours.

Despite the bad weather I'd been able to receive the periodic broadcasts. Had I needed to transmit, however, I'd have had trouble, with so much static. Flying in the top station, though, I really felt I was doing the job I was trained for, both wireless op and air gunner at the same time. I was to do eight more ops on the Hampden, but only one down in the tin.

On 4 January 1942 we did an eight hour flog laying mines off Brest but had to bring our bombs back – at that stage of the war we still had to think about dropping our load blind over Germany, to do so over France would have been unthinkable.

I returned to Brest on 25 January, with our flight commander, Squadron Leader Bennett, DFC. It was a mixed bag of a trip, so that although the target was brightly moonlit and we were able to run up accurately, we had to break off and take evasive action when a Messerschmitt Bf109 closed with us. We actually fired at it, but inconclusively. Once again, therefore, we had to bring our bombs back, this time landing on a snow-covered runway eight hours after getting airborne.

On my third visit to Brest, on 27 January, and despite hazy conditions, we bombed some cruisers in the harbour and after landing found a six-inch rent in our starboard wing, flak having narrowly missed the petrol tanks.

The next trip was to Bremen, on 10 February 1942, but we had to settle for bombing our secondary target, Wilhelmshaven, and even then, although we dropped successfully, the flak flashes masked those from our bombs.

Two days later, on 12 February, we were hurriedly summoned to a midday briefing and tasked to lay mines in the path of three German cruisers – *Scharnhorst, Prince Eugen* and *Gneisenau* – who were using bad weather to make a run up the Channel from Brest to reach their home bases: the Channel Dash, as we were to know it. As I was kitting up, however, and grinning at the cursing of Brian Hunter, a fellow WOp/AG who'd not only heinously taken his flying boots from the locker room but left them in his billet! I was stood down because my aircraft had become unserviceable so I offered him mine. Brian stopped his cursing, accepted with alacrity and moments later, now clear of disciplinary embarrassment, trotted off to his aircraft. Hours later his Hampden, together with two others from 'B' Flight, came down in the sea, his body being washed up on a Dutch beach two days later. In all, the RAF would lose 42 aircraft.

My immediate problem, though, was that I was now short of flying kit myself. And flying boots were not only 'valuable and attractive' but hard on the pocket to replace. Finding myself on the Battle Order for 16 February, I had to report my loss to the flight commander. However, on hearing the circumstances, he authorised me to take possession of Brian's flying boots, waiving any disciplinary action. They turned out to be a size too large, but that was all to the good, for it meant I could wear an extra pair of socks, and have slightly less icy feet.

When we eventually heard that Brian's body had been found I did have the whimsical notion that my name and number on the boots might have led to me being declared killed in action. He would, though, have been wearing his identity discs. As it was, I wore his boots on every op after that. And to this day, I mourn him. As indeed, I mourn the other 955 aircrew of No. 49 Squadron who failed to return.

Fully-equipped then, on 16 February 1942 I flew with Sergeant Frank Slingo on a 'Gardening' sortie – laying mines – off Heligoland, landing after six hours. Next, on 4 March, flying with Pilot Officer Jeffreys, with whom I was to fly eight Hampden ops, the target was Essen, but just over an hour out our intercom broke down – I recall the set was the A1134A: the odd things that stick! – so we had to abort the op, and drop in at Waddington.

On 28 March 1942, once more flying with Sergeant Slingo, it took nearly nine hours to raid Lübeck, a port city on Germany's Baltic Coast, dropping a strangely-mixed load of incendiaries and leaflets: my logbook, I see, records obscurely, 'Burner: Lübeck'. Certainly, at debriefing we reported seeing widespread fires. Twelve bombers were lost, 5.5% of the force employed.

In fact, this was one of the 'experimental' raids following the amended Area-Bombing Directive of 14 February 1942 in which Air Ministry – the government – tasked Bomber Command with lowering the morale of both the enemy workforce and the populace by bombing German cities. 'Butch' Harris, having spoken of Lübeck's docks and the nearby submarine-making facilities, observed that the city was 'more like a fire-lighter than a human habitation'. Much later we were to discover that the raid caused the first of the firestorms.

On 5 April I flew another trip with the flight commander, when we dropped high-explosive bombs and leaflets on Cologne but were unable to see our bomb bursts through the nine-tenths cloud cover. It took us nearly seven hours, and was to be my last Hampden op. Not my last Hampden flight, however, for on 13 April I cadged a lift to Finningley when I went on leave.

During my time away others continued to fly Hampden ops, not least Frank Slingo, with whom I'd been to Lübeck. For on 18 April he and his crew failed to return from laying mines off the North Frisian island of Terschelling. Theirs was the last No. 49 Squadron Hampden crew to be lost. And their Hampden, AT217, was the one I'd grabbed a lift on just five days before ...

For many months we'd known that the first of the much-vaunted new bombers to roll off the stocks was to be the Avro Manchester. This was another twin-engined type, but much more advanced that the Hampden which, we all felt, had come to the end of its time. We were highly gratified then, when we began to receive the Manchester in mid April 1942. I dare say we'd have been rather less pleased had we known how disastrous its engines would be. Rolls Royce don't make many mess-ups but their Vulture came close. Yet, speak as you find, and on my first Manchester flight, on 27 April 1942, I likened it to going from a Ford Ten rattler to a Rolls Royce saloon. By then I'd been put in charge of 'B' Flight's WOp/AGs, so over the next week or so I not only screened new chaps but flew on training sorties to convert myself.

*The Avro Manchester*

I did my first Manchester op on 2 May, carrying out a 'Nickel' – leaflet – raid on Rennes. In fact, it was a washout, for our direct-reading compass went unserviceable and we were unable to locate our primary target, dwelling until just gone midnight, and then dropping the leaflets blind from 10,000 feet. We landed back at Scampton after six and a half hours. My second Manchester op, on 8 May, was a mine-laying sortie in Heligoland Bight. The weather was fine, not too cloudy, not too clear, and we could see our mines entering the water.

What pleased me far more, however, during those early Manchester ops, was the contrast with the Hampden, for from my station, just aft of the main spar, I could go forward, past the navigator to the pilot's station, and aft back to the tail. Then again the wireless op's position had a narrow, but ample, desk, and was so positioned that I could pass notes to the navigator. I also had the new Marconi transmitter-receiver T1154/R1155 – with its coloured tuning knobs –, a vast improvement on the Hampden's gear.

Further, not only was the trailing-aerial reel to hand – dangling the wire aerial below the aircraft considerably improved the set's range – but heated engine air flooded in beside me, giving me the most comfortable place in the aircraft.

And there was more, for by standing up and stepping right I could not only get an all-round view from the astrodome, but manipulate the directional loop-aerial to obtain wireless bearings.

May 1942 was a bad-weather month during which we briefed for seven targets only to have the sorties scrubbed. On 30 May, however, we got airborne to raid Cologne. It was to be a red-letter day for the bombing campaign and would be trumpeted by the press as the first thousand-bomber raid, and evidence that we were finally taking the war to the enemy. Our squadron supplied thirteen Manchesters, while our Scampton neighbours, No. 83 Squadron, sent twelve of their newly-received Lancasters.

Crews had begun to stabilize now, and I continued to fly with Pilot Officer Jeffreys, on this occasion receiving the green light to take off at 2306 hours. Conditions were excellent, with no cloud over the target, although when we arrived there were a great many fires and columns of smoke. There were also many searchlights, but little enough flak. We got a good sighting, and dropped accurately, actually seeing our bombs burst. We landed back after nearly six hours and the raid was rated as 'successful in all respects'. However, of the 1,047 aircraft employed, forty-one failed to return, including two of No. 49 Squadron's Manchesters.

On 1 June 1942 we got airborne on the second one-thousand-bomber raid – in fact, 956 aircraft –, this time, for Essen. We made our bombing run – the run-in heading, I recall, was 090° true –, at 0203 on 2 June, releasing from 9,000 feet. Again, the weather was clear and we saw our bombs burst accurately, adding to the fires already burning. I remember being particularly struck by the lack of opposition, even so, one of the squadron's aircraft did not return.

This was to be my last Manchester op, though No. 49's Manchesters would raid on until 25 June, when they attacked Emden.

On 13 June 1942 I was put in charge of all the squadron's WOp/AGs, and was given responsibility for vetting and instructing new arrivals. And on 14 June 1942 I flew a one hour thirty-five minute circuit detail with a pilot I'd first flown with some three months back, on 4 March, Pilot Officer J.K.M. Cooke. Since then he been promoted to flying officer and been awarded a DFC. The renewed association was to be among the most significant of my life.

Over the next few weeks we flew on several training sorties together. I thought nothing of it, therefore, on 9 July 1942 when he told me the two of us were to fly to Swinderby, near Newark. On landing, however, he said, 'Get your stuff out of this heap, we're leaving it and collecting a Lanc.'

This was typical of 'Cookie's' approach. He was a little older than me, and what today we'd call laid back, with a very dry, laconic humour, and a slight speech impediment. Some considerable time later, following two particularly harrowing trips on a Lanc, he stamped to where the groundcrew awaited us.

'T-tell me, Ch-Chief,' he said seriously. 'This is a four-engined bomber, isn't it?'

Chiefy, and all the groundcrew, pricked up their ears, for though used to indulging aircrew, they knew most of us could count to four.

'Then how is it that on the last t-two ops I've had to come back on th-three?'

To his crew, if he had to chivvy us, it would be, 'You clueless clots, pull your f-fingers out!' And after a trip during which I'd pulled out all the stops, when he said quietly, 'Good show, Sergeant,' I felt more than adequately rewarded. Certainly, I saw him as iconic, and worried as I invariably was on ops, during the eight I flew with him I always felt secure.

On that first trip back to Scampton – by then he'd become a flight lieutenant –, he had me hold the throttles forward for him until we got airborne. And that was my initiation to the Lancaster.

*The Avro Lancaster*

So much has been written extolling the Lancaster. 'The Manchester with four engines and the extended wingspan'; the 'Flying Legend'; 'As good to work on, as to fly in'. Its reputation is unassailable. Anything I could add would be inadequate. 'The aircraft without vices ...' But what I truly feel about the Lanc is inexpressible. And I'm quite sure I'm not alone in that.

For most of July 1942 I was busy helping with the conversion, but on 7 July I was interviewed for a commission by Group Captain Whitworth (later to command No. 617 Squadron). Coming down to earth, once more, however, on 31 July I flew my first Lanc op with Cookie, taking off at 0100 hours to raid Dusseldorf, and landing safely four hours later.

Then it was back to training again, until on 15 August we set off for Dusseldorf, only to have two engines run rough. Forced to turn back, we dropped four 2,000 pounder high-explosive bombs on the alternative target at Rotterdam, landing with an engine feathered after just two and a half hours. During the rest of August we visited Osnabrück, the islet of Flensburg, and Frankfurt, each op taking between four, and four and a half hours. The raids on Flensburg and Frankfurt saw the debut of Pathfinder Force, but due to shifting winds, neither was that successful, the Frankfurt raid leading to the loss of 7.1% of the aircraft involved.

In September we raided Saarbrücken – where ground haze led to scattered bombing –, then Bremen, and Essen. And on 19 September I got airborne with Cookie to Munich, a nine-hour flight which was to be my last with him, he and his crew – bar me – being transferred to Pathfinder Force. By this time Cookie had become a squadron leader and received a bar to his DFC.

I have to admit that with his departure I felt bereft. I was also a little hurt that I wasn't to accompany the rest to the Pathfinders. I quickly realised, however, that having been on ops for a full year, my tour was nearly up, so the Pathfinders wouldn't get full value from me. As for extending my tour, nobody asked me, obviously realising that not only was I married but indeed, the proud father of a brand new baby.

I flew my next op with a Sergeant Jimmy Thom, a Scot, I recall, raiding the Dornier factory at Wismar, on the Baltic Coast. Then, on 15 October 1942 we bombed Cologne, when, although all our squadron's aircraft returned, the main force lost eighteen bombers.

The Cologne trip was singular in ushering in a series of flights on which I was ordered to break radio silence and get bearings, fixes, and courses to steer (or QDMs, in the 'Q' brevity-code we used). Not all of these involved me actually transmitting, for fixes and bearings could also be taken using the loop, directional aerial: turning it to find a null position, and passing the result to the navigator. However, as I'd never been called upon to do so before I must assume that Cookie's navigator had been just up to scratch as Cookie.

On 19 October I was summoned to Air Ministry and offered a commission as a signals officer (technical). I refused it, however, in favour of becoming a commissioned air signaller.

I did what was to be my final op on 24 October 1942 when we got airborne at noon for a daylight operation to Milan. We'd been engaged most recently in high-level bombing, but this was to be a low-level raid by 88 Lancasters from No. 5 Group.

Acting independently, the squadron flew south from Scampton, crossed the Channel, located the River Loire, then turned port to Lake Annecy.

Here, we rendezvoused with the rest of the force before flying onwards through the Alpine peaks towards Milan. Positioned in the astrodome I had the unforgettable experience of looking forward to see a big, white, full moon and aft to see an enormous orange sun, both at eye level, while down in the now dusk-softened valleys lights twinkled, showing that there was no black-out here.

As we approached the target we let down to 4,500 feet, descending through cloud, to emerge just as a Stirling crossed below us, scaring us rigid. We bombed accurately, the whole force clearing the target within eighteen minutes, after which we took a direct line home, having to avoid just two flak concentrations. Worried about petrol as we coasted inbound we put down at RAF Upper Heyford, in Oxfordshire. Another squadron aircraft, though, crashed on the South Coast, killing the crew. We had been airborne for a full nine hours.

In the next week we did some local flying, and were twice briefed to raid Stettin, only to have both ops scrubbed. Expecting to be tasked with another, I was sent, instead, on an end-of-tour leave. The Milan op, I was told, had been my last. In fourteen months I had done twenty-six operations on three different bomber types, and flown 148 operational hours.

Fourteen months before I had arrived at Scampton with Pat Maloney. Now, coincidentally, we were to be posted away together, Pat to Lossiemouth. He was to volunteer for another tour, however, but on 18 August 1944 he and his crew baled out over Lincolnshire, and Pat, by then a DFM and a flight lieutenant, was killed. The rest of his crew survived, only to be lost on another op.

On 12 November 1942 Scampton paraded for His Majesty King George VI, and next day I was posted to RAF Pershore, in Worcestershire.

I now moved into the Signals world as a staff instructor, joining No. 23 Operational Training Unit (OTU) where my job was to supervise air signallers as they joined up with crews and learnt to operate first-line aircraft. To this end I put up an 'S' (for Signaller) brevet myself. And on 19 December 1942, my commission came through: the papers had been routed to the technical branch, and had been sitting on some desk. My appointment, therefore, was backdated to 7 July 1942, bringing six months' back pay!

It was all go now. On 7 January 1943 I was promoted to flying officer and became chief ground instructor, and a month later, as an acting flight lieutenant, I moved across to Pershore's satellite, RAF Stratford (formerly Atherstone), in the dual role of Chief Signals Instructor and Deputy Chief Ground Instructor for all aircrew. I was also appointed Officers' Mess Secretary. Another responsibility to come my way was station discipline.

This turned out to be potentially onerous, for all the students were Canadian and French Canadian, and commissioned, though few had any notion of how an officer was expected to behave. The nettle had to be grasped. So, concentrating initially on smartening them up, I reverted to my Church-Lads'-Brigade-drill-squad persona, and as each fortnightly intake arrived drilled them for thirty minutes, non-stop, daily. Basically, of course, they were great material, and after a couple of sessions, responded well.

The same couldn't be said for some of the veterans who resented my rapid promotion. In particular one 'O'-brevet navigator's loud obnoxiousness began to make life rather difficult. Until he failed to pay his mess bill. When, as mess secretary, I inadvertently-audibly taxed him with it in the crowded anteroom. After which I had no more trouble with him.

April 1943 opened with a shock when Cookie turned up as my new station commander. Now a wing commander, he had added a DSO to his DFC and bar: he and the crew had done particularly well on Pathfinder Force.

Shaking hands, he demanded, 'Where's your DFM?' And when I showed my puzzlement, his lips thinned. 'You were put up twice, to my knowledge.'

Nor did he let it go, for a day or so later he came back, still concerned. 'I've just checked with the *London Gazette*, and they haven't missed it.'

I was delighted, a year later, on 8 June 1944, to be gazetted for a mention in dispatches. What happened to the Distinguished Flying

Medal recommendations, I never did find out. Possibly misrouted like my commission, and sitting still on some dust-covered desk ...

My next move, on 18 January 1944, took me to RAF Penrhos, Caernarvonshire, where I completed the six-week Special-Category Signals Leaders' course. My posting, on 15 March 1944, was to No. 24 OTU at RAF Honeybourne, in Worcestershire, as Chief Signals Officer; also Officer Commanding the wireless and radar schools; also Officers' Mess Secretary, also Entertainments Officer: organizing station dances, in particular. Wearing all my Pooh-bah-like hats, in mid April, I shifted to Honeybourne's satellite at Long Marston, near Stratford.

By VJ Day – 15 August 1945 –, all the Canadians, staff and pupils, had been repatriated, but before that, in July 1945, Long Marston closed down. On 3 July 1945, therefore, I was posted as Chief Signals Officer to No. 26 OTU, at RAF Wing, in Buckinghamshire, moving a month later to its satellite at Little Horwood, near Buckingham.

My final move, though, on 13 September 1945, took me home, for I was posted to the Bomber Command Instructors' School at RAF Finningley, as Senior Staff Lecturer on all aspects of air signalling, including radar countermeasures: I was running, in effect, the Central Flying School for air signallers!

Having been there for some weeks, I was called before the commandant and asked if I'd like a permanent commission. This was very flattering. Particularly to a non-grammar-school type like yours truly. With a permanent commission, the sky, it was hinted, was the limit ... But, less reluctantly than Pooh-bah, I curbed my aspirations, and politely declined. And just as well, for another chap I knew who accepted a similar offer found himself on the next trooper out to the Far East! Gladys and I were much more interested in our second son, who was just graduating to a pram.

On 27 September 1945, I had my last RAF flight, navigating a Mosquito from Finningley to Abingdon and back. And on 27 November I began my demobilization leave. I left the Service on 27 February 1946.

Foremost among the problems awaiting all of us returning to civvy street, was earning bread for the family. The years in the Service, however, had shown that I was lucky. Luck that held when, pushing baby Raymond through town, the treasurer of the local council, recognising me, asked how I was getting on.

'Fine,' I told him. 'Except that I don't have a job.'

He pursed his lips. Then said, 'There's little enough on offer, with people flocking back from the forces. But if you'd consider a temporary position ...'

I would, and did, and with alacrity. They started me off in the drawing office where, at just over four pounds a week I was getting a lower wage than any labourer. Then I moved into housing repairs – on a temporary basis. After which I became a temporary clerk in the treasurer's department. Indeed, I wonder now if I was ever formally made permanent.

As the years went by, however, I studied local-government accounting and administration and passed examinations in both Sheffield and London. Then qualified, I went on to make a career in local government, rising to the post of Deputy Chief Financial and Rating Officer at Adwick-le-Street Urban District Council, joining Doncaster Metropolitan Borough Council on reorganisation in 1974, before retiring in 1978.

Having left the Service I did not altogether sever my ties. Early on I helped set up the Doncaster branch of the RAF Association, and later became a member of the No. 49 Squadron Association. There were to be many happy gatherings. But sad ones too. We had lost so many comrades. Inevitably the years were to take yet more.

Cookie died in 1967. And in 2008, after she had suffered far too much discomfort, my Gladys passed away. Visiting Pat Maloney's grave, I discovered it to be covered in vegetation ... And always nagging is the opprobrium visited upon my Bomber Command comrades since the war ended.

'You should never have bombed Dresden.' a German said to me, not that long since. On the other hand, my hearing is not as sharp as it was.

So did he say Dresden, or was it, perhaps, Coventry, or Warsaw, London, Portsmouth, Rotterdam, or Sheffield?

Ironically, my hearing aside, the years are proving increasingly kind to me. I have been honoured by a Lancaster flypast; given a standing ovation; feted at royal garden parties; addressed crowds at commemoration ceremonies; taken the Remembrance Day salute; been the guest at civic receptions; and freely admitted that there were times on operations when I was scared to death.

I am so pleased to know that you are celebrating your one hundredth birthday on 22nd April, 2013. I send my congratulations and best wishes to you on such a special occasion.

Elizabeth R

Flight Lieutenant Eric Clarke

*Left: Eric Clarke, Aviating, 2013. Right: Centenary*

Recently I accepted the newly-instituted Bomber Command clasp from a very senior Service officer. Had Churchill not turned his back on us, would all those who have passed on received yet more recognition? the recognition I believe they deserved. I have survived so much. Perhaps, then, I shall survive long enough to see my comrades get their just reward.

*Eric Clarke, 2013*

## Squadron Leader Herbert Nevil (Bluey) Mottershead, MBE, DFC, pilot

I was immediately bowled over by a WAAF busily clicking away at her keyboard. Her name, I was to discover, was Kaye. Utterly bemused, I uttered the first words that came to my tongue. 'You're wearing too much make-up.'

*Nevil Mottershead, flight cadet, Georgia, 1942*

My family farmed at Chelmarsh, south of Bridgnorth, in Shropshire, but although I had a great affection for the land, I decided to seek another way of life. Having spent some time at an electrical shop in Kidderminster, I got a job with ICI's Metals Division, in Birmingham, working in the strip mill.

When war broke out I was seventeen, and although I joined the local Home Guard, I was quite satisfied with my job. Indeed, I rather think, as I approached eighteen, I would have found that I was precluded from call up, being in a 'reserved occupation'. In August 1940 however, a bomb aimed at an airfield, fell on a pub where my best friend was drinking. Some time earlier he'd joined the RAF as trainee aircrew. He did not survive the raid. Fate has a way of changing our lives, and this event heralded a major change in mine. On the spot I determined that I too would join the RAF and do my best to even the score.

I knew little enough about the requirements for fliers. In 1933, or 1934, perhaps, during a family holiday at Southport I had scraped together money enough to buy a flight in a Fox Moth, and had never forgotten the thrill of it. Then again I believed I was academically acceptable, having done well at Bridgnorth's celebrated grammar school. And I was certainly fit enough, for not only had I cycled to and from school, but on moving to Birmingham I'd taken to cycling there on the Monday and back again on the Saturday afternoon. In January 1941, therefore, at the age of 19, I went to Shrewsbury to apply to join the RAF as a pilot, and was subsequently sent to Cardington, in Bedfordshire, for assessment.

The medical examination was searching, but I was passed fit. I also seemed to get on well in the interview. Even so I was relieved to discover that I had been found suitable for training as aircrew. Whether I had the aptitude to be a pilot could only be finally decided, I was told, once I'd been checked out in the air.

On 7 July 1941 my papers came through and I reported to Lord's Cricket Ground, at that time the main Aircrew Reception Centre. My arrival, however, coincided with a blockage in training, accordingly I was sent to RAF Scampton, near Lincoln, to kill time. In fact, managing to get myself airborne in a Hampden bomber during my stay, re-whetted my appetite for flight. And at the beginning of September I was back at Lord's.

My first real step onwards came in early October 1941 when I was sent to No. 7 Initial Training Wing at Newquay, in Cornwall. Here, courses of aircrew cadets were accommodated in hotels while drilling and doing physical training, and being introduced to a range of aviation subjects.

A really critical phase came on 10 December 1941 when I was called forward to RAF Booker, near High Wycombe, to No. 21 Elementary Flying Training School. This unit had a secondary function as a grading school, with pupils allowed twelve hours' tuition in a one-hundred-horsepower-engined Tiger Moth to see if they would make pilots. I actually did just over twelve hours with a very dependable instructor who diligently took me through the elementary flying syllabus – with a break for Christmas. At the end he declared himself well satisfied and recommended me for a full training course. I was ecstatic. And only a little puzzled that he'd never sent me solo ...

The next move was to Heaton Park, in Manchester, to await a passage to the United States, where I was to do my flying course. I waited here until late January 1942, when my contingent was entrained to the Clyde to board *RMS Ausonia*, a former Cunarder which had been converted into an armed merchantman but doubled as a troopship. On this occasion it did not wait for a convoy but set off at top speed with a lone Polish destroyer as escort.

To say that we were relieved when we arrived at Halifax, Nova Scotia, on 4 February, probably says all that needs be said about the crossing. But I can still visualise clutching the rail – anything to avoid the stench of vomit below – and seeing our destroyer escort literally disappearing between mountainous waves for minutes at a time. On disembarking, to stumble aboard a train for the day-long journey to Royal Canadian Air Force Monckton, a holding camp, was like a gift.

As was the food, once we'd regained our land legs. For after over two years of austerity and rationing at home we found ourselves feasting upon such delicacies as snow-white bread, and honey, and in unlimited quantities.

They held us at Monckton for some three weeks, occupying us with drilling and with lectures, though our sights were set on the next stage, which turned out to be a three-day, two-night train journey to the south-eastern American state of Georgia. And specifically, to Turner Field, located in the south-west of that state.

We found that we were to be taught, in the main, by civilian instructors, at what were essentially, commercial flying establishments. And I say, in the main, to take account of a Pilot Officer Parry who, just months before had been a cadet like us but on gaining his wings had been asked to stay on as an instructor.

One of the first things they did was to kit us out in light khaki drill, the weather being unfailingly hot and dry. For that, of course, was the big advantage of doing our training overseas, the settled good-weather conditions affording us the continuity so important in learning to fly: good weather, and back then, not having to worry about enemy intruders, or straying into the trigger-happy ack-ack guns and balloon barrages of Britain's defences.

We began our flight training on Boeing PT-17 Stearman biplanes not too unlike the Tiger Moth, except for their 220 horsepower Continental engines. I suppose this was to settle us in, for a month later we moved across the state line to Lakeland Field, Florida, where on 18 April 1942 I finally did my first solo.

On 2 June we moved back to Georgia, to mid-state Cochran Field, where we flew the BT-13A Vultee Valiant, a low-winged, fixed-undercarriage monoplane with a continuous canopy beneath which pupil and instructor sat in tandem, and a 280 horsepower engine. Though essentially a basic trainer it had enough blind-flying instruments to introduce the pupil to bad-weather operation.

**BT-13 Vultee Valiant**

Early August 1942 saw us flying a variety of types at Moody Field (Lake Park Field), Valdosta. First, there was the North American AT-6 Texan, which we knew as the Harvard, similar to the Valiant but with flaps and retractable undercarriage and a 650 horsepower Pratt & Whitney Wasp engine. Then there was the Beechcraft AT-10, twin-engined, with two 375 horsepower Lycomings, and two other twins, the AT-9 Curtiss, and the Cessna AT-17 Bobcat, both having two 650 horsepower engines, the Curtiss being quite difficult to fly.

The instructors really knew their stuff, part-wise-cracking, part-dead-panning us through the syllabus. I recall quite late on when I was probably getting a bit too confident, and we got airborne in a Beechcraft. The take-off into wind, with both engines pulling evenly, gave no problem. On attempting to turn after getting airborne, however, the ailerons failed to answer. In the course of panicking I suddenly realised that by slapdash pre-take-off checks I'd forgotten to remove the locking pin. Surreptitiously reaching down and doing so, I found myself with instant full control, and breathed a heartfelt sigh. It was good to get away with something, and more especially, to do so under the eagle eye of the instructor.

Then the slow drawl sounded in my ears, 'You won't do that again, will you ...'

In time, we flew through the gamut of straight and level, medium turns, stalls, spins, circuits and landings, forced landings, steep turns, loops, barrel rolls, slow rolls, and stall turns. We also practised manoeuvres less familiar to the RAF, chandelles, pylon eights, lazy eights, and flick rolls.

In fact, these were more procedural exercises than aerobatics. The chandelle, for instance, required you to fly level at a given speed, begin a roll into a medium rate turn, then pull up, increasing and decreasing power, pitch, and angle of bank as called for in order to level out flying in the opposite direction but on the very brink of the stall. It was, in fact, a stylised version of the First World War air-combat reverse-turn tactic.

Pylons were, essentially, a pair of masts on the ground around which one flew a figure of eight, varying the bank angle depending upon the wind. Again, the simple figure of eight was stylised, so that in one variation the pylons had to remain fixed as seen from the cockpit.

The lazy eight was rather akin to pulling up as if for a loop, but winging over into a dive, then repeating the evolution in the other direction; flick rolls, in contrast, called for a horizontal incipient spin – initiated by pulling hard against a bootful of rudder, then checking before auto-rotation (a spin) could develop. All were probably far easier to do than to describe, and all were fun. Except that they had to be done precisely.

Another thing strange to RAF eyes is that flights were timed to the minute, so that instead of being rounded up – thirty minutes, forty-five minutes – log-book entries recording American flights read, thirty-two minutes, forty-seven minutes, and so forth.

We gradually moved on to more advanced flying, to lengthy cross-countries, to night flying, and to a surprising amount of instrument flying. Indeed, although it never occurred then, the fact that our course were introduced to twin-engined types – and therefore to asymmetric flight: flying on one engine – and did quite so much flying blind on instruments, suggests that we must have been earmarked for the new heavy bombers the RAF was so desperate to get crews for.

They worked us hard. But they also gave us time off. And as the locals made much of us, and as we liked them, we seemed set to have a pleasant stay. We were young, of course, and getting all geared up to go to war, so we'd been warned – as representatives of Britain – not to engage in any form of 'hanky panky'. Fate, however, had its own agenda.

Some months earlier, back at Cochran Field, I'd decided to spend some off-duty time visiting a region called Heaven Sent, in the Tallulah Gorge State Park. I'd only gone a short way, though, when a car stopped and offered me a lift. To shorten an account which pains me so deeply still, let me just say that the driver was the most beautiful girl. Her name was Marise, and she was as lovely as her name. Her family, just like mine, farmed, so we had a common bond from the start. And from the start we got on well together. But, all too soon my group received notice to move to Moody Field. And so, remembering that, by British standards, Georgia is vast, Marise and I were forced to part. Not that we were too devastated, for there would be extended weekend passes, and end-of-course leave, and we were young ...

At Moody Field time had sped by as we'd flown the Cessna and Beechcraft twins, and the Harvard which, unwieldy as it may have looked flew beautifully, handling like a baby. Only out of the blue I received a telegram from Marise's family to say that she had unaccountably fallen desperately ill. I was concerned, but hopeful, for we had so many years before us. Only to have my world knocked askew when a second telegram advised me that she had died. Further, that the funeral – as is the custom there – was that very afternoon, and to be conducted so far away that I hadn't a hope of attending.

To say that I was devastated does not begin to meet the case. But the course progressed, and on 9 October 1943 I received my silver, American-pattern wings. I also received an offer that would have delighted me had Marise still been alive, that of staying on as an instructor. In the circumstances, however, I could not stomach the thought of being in America without her. And so I opted for taking the – for me – drear and desolate road via Monckton, New York, and Liverpool to No. 7 Personnel Reception Centre at Harrogate, where I was allotted a spell of not-that-welcome leave.

*Silver American pilot's wings, against a c.1934 Fox Moth*

On 15 December 1943, I resumed training, reporting to No. 6 (Pilots) Advanced Flying Course at RAF Little Rissington, in Gloucestershire, to fly the twin-engined Airspeed Oxford. Not the most inspiring of advanced trainers, and being British built, one in which I had to get used to pushing the throttles forward for more speed rather then pulling them back, as on American aircraft.

I was also beginning to learn to fly with other crew members, a navigator, certainly and a wireless operator. Equally importantly I was learning to contend with European flying conditions; not only an urban sprawl unlike anything we'd met in the States but also abysmal weather. It was as well then that I was sent to spend time with Little Rissington's lodger unit, No. 1523 Blind Approach Training Flight, where I gained experience in using low-visibility approach-to-landing aids.

Even so, having been sent solo to collect a new aircraft, I was dismayed to find low cloud blotting out the ground below me. Further, only then did I realise that a radio had yet to be installed. Eyeing the fuel, which was not overgenerous for what was supposed to be a short ferry, I could see only two courses of action. The first was to let down blind and hope to be well above the ground when I broke cloud: though even with my limited experience I regarded this as a non starter. The other was to resort to my parachute and bale out; and this I did not relish. Only just at that moment something decreed that another aircraft should float before me, and one, moreover, that seemed to know where it was going. Hurriedly closing into loose formation, therefore, I descended in its wake, to find myself at RAF Madeley, near Hereford. And the 'something' that had done the so-timely decreeing? Fate again, could it be?

All in all it was a posting which concentrated the mind. Possibly, too, one that to some degree helped moderate the grief.

*Sergeant Pilot Nevil Mottershead, 1943*

The next move was to No. 15 Operational Training Unit (OTU), first at RAF Harwell, in Oxfordshire, then at RAF Hampstead Norris, near Reading, to learn to operate the Vickers Wellington. I have to say, however, that while 'The Wimpy' was revered by many, I never liked it, not the way its fuselage twisted nor the way its wings flapped. Mind you, I must concede that these particular machines had done sterling service. Only rather too much of it, so that the airframes were weary and the engines so overworked that Unit Flying Orders forbade putting them to the stress of overshooting: that is, of piling on the power to go round again after a misjudged approach ...

On 17 May 1943 we finally began to see the end of the training road when we progressed to No. 1658 Conversion Unit, at RAF Riccall, near

Selby, in Yorkshire, to fly the aircraft we were to take to war, the Handley Page Halifax. Perhaps I should put it on record that, from the outset, the 'Halibag' suited me just fine. It was comfortable, and if some thought it a beast, it was a powerful beast. There was another four-engined heavy called the Lancaster, but whereas that could drop bombs, and on occasion carry a passenger or two, the Halifax could do virtually anything that was asked of it: supply dropping, para-dropping, trooping, covert and clandestine operations, maritime patrols, anything …

While on Wellingtons, along with my navigator and wireless operator/ air gunner, I'd picked up a straight air gunner or two, but now I required a bomb aimer and a flight engineer, so that as we settled into working together, and progressed to exercises each of which more nearly mirrored an actual operational sortie, my all-sergeant crew comprised:

Herbert Nevil (Bluey) Mottershead, pilot
Dennis Austin (Di) Jones, navigator
Alan March (Glen) Glendinning, air bomber
Donald (Don) Sidney Hawkes, flight engineer
Charles (Chick) McKinnon, wireless operator/air gunner
Thomas (Tommy) William Edwards, air gunner (mid-upper)
And for rear gunner I shall nominate:
William (Bill) George Martin, air gunner (rear turret)

I say I nominate Bill because, in one way or another I was to fly with fifteen different air gunners during my tour of ops. None died, or was physically injured in action, but Bill was killed in a bizarre accident when the flight commander borrowed my crew for an op. Somehow, while still at dispersal, the wing co put on power, and swung forwards, not realising that Bill was out of the turret, and in the path of the tailwheel …

A prime purpose of OTU was to have crews gell together, for the time was fast approaching when each man would have to rely implicitly upon the next. In our case the degree to which we'd gelled was demonstrated when

I took everyone roaring down the runway, only to realise that nothing was registering on the airspeed indicator. I knew at once that I'd forgotten to take the cover off the tube that fed air to the instrument!

It was too late to stop, so I had to get airborne, after which, with the aid of flight engineer Don, I felt my way around the circuit, keeping the speed up with more than the normal application of power, and even more on the final approach. I was particularly careful to come in fast, anything to avoid a stall, but I must have come in very fast indeed, for I bounced hard, then slowed only gradually, and in a series of lowering hops all the way down the runway.

Turning clear at the end – I'd long since confessed, and we'd had a hurried crew discussion – I halted the aircraft side-on to the control tower, and Don and one of the gunners got out. With one standing on the other's shoulders they had just managed to pull off the offending cover and turn back towards the aircraft, when the wing commander drove up.

'I should think you *would* have your flight eng check the undercarriage,' he fumed, 'after an abysmal arrival like that ...'

On 29 May 1943, towards the end of the conversion course, I flew as supernumerary to another captain on an operation to Wuppertal, standing at his shoulder for four and a half hours while greedily gathering impressions of the way things were done. And on 15 June, now operations-ready, the seven of us joined No. 158 Squadron, then stationed at RAF Lissett, near Bridlington, in Yorkshire.

As a settler, we flew a 'Bullseye' sortie, flying out towards the enemy coast to create a bit of a distraction for a real raid coasting out elsewhere. Before that, though, now fully checked out as an aircraft captain, and having been recommended from the start, I was commissioned. There was no course, I was merely given a voucher for the nearest Austin Read, or whichever, got myself fitted with a smoothy uniform, then carried on as before. Nor was there a problem with the crew. I remained 'Bluey' in the air and off duty, and became 'Sir' whenever Service etiquette demanded. For in wartime, certainly, aircrew interaction was nearly always seamless. So that, later, during a period when losses were particularly heavy, Flight Sergeant Dave Lister – due to be commissioned anyway – was the only captain left to act as flight commander, so in an instant translation, he became a temporary squadron leader.

A rather weird bit of fatefulness associated itself with my own promotion, for late on in our tour, when I had months since left the crew billet for the officers' mess, my crew, reluctantly drawn, told me that every subsequent incumbent of my former bedspace had failed to return from ops ...

Mention of losses brings the reflection that operational fliers grow used to being asked what ops were like. Which invariably means, how could you stand it, facing those odds, night after night, especially as, by virtue of your calling, you were numerately literate, and when the empty spaces were there to be counted in the mess ... We normally plead our youth, the innate belief that 'it won't happen to me', and that we were too busy to be over-concerned. I have to say, however, that although ops had commonalities, each was different, and each man saw them with different eyes.

To exemplify this, our first op as a crew, on 21 June 1943, was to Krefeld. Having already done an op as a supernumerary I was able to record that the searchlight defences were only weak, but that the flak was moderate. As indeed it was. Certainly it holed us, though not seriously. That said, most of us seemed happy enough as we powered away from the target in a shallow dive, very much on the qui vive for fighters, but otherwise with a sense of relief now that our first op as a crew was behind us.

For the rear gunner, however, it was the target that was behind him. So for the best part of fifty miles his scan for night-fighters took in not only the conflagration on the ground, the searchlights periodically snapping together in a deadly cone, and the flak bursts, but also the prolonged and red-cored flaring as stricken bombers spiralled down to earth. As the rest of us left de-briefing for the mess, and breakfast, he held back. 'No, Bluey,' he told me, 'ops aren't for me.' And that was the last we saw of him.

Losses now became an integral part of our lives. All we could do was try to employ the lessons we had learnt from our increasing number of ops. Just as I had flown as a supernumerary, so another new captain flew with us. Indeed, he accompanied us twice. He then captained his own crew, and was shot down on their first op. All you could do was try to hone your own operation.

Bill Bolam, for example, took a brand-new Halifax to Hamburg, but due to what could only have been a navigational error was a full fifty miles from the protection of the bomber stream when night-fighters got him. And Ken Larkan, en route to raid Essen, suffered a malfunction as he crossed the Dutch Coast such that nobody would have criticised him for turning back. Instead, he and his crew decided to press on, and having fallen behind the stream, were similarly singled out by fighters, only the rear gunner surviving.

Yet had the flak that holed us on our first crew op over Krefeld been an inch one way or the other, all the expertise in the world wouldn't have saved us. As for night-fighters, it happened that, for all that we saw them on most ops, and although over Berlin I stared down at another Halifax being chased by one, we were never actually attacked, nor did any of our gunners have cause to open fire. And that, should I say, was just how we wanted it, for once let fly with tracers and every fighter within miles would know where you were.

Not expertise, then, but just luck? Or Fate, perhaps?

There were also losses of a different sort. As on 2 July 1943 when a thousand-pounder bomb exploded as it was being loaded onto a trolley, killing six airmen. A seventh, Aircraftman David Owen, dragged one dying man out of the flames, then drove three laden bomb trolleys clear. He was awarded the George Cross for his bravery. And a very well deserved decoration. But then how often non-fliers deserved awards, and how seldom they got them!

I have to confess that, throughout that mix of tragedy and heroism, having just returned from ops, I slept an undisturbed sleep.

Once embarked upon our ops tour in mid June 1943, we were regularly employed until April 1944. Many of our tasks were located in Germany's industrial Ruhr. So, we raided the synthetic oil plant at Gelsenkirchen (I recorded, 'heavy barrage hit several times'), the chemical plant at Leverkusen, the Krupps conglomerations at Essen, steel plants at Mulheim ('predicted high flak at 20,000 feet') and the U-boat accumulator factory at Cologne.

Early on, raiding Wuppertal, I recorded, 'hundreds of searchlights, we were coned for thirty seconds, fighters very active'; and that Mannheim had been 'a good prang'. We also visited, and revisited on occasion, Aachen, Hamburg ('a poor trip, many electrical storms, 10/10 – total – cloud over target'), Nuremburg, Kassel ('coned on the run in, a good prang'), and Berlin ('Flares dropped by a plane to light up our aircraft' – undoubtedly a night-fighter flare, but there was no attack). We raided too Montbéliard, Montluçon (the Dunlop tyre plant) and Cannes (a rail target, 'bright moonlight, a good prang'), and flying further afield, industrial sites in Milan.

Having visited a target, of course, we rarely got the full picture, although I believe Command did their best to be honest with us. When we raided the Peugeot works at Montbéliard, bombing at just 5,000 feet in a clear sky with only light flak and none over the actual target, we knew we'd done our job, but only after the war would we learn that while some thirty bombs had hit the factory, by far the majority had been dropped short, on the town.

On 17 August 1943, however, we took part in what was always held to be not only a successful but a particularly significant raid, this one on the V1 Flying Bomb and V2 Rocket development site on Peenemunde with a total of 596 aircraft taking part, including 218 Halifaxes. A moonlight night was deliberately chosen, and there were three very specific targets: the living quarters for the technical workers and scientists; the experimental site; and the works. Then, to ensure maximum effectiveness, the Pathfinders moved the markers from target to target as the raid progressed.

A diversionary attack had drawn off most of the enemy fighters, but they returned as the third and final wave bombed, some using for the first time their upward-firing cannon. We probably knew, therefore, that forty aircraft, including fifteen Halifaxes had been lost, 6.7% of the force. But only very much later would we discover that a hastily-corrected marking error had led to a labour camp being bombed, with many Polish casualties. Overall, however, the planners would have been heartened to learn that German sources held the raid to have put back the V2 Rocket operation – and therefore the deluge planned for London – for a good two months.

*A section of No. 158 Squadron's Battle Order for Peenemunde,*
*17 August 1943*

As our tour progressed, and my experience level grew, my logbook reflects how much more critical I became. On our twenty-sixth op, to Leverkusen, for example, I recorded, '10/10 cloud at 12,000 ft over target, PFF boobed, only four green TIs seen.' However, awry as things had been, we'd had no option but to trust that the few target indicators (TIs) dropped by Pathfinder Force and still evident when we reached the release point were accurate.

Even so, by this stage of our tour I had long changed from celebrating 'good prang', to recording instead, 'no damage' (sustained by us, that is). And perhaps with good reason.

For on our twenty-second op, raiding Mannheim, just as we were on our bombing run, an incendiary dropped by an aircraft above us fell on our port-inner engine and exploded, wrecking the motor and showering us with debris. Fortunately we were able to feather the propeller, but even with the bombs gone I was unable to maintain height. Indeed, the aircraft did not stabilise until we reached 5,000 feet, and even then we could only make a 140 mph cruise, rather than something above 220 mph. It had been a long, fraught way home, badly damaged, in hostile skies, and alone.

Perhaps that, coming on top of the cumulative stress, had taken more out of us than we realised, and perhaps the CO had begun watching us because of it. At that time the 'standard tour' of thirty ops was still not fully established, and the decision regarding when a crew had done enough was very much in the hands of the commanding officer. So it was that when we returned from our twenty-seventh op, a quite harrowing trip to Berlin, he met us at de-briefing. 'That's enough for your lads, Bluey. Many thanks. As of now you're stood down from ops.'

And so we stood down. To date I'd flown a total of 635 hours, been promoted to flight lieutenant, and been awarded the Distinguished Flying Cross. Our expectation was that we'd be rested for three months or so, probably instructing somewhere, and then be called back for an obligatory – but final – second tour. As it happened, this was not what postings – or good old Fate – had in store for me, and in fact, my operational flying days were over. But though I might have thought so as I cleared from Lissett, it was to be far from my last association with No. 158 Squadron.

*No. 158 Squadron personnel with Halifax Mk.3 LV907 F-Freddy,*
*or* **Friday the 13ᵗʰ**. *After my time, this aircraft flew 128 operational*
*sorties, and is commemorated by a replica in Yorkshire Air Museum*

As I say, I might well have been posted to an OTU to instruct raw crews, and then been called back for a second tour ... But that is to speculate. For on 15 April 1944 I was required to report to No. 8 Group (Pathfinder Force) Headquarters at Castle Hill House in Huntingdon.

No. 8 Group had been especially set up to control the specialist squadrons whose operations had given potency to the relatively ineffectual bombing tactics of the early war years. The electronic aids which underpinned this advance had virtually all been developed by the Telecommunications Research Establishment (TRE) which was currently at Malvern. My new job, as I learnt in the course of a day's briefing, was to become a controller of one of the paired stations of the Oboe blind-bombing system, itself a major fruit of TRE's boffins. To learn my new trade I was sent for three weeks to the Worth Matravers Oboe station on the Dorset cliffs near Swanage, visiting between times an associated station, 'Tilly Whim', at Durlston.

My job would be to supervise the team of airmen and WAAFs who actually operated the system, from the radio (wireless/radar) mechanics, through all the communications staff, to the plotters who, like fighter controllers, gave me and my assistants a visual picture of what was happening on a table map. To do this, it was necessary that I had a good grasp of how the system worked.

Getting this grasp was helped by simplifying the system. One started, therefore, by imagining the very narrowest of radio beams being sent from a controlling station (the Cat station) to pass over a target which, as with a Ruhr factory, might be up to 300 miles distant. Such was the accuracy with which the beam was directed, and so narrow was it, that a Mosquito flying along it at 30,000 feet would pass over the target with a lateral error of just fifty-two feet.

The system then told the Mosquito when to release its bombs to hit the target. To do this it utilised a second station (the Mouse, or Releasing, station) which sent its own beam to cross the Cat station's at the bomb-release point. On reaching this coincidence of beams the Mosquito would release its bombs. And this at night and regardless of there being ten-tenths cloud cover over the target.

That amount of detail would have satisfied me. Though I knew full well there were no beams as such, only radar pulses sent from both Cat and Mouse stations and automatically returned from a black box in the aircraft known as a transponder.

In fact, the way the system worked was that when Group advised of the night's objective a 'master range marker' would be set up on both the Cat and the Mouse radars corresponding to the precise distance to the target. A team at the Mouse station would then feed a device called 'Micetro' with the relevant parameters required to release a bomb at 30,000 feet from a Mosquito doing perhaps 250 mph, the bomb curving forwards and downwards through possibly changing winds and temperatures, to hit the target.

The operating procedure, again, in essence, was for the Mosquito to navigate to within fifty miles or so of the target, fifty miles equating to some ten minutes' flying time. This fifty-mile point was regarded by all three agencies – Cat, Mouse, and aircraft – as the start point for the controlled run. By then the aerials at both ground stations would have been tuned to show the Mosquito as a blip on their screens, leaving the electronics to compare the changing relationship between blip and master range marker.

Approaching the start point the pilot would have picked up the radar pulses from the Cat station in his headset. If the electronics showed that he was to the left of the master range marker, he would hear morse dashes; to the right, morse dots. However, once he was aligned with the master range marker he would hear the note that had been likened to that of an Oboe. That the track to be followed – 'not as wide as a Mosquito', even at 300 miles – was the arc of a great circle is academic, for all he had to do was pressure his rudder to stay within the 'oboe' howl.

The Mouse station, meanwhile, was transmitting pulses which were received by the Mosquito's navigator. These counted down to the release point, culminating in five morse dots and a long dash, the end of which was the executive signal. The navigator (with bomb doors already open) would press the release button and the bombs would fall away. Pressing the bomb release would also break the link, so permitting Cat and Mouse to turn to controlling the next Pathfinder in the train: the system was capable of controlling three aircraft an hour, though two was a more normal figure.

It was all very clever, and what is more, it worked. And while understandably noncommittal to a life outside ops, I could see that this was a very worthy field. Pointless, after all, continuing to send out all those aircraft, carrying all those bombs, and risking that many aircrew, if the force could neither find the target nor hit it if they did find it.

On 9 May 1943 I reported to RAF Winterton on the North Lincolnshire coast, near Great Yarmouth, to begin my life as an Oboe, Cat-station controller. Five months later, I switched to our Mouse station at Hawkshill Down, near Deal, in Kent. Although, while that is how we used them during my time, either could have acted as Cat or Mouse.

I served there for the rest of the war, leaving for Castle Hill House, and headquarters, in mid August 1945 where I remained until late December

1946. And on 1 January 1946, I reported to RAF Elstree, finishing my service on 12 February 1946.

I must retrace my steps, however, to the most significant occurrence in my life, back to relatively early days at Winterton. With the growth of the unit, the RAF had taken over many of the beach chalets. One of these now housed the teleprinters used to maintain communication with, not only No. 8 Group and our Mouse station at Deal, but with all the other units we needed to contact. Entering on this particular day, I was immediately bowled over by a WAAF busily clicking away at her keyboard. Her name, I was to discover, was Kaye. Utterly bemused, I uttered the first words that came to my tongue. 'You're wearing too much make-up.' Hardly an approach to be recommended. But one that, to date, has led to sixty-eight happy years of companionship and marriage.

A major interest in my life since those days has been promoting the No. 158 Squadron Association, ably supported in later years by my daughter, Alison, who, besides acting as secretary and accountant, has expended an enormous amount of effort in collating records. I would say that it is not a little due to Alison's good offices that in 2012 Her Majesty saw fit to confer upon me the honour of Member of the British Empire. An honour to add additional lustre to a squadron, No. 158, whose number, reversed to read 851, reflects the number of personnel killed in the service of the nation: 850 airmen, and Sergeant Olive Morse, a WAAF meteorological observer who was killed while passengering on a training flight.

Following the war it was as if that nation had cast aside Bomber Command, along with all its squadrons and all its personnel, not least its dead. Nor does the 2013 award of a paltry Bomber Command clasp – as opposed to a medal – assuage the slight. But a squadron with such an illustrious record as No. 158's can weather such pettiness. After all, when it was needed, in the hostile night-time skies over Germany, it weathered far worse.

*No. 158 Squadron Memorial, Lissett, 2009*

*Awards*

*Squadron Leader Nevil Mottershead, MBE, DFC, 2013*

**Warrant Officer Ted Cachart, wireless operator/air gunner**

On 28 April 1943, despite never having fired a shot from the air, I sewed up an Air Gunner's brevet on my left breast. More, I was now a sergeant. And more still, the youngest ever wireless operator/air gunner in the RAF!

*Aircraftman Class Two Ted Cachart, RAF Warmwell, 1942,*
*aged seventeen*

I was born in June 1925 at Gorlston-On-Sea, in Norfolk, but grew up in North London. In 1938, having won a scholarship, I began to train as a chef at the prestigious Westminster Hotel and Catering College. After a year, however, when the building was requisitioned as an emergency hospital, I began to ponder the inevitable conscription. Cautionary tales from two soldier brothers put me off the army. The Royal Air Force's glamorous posters, on the other hand, were persuasively attractive. In the interim I served as a fire-watcher and runner for the Air Raid Precautions Service, and equipped with whistle and steel helmet, and a segment of motor tyre to protect my shoulders from falling shrapnel, patrolled the pre-dawn streets for incendiary bombs.

Enquiries showed that although I could escape army call up by volunteering to fly, I had to be at least seventeen and a quarter, even with parental permission. In March 1941, therefore, driven by an emergent bent towards self-reliance, I used a laddishy vague approach to persuade both dad and our priest to sign and witness the official forms. Having then declared my date of birth as 1923 – as opposed to 1925 –, I began the application procedure.

Just weeks later Dad was surprised, but pleased, when I told him that a preliminary selection board – as I termed it – had found me suitable to train as a wireless operator/air gunner. In fact, on 13 May 1941, a month before my sixteenth birthday, I was attested into the RAF.

While waiting to be summoned I joined the Air Training Corps and made a start on drill, aircraft recognition, and the morse code, achieving a sending, and more taxingly, a receiving speed of four words a minute. Naturally, the arrival of my papers in September 1941 called for some earnest wheedling, but dear old dad let things stand, and I duly reported to No. 5 Personnel Dispersal Centre at RAF Padgate near Warrington. Here, aspirant aircrew were kitted out, jabbed, re-examined medically, drilled, and generally run about before being packed off to No. 9 Recruit Centre at Blackpool, where training proper began.

During our three month seaside stay we were accommodated in the profusion of boarding houses that had drawn the RAF to this location, drilled on the promenades, and marched, in threes – as opposed to the recently abandoned, but time-hallowed, fours – to various venues for technical training. Add on youth, fresh sea air, and daily physical training in Stanley Park, and it is hardly surprising that my abiding memory of Blackpool is of constantly being hungry.

As we were destined to be wireless operator/air gunners, morse code loomed large, with lessons in Blackpool's draughty, and totally unheated, tramsheds, and periodical tests in the ballroom above the Burton Tailors, the goal being to work at twenty-two words a minute. Greatcoats did nothing for our feet, which got steadily chillier, while keying dits and dohs precluded gloves, so that our fingers froze. Notwithstanding which we duly passed a progress test at twelve words a minute and were rewarded with seven days' leave.

I can tell you it was a very proud Ted-the-Lad who walked indoors resplendent in RAF uniform with shouldered kitbag and wearing the distinctive trainee-aircrew white flash in his side-cap. But one who was to become acquainted only moments later with the invariable formula, 'When do you go back?' Never, ever, 'How long have you got?'

With leave over I reported to No. 2 Radio School at RAF Yatesbury, in Wiltshire. This was a massive, wooded-hutted encampment, made memorable by the ablutions having only cold to tepid water and meal queues so long that laddie-lads like me could join early, scoff at leisure, then re-join for seconds.

In hutted classrooms we studied wireless theory and learnt to operate the by-then venerable airborne transmitter-receiver T1182/R1183, which required coils to be swapped for every frequency change. At the same time we plugged away at morse, not least mentally transcribing any notices we saw, until in March 1942 we finally met the required standard: twenty-two words a minute when sending and receiving plain language, and twenty-five handling five-symbol groups. The achievement entitled us to wear wireless operators' sleeve badges: a hand grasping lightning darts. It also meant an increase in pay from two and six a day to four shillings (12.5p to 20p!).

At this juncture we should have started our flying training, except that one of the system's bottlenecks intervened and we were dispersed to 'make ourselves useful'. While many found themselves used as dogsbodies, I fell on my feet by being attached to No. 1497 (Target Towing) Flight at RAF Warmwell, in Dorset.

The flight used Westland Lysanders to drag tubular canvas sleeves – drogues – as air-firing targets, the tug flying level above the nearby Chesil Bank, a singular spit of gravel running for 18 miles south-eastwards from West Bay to the Isle of Portland. Spitfires and Hurricanes would run in and let fly, each aircraft's bullets being treated with a wax coating to leave a distinguishing colour. The used target would then be dropped to a ground party who recorded the colour and number of the holes, if any. And I add the caveat, 'if any', advisedly, for such scores as two and three percent were deemed wholly satisfactory!

Although nominally assigned to the wireless section, I attracted the attention of a madcap Polish fighter pilot on a rest tour. Discovering that my white side-cap flash denoted a flier he declared, 'When I fly, you fly.'

Next morning, accordingly, he took me up in one of the unit's nippy – 226 mph – Miles Masters and threw it all over the place, finishing by skimming the length of Chesil Beach. After landing I have to admit that I brought up my breakfast. But I was hooked. Using laddish guile again, I had a drogue operator check me out, after which I flew, and he collected the few pence a day flight pay, so that on being recalled I had amassed fifty hours in the air.

The flying was always potentially hairy, but one day two of us were simply strolling by the fuel store when a tanker burst into flames, engulfing the driver. We grabbed fire extinguishers, jumped onto the store's sloping roof, and played foam on him until he was pulled free. He recovered, and we were duly praised. Though when the fire crew showed us how close the store had been to going up beneath our feet we sobered somewhat. But only somewhat, for at seventeen one thrived on Boy's-Own-Paper stuff.

The backlog cleared, only our expectations of finally starting flying training were dashed when we were sent to London for a three-month course centred on the new Marconi transmitter-receiver, the T1154/R1155. This was not only a lot more powerful than its predecessor but far easier to use, all the frequency changing being done by yellow, red, and blue controls. Additionally, frequencies could be pre-set – or click-stopped, as we said –, allowing stations to be found by touch, even in the dark.

*Albert Court, Knightsbridge*

Our accommodation, Albert Court, in Knightsbridge, behind the Albert Hall, was nothing less than splendiferous. Notwithstanding which, discontent blossomed, in retaliation for which our late passes were restricted to 2230 hours (half ten at night) instead of midnight (or 2359 hours, as the Service has it). And so our mutinous mutterings escalated. Before long, however, we were assembled before a flight-sergeant. Helped up onto the top of a telephone box, of all things, he wasted few words.

'You want to get into the war. And you think you're old sweats. But I know the ropes better than the lot of you. So, if you want get off something, then find an excuse and see me for a haircut chit. If you're late back off pass, then don't get caught.'

The 2230 hours restriction was removed. And harmony, together with good order and discipline, was restored.

We finally moved on in January 1943, reporting to No. 4 Radio School at RAF Madley, near Hereford, where we practised sending and receiving from twin-engined de Havilland Domine biplanes and single-engined Percival Proctors. After that it was off to No. 1 (Observer) Advanced Flying Unit, at RAF Wigtown, near Dumfries, where we put the final polish on our airborne operating skills in Avro Ansons.

On finishing there, we became aircrew wireless operators. But the WOp/AG had the dual role of air gunner, so in April 1943 we progressed to No. 7 Air Gunnery School at RAF Stormy Down, in North Wales, where we studied aircraft recognition, blasted off at clay pigeons with shotguns, and became thoroughly familiar with the Browning 0.303 inch calibre machine gun. Next, taking turns at a rigged-up turret mounting two Brownings, each of us fired 200 rounds at a model aeroplane running on a circular track.

I can only presume that wireless-operator casualties had caused a shortage, for on 28 April 1943, despite never having fired a shot from the air, I sewed up an Air Gunner's brevet on my left breast: a half-wing bearing the letters 'AG' (wireless operator/air gunners were distinguished from common or garden AGs, of course, by the signals flashes on our sleeves). More, I was now a sergeant. And more still, the youngest ever WOp/AG in the RAF!

*Sergeant Ted Cachart, wireless operator/air gunner, 1943, aged seventeen*

Before moving to the penultimate training stage, we were granted another leave, when I was dismayed to see the perturbation with which both mum and dad eyed the brevet I was so proud of: there and then I resolved not to tell them when I began to fly on ops.

With leave over, I reported to RAF Hixon, Staffordshire, then hosting Bomber Command's No. 30 Operational Training Unit (OTU). Hixon still had the ageing, twin-engined Vickers Wellington, which called for a five-man crew (at Hixon, that is, it varied at other OTUs). Accordingly, all course members were herded into a hangar, and directed to mingle. Within minutes I was approached by a pilot and a navigator, both Canadians, after which the three of us picked out a bomb aimer and a rear gunner, the crew, as formed, comprising:

Flying Officer John (Johnny) Young, Royal Canadian Air Force (RCAF), pilot

Flying Officer Jack Scott (Scotty), RCAF, navigator,

Sergeant (to become Pilot Officer) Les Orchard, RAF, bomb aimer,

Sergeant Ted Cachart, RAF, wireless operator/air gunner

Sergeant Len Crossman, RAF, air gunner (Len manned our rear turret).

The three-month OTU course was designed to meld us from five individuals into a team, starting with circuits and bumps to get Johnny's eye in, then progressing to more and more ambitious navigational exercises during which each crew member honed his own speciality.

That flying was chancy by its very nature was brought home to me one night when a Wellington overshot the 'drome, crashed nearby, and began to burn. Two of us ran to give assistance, only to confront an inferno. Dolefully, with heat-exploded bullets whistling about us, we turned away – to discover the crew whooping it up in the night-flying canteen. On impact they had scrambled out on the far side from us and made off into the darkness.

We completed the OTU course on 17 August 1943, by which time I had logged some 200 flying hours, and celebrated my eighteenth birthday. A month later we began the final training stage, reporting to No. 1660 Heavy Conversion Unit at RAF Swinderby, near Newark, to learn to operate four-engined heavies. To do so our crew had to be supplemented by a flight engineer, Flight Sergeant Alan Vidow (RAF), and another gunner for the mid-upper turret. Best, however, to omit the latter's name.

After two trips on the Handley Page Halifax, during which Johnny and Alan familiarised themselves with four-, three-, and two-engined handling, we flew fourteen details on the 'Dream Machine': the Avro Lancaster. It was 20 September 1943 when I first got airborne in her, and as those four so-singular-sounding engines throbbed through my fibres, so I fell in love. As I remain, to this day.

**Left to right:** *Flying Officer Jack Scott (Scotty), Royal Canadian Air Force (RCAF), navigator (half-obscured); Flying Officer John (Johnny) Young, RCAF, pilot; Sergeant (to become Pilot Officer) Les Orchard, RAF, bomb aimer; Flight Sergeant Alan Vidow, RAF, flight engineer; Sergeant Ted Cachart, RAF, wireless operator/air gunner; Sergeant Alan 'Spud' Mahony, Royal Australian Air Force, air gunner (mid-upper); Sergeant Len Crossman, RAF, air gunner (rear turret).*

We flew thirty hours on that course, and on 13 October 1943, reported to RAF Fiskerton, just east of Lincoln, to join No. 49 Squadron, a first-line bomber squadron in No. 5 Group. Or as I would put it, the foremost squadron in the whole of Bomber Command.

To settle us in we were set to flight testing the Lancasters scheduled for the night's operations. We also flew various navigational exercises, and some radar-training sorties. Finally, Johnny flew on an operation as a supernumerary, observing another crew. But even when our own crew was cleared as fit for ops, bad weather intervened. It was not until 2 November 1943, therefore, that we appeared on the Order of Battle.

By then we'd seen No. 49 take part in four major raids, on Modane, Hanover, Kassel, and Leipzig. We had also seen them take losses. Losses which had suddenly ceased being BBC statistics, and become personal. On the other hand we were young, and all holding the same inner assurance: it won't happen to me.

Even so, the day of our first op saw us going about in a rarefied state of mind. We carried out our own night-flying test, handed the aircraft to our groundcrew as satisfactory, then tried to get some rest. For my part I got very little, tossing fitfully until it was time for the pre-op meal. After that came the various specialist briefings, signals for me, followed by a main briefing for all crew members.

We heard that the weather was reasonable, and were told about fuel and bomb loads. Pilots and navs made notes of the heights and speeds at which to fly, and the courses. We learnt too that the target was Düsseldorf, in the Ruhr – 'Happy Valley', to the initiates. And on emerging, now bundled in flying kit, we were driven out to the dispersals.

'U-Uncle,' our WAAF driver announced. 'Don't be late back, boys.' Her name, we knew, was Dot Everette.

Nerves settled somewhat as we concentrated on our on-board preparations, tensing again as Johnny carried a power check, then let off the brakes. Standing in the astrodome I could see the triple towers of Lincoln Cathedral directly ahead, until the nose lifted, sweeping them from sight. Clambering down, I logged the take-off time: 1705 hours.

My primary task on operational sorties was to copy the broadcasts sent every thirty minutes by Command. These might concern changes of target, or routings, or even a cancellation. Otherwise, as strict radio silence was enforced, I was far more use in the astrodome: with hundreds of unlit bombers, each navigated independently, but all heading for the same place, and in pitch darkness, a good lookout seemed only politic.

On that first op everything was so novel that I even found the flak thrilling. There were the searchlights sweeping the sky, the fires already burning below, and the flashes of bombs dropped from aircraft ahead of us in the stream. Then came the tenseness as Les guided Johnny over the last couple of miles, his curt advisory, 'Bombs gone', and the upward surge as U-Uncle was lightened of its load.

We landed back at Fiskerton at 2200 hours, appreciatively handing over Uncle to our groundcrew. In retrospect, I realised that I'd had a sense of detachment throughout, as if the metal fuselage had been a secure cocoon.

'We bombed from 21,000 feet,' Johnny summarised at de-briefing, 'aiming at the green target markers, but didn't see our bombs explode because of mist and smoke. We also dropped seventy-two bundles of Window. On the down side, our Gee went u/s': 'Window' being foil strips to confuse the German radars; 'Gee' being a navigational aid which, just reaching far enough to cover the Ruhr, furnished navs with a positive position all the way to the target, so supplementing their air plots which were created using always-suspect winds and deduced reckoning.

'Thank you, Gentlemen,' said the WAAF intelligence officer, as we shuffled to our feet, 'enjoy your sleep.'

*A fragment of radar-obscuring Window*

Certainly I enjoyed mine. And when we awoke to find that two squadron crews had failed to return I realised that not once had I given a thought to the danger or, for that matter, to what our bombs were falling on.

That was my reaction. Our mid-upper, however, had decided that ops were not for him. And in the way that such things were arranged, we never saw him again. The judgement that would have been passed on him – lack of moral fibre (LMF), together with the stripping of rank and brevet –, was drastic but, I still believe, essential, to prevent the demoralisation of others.

Off duty, beer helped with morale. As did female company, of course. Not that it paid to be too complacent about the attraction of an aircrew brevet. As when a particular charmer, Betty Wilcox – a friend of our airfield driver, Dot Everette –, ascertained that I had to do with Lancaster N for Nan. In fact, Nan had been allotted to us only days before, but Dot had already christened her 'Nancy Pants', and even fashioned a rag doll that dangled now from the canopy above Johnny's head.

'Well,' Betty told me, 'our house is behind your dispersal, so would you ask your pilot to turn Nan side-on before he runs up? As it is, you're dirtying our washing.' Accommodating the request earned the crew a permanent invitation to tea, and in Betty and Dot, gained me two life-long friends.

Other social encounters paid dividends too. As when Johnny fell into conversation with an Australian air gunner, a crash survivor without a crew. The result being that Flight Sergeant Alan 'Spud' Mahony, Royal Australian Air Force, joined us as our mid-upper.

Although our second op, on 2 December 1943, took us to Berlin, the trip itself proved uneventful. We returned, however, to thick fog. Fortunately, Fiskerton possessed FIDO (Fog, Investigation and Dispersal Operation), a system in which petrol was piped along each side of the runway and set alight; as heated air could contain more moisture, so the fog thinned. From the astrodome I watched us sinking down through billowing smoke and residual mist towards the flame-limned runway, then running its length through a virtual tunnel of fire. It was mind blowing!

*Daylight test of FIDO at Fiskerton, 1943*

Bad weather kept us grounded until 16 December 1943 when we visited Berlin as part of a 483-strong all-Lancaster main force, led in by Oboe-equipped, Pathfinder Mosquito target markers; Oboe being an electronic aid in which the user flew along a beam to the target, then released the load on a signal.

Our crew bombed accurately from 22,000 feet, sighting on the very centre of the green target indicators. Yet it was a disastrous night, with twenty-five Lancasters downed by the defences, and another thirty-two lost trying to land on their fog-bound east-coast bases: few stations had FIDO!

We flew our fourth op on 20 December 1943, to Frankfurt. Finding nine tenths cloud, the Pathfinders were unable to lay the ground markers we expected, but Les bombed on re-laid yellow target indicators, doubly proving their accuracy with H2S, the ground-mapping radar – No. 49 having been among the first of the main force squadrons to receive it.

Others were not so well equipped, besides which the Germans had set both decoy fires and bogus markers. Additionally we saw stark evidence of the never-to-be-solved phenomenon of bombing short, or 'creepback', in which successive crews dropped ever earlier on either markers or conflagration. We also saw numerous flares indicating night-fighter activity. Certainly, forty-one of the 650 aircraft employed failed to return, 6.3% of the force. Or put less clinically, at least 287 aircrew.

We were warned for another Berlin trip on 23 December 1943, but Nancy Pants took sick. Our enforced stand down, however, brought no relief, only the most enervating sense of anti-climax. We'd steeled ourselves – to no purpose. And the balance of thirty ops remained to be done. That night fifteen of the 390 bombers engaged were lost, though none from the squadron.

On Christmas Eve there was a Command-wide stand-down from operations, but only because Germany was under ten tenths cloud. Most personnel descended upon Lincoln, but reasoning that the pubs ran out of beer by nine, a couple of us stayed in the Sergeant's Mess bar. It was not a wise decision, for the silly mixture we decided to drink set me off on a monumental, and utterly uncharacteristic, bender. At some stage I hurt my knee, an injury which, a day or two later, put me into station sick quarters.

To be hospitalised through my own fault was chagrining, for on 29 December 1943 Nancy Pants was among 700 bombers to re-visit Berlin. Aware that my crew were at risk, I experienced that form of nervousness that must have become habitual to anyone related to operational aircrew. In fact, all Forty-Nine's aircraft returned safely. Command, though, lost twenty.

I was released from sick quarters on 1 January 1944 in ample time to brief for yet another visit to Berlin. The squadron put fourteen Lancs over the target and all returned safely, despite fighters pressing home attacks on two. As for us, our H2S mapping radar failed halfway there, and as layered cloud precluded our getting assistance from either stars or ground features, Scotty was forced to rely on deduced reckoning. The single visual pinpoint we eventually got put us miles off track, but after a hurried crew confab we decided to press on, only too aware that, having been scheduled to bomb with the last wave, arriving twenty minutes late would rob us of herd protection. Weirdly, however, there was no flak, no searchlights, no fighters, no nothing. We concluded that the Berlin controllers, deciding that the raid was over, had stood their defences down.

Not Hanover's, however, for as we passed, a prolonged encounter with predicted flak – specifically-aimed – made Jerry's venom all too personal. The skipper, though, pulled out all the stops and we lost nothing more than an inch or so from a propeller tip.

We were lucky, but twenty-eight of the 421 Lancasters engaged failed to return, many falling to Messerschmitt Bf110s using their 30 mm calibre *Schräge Musik*, upward-firing cannon.

We arrived back to find settling-snow falling at Fiskerton, and made a second FIDO landing. But as Dot drove us back to debriefing we eyed the weather kindly, certain that there would be no ops that night.

Except that, as we slept, everyone else on the station was out with shovels and brooms clearing the main runway. When we awoke, therefore, it was to stumble off to yet another Berlin briefing.

Just before midnight on 2 January 1944 Johnny lifted Nancy Pants off the minimally cleared strip of Fiskerton's main runway. It was my sixth op, the seventh for most of the rest, although Johnny had also done that supernumerary trip with another crew. As always, our groundcrew had stowed their side-caps inside the entrance door: barred from coming on ops, they were with us in spirit.

Overextended from the night before, Bomber Command could only muster 383 aircraft. Of these, just 311 claimed to have reached a cloud-covered Berlin, with ice forcing many to jettison some of their load in order to reach the designated bombing altitude.

In Nancy Pants we were sixty miles from the target at 20,000 feet when Scotty called for the run-in turn. I was steadying myself as Johnny banked right, when the most tremendous impact flung me from my seat.

The radio lead tugged away my helmet, cutting my intercom connection, and depriving me of oxygen, but I scrambled up to a luridly lit astrodome in time to see the starboard wing peel away outboard of the inner engine. Frantically eyeing its passage I glimpsed the Lancaster we'd evidently collided with, still far too close, but rapidly falling away.

By now we too were diving steeply, the rising air shriek stultifying the mind. Back at Swinderby we'd made a competition of emergency evacuations. Now, automaton-like, but only too sentient, I found myself heading aft, unaware that I'd clipped on my parachute.

I'd just negotiated the main spar when I was pinned into position as flight-engineer Alan helped Johnny haul the aircraft bodily from its nosedive. Then, as we levelled, and the 'g' force lessened, I forced myself rearwards again, registering that Spud's turret was empty. As called for by the drill, he and Len were awaiting me at the latched-back entrance door. Without hesitation I crouched on the sill, and rolled myself headlong into the night.

Seconds later, swinging sickeningly beneath the canopy, the sight of Nancy Pants receding as if in normal flight, panicked me into thinking I'd jumped precipitously, that I'd face court martial charges for abandoning without an order ... This, of course, was shock. And thank goodness for it, for far worse could await, with German citizens giving short shrift to 'terror fliers' who fell into their hands ...

Because the WOp/AG's station was overheated by ducted engine air I habitually flew in nothing but sweater, battledress, and flying boots. Nor, for ease of tuning the wireless, did I wear gloves. The protracted high-altitude descent, therefore, through sub-zero temperatures, buffeting winds, and sleet, was absolute misery. Becoming desperate, I sought relief for my fingers by alternating my wet, freezing-cold hands between the parachute risers and my trouser pockets.

Nor did things improve when I crashed through the upper branches of a tree, to hang suspended in pitch darkness, heaven's knew how far up. Eventually, having created a swinging motion, I grabbed the trunk, banged the release box, and slid, eyes closed, to the ground – barely four feet below.

Cold, soaked through, shivering violently, and too shocked even to be apprehensive, I began to walk, knowing that I was in desperate need of succour. My progress was slow and befuddled, but I recall sliding down a forested slope, and reaching a fire break. And an eternity later standing by a farmhouse door.

Rousing the inmates took some persistence, but when the door opened I tendered my unsheathed scout knife butt first to show I was no threat. After an initial period of mutual awkwardness, the farmer and his wife could hardly have been kinder, particularly as they were mourning a son lost on U-boats. I was given a blanket and a drink while their daughter summoned the burgomaster – the local magistrate.

Eventually a Luftwaffe escort drove me to a nearby airfield where the duty NCO shared his rations with me, then locked me in a cell, and went off duty. I was wary later that morning when five Luftwaffe officers packed into the cell. They were not interrogators, however, but fellow operational fliers.

'You are lucky,' one smiled. 'Your war is over. We have to fight on.'

That afternoon I was taken to Trollenhagen airfield, some seventy miles north of Berlin, where I was interviewed by the commanding officer. My scout knife lay before him. Why carry such a vicious weapon, he wanted to know.

'To open the in-flight ration cans, Sir,' I told him truthfully. 'The fresh orange juice ...'

Once in possession of my basic details, he sent me to a holding cell. I got no sleep, it was so cold, and as the shock lessened I agonized increasingly over the crew. I was enormously bucked next morning, therefore, when Spud, Len, and Les were placed in neighbouring cells, Spud on a stretcher, having damaged his back. Scotty and Alan arrived after that, and Johnny a day later, having had a dislocated shoulder put back. The crew we'd collided with, it transpired, hadn't stood a chance.

The seven of us were then entrained to Frankfurt, overnighting in a Hamburg jail, our escorts taking precautions throughout to restrict the civilians to verbally reviling us. Later, passing mile after mile of bomb damage we could understand their hostility. Certainly it made me wonder anew at the kindness of those Germans we'd come into personal contact with. But I recall too, throwing away a fishcake from the journey rations that wasn't to my taste. It would be a long time before I was that cavalier with food again!

Our destination was the Dulag Luft – Luftwaffe transit camp – at Oberusal. The unit's function was to extract intelligence information, but they'd had hundreds of run-of-the-mill aircrew through their hands, and didn't bother overlong with us. They did send the 'Red Cross' official to see us, however. He assured us that once we'd completed his form, Geneva would be able to let our loved ones know we were safe. When we filled in nothing more than number, rank, and name, he went into a not-that-convincing tantrum, then sloped off. Besides that we had daily, hour-long questioning sessions in which regurgitating our personal details, and being a rank-and-file crew, proved sufficient.

Kept in isolation from each other, the routine was boring, though the guards broke their own tedium by playing with the heating, first making us shiver, then sweat. And although the food seemed abysmal, with watery soup, thin coffee, and even thinner black bread, we were soon to discover this to be pretty standard Prisoner-of-War (POW) fare.

We were kept in isolation for just a week, then held in the transit camp until there was a large enough party to be moved on. At which point Johnny, Scotty, and Les were taken off to Stalag Luft 3, an officers' camp, while the rest of us were packed aboard cattle trucks for shipment to Stalag 4B, an other-ranks' camp, at Mülhberg, between Liepzig and Dresden.

Although Mülhberg held a thousand airmen, it was essentially for army POWs, at that time, 16,000 of them. Living conditions were cramped, with

200 men, triple bunked, to every hut, with a single stove in each to serve for both heating and cooking.

It had long been realised that the German-issue rations were insufficient by themselves, fortunately, Red Cross parcels filled the gap. The contents of these varied, but they always contained chocolate, dried fruit, eggs, sugar, and compressed oats, for porridge: very filling. There was also Klim dried milk – Klim, of course, being milk spelt backwards. This came in tin containers which, themselves, proved infinitely useful. And let's never forget the cigarettes which were additionally valued for bargaining.

Life was humdrum. But after two months the monotony was disrupted for me by a summons to return to Dulag Luft for 'further questioning'. Speculation ran rife among the Jonahs. But I was so fed up with Mülhberg that any change was fine by me. Nor was I unduly concerned, for by now any untapped gen I might have was months out of date.

The renewed interrogation took the form of daily two-hour sessions during which a highly aggressive officer kept me standing as he pressed for details about a radio gear found in the wreckage of Nancy Pants. After five days another officer took over, adopting a gentle posture, allowing me to sit, feeding me cigarettes, and posing his questions in a friendly tone, though never straying far from the mystery equipment.

I didn't have to play that dumb. I knew the set had some radar-jamming function, but it had been installed while I was in sick quarters, so all I knew was that as we crossed the English coast outbound, I had to throw a switch, and see a red light; that if this flashed, I was to switch off, wait fifteen minutes, and switch on again. Easy then, to maintain that I knew nothing whatsoever.

On day ten they gave up, the kindly interrogator smilingly telling me that instead of returning to Mülhberg I was to go to a Stalag Luft, an air force camp.

My new home was Stalag Luft 6, at Heydekrug, in Lithuania. When I arrived, after an interminable ten days in a cattle truck, it held only just over

6,000 kriegies – *kriegsgefangener*: POWs. It was also far more organised than Mülhberg. There were three compounds, British, American, and a joint British-American one, with a mixture of permanent barrack blocks, wooden huts, and as the population increased, tents. There were recreation rooms, a chapel, a theatre, and a sports field. Each hut had a leader who could put forward grievances, while a 'Man of Confidence', selected by the POWs and approved by the Germans, was able to ameliorate our lot considerably.

Gratifyingly, food was reasonable, for Red Cross parcels never failed to arrive. So, what with sports, study courses, hobbies, and gentle guard baiting, time passed. One of the many drawbacks, of course, even before the influx from more easterly camps, was that of never being alone.

Thanks to a clandestine wireless receiver, we were well aware that the influx reflected the ever-quickening tempo of the Russian advance. Indeed, by 13 July 1944, when orders came for us to move out, we were 10,500 strong.

This time just two days of cattle-trucking deposited us at Stalag 357, near Thorn, in Poland. But only a month later we were transferred to Fallingbostel, near Hamburg, where conditions were poor even before January and February 1945 brought atrocious weather and a serious breakdown in the delivery of Red Cross parcels. Then, in March 1945, with not the slightest improvement in the weather, we were abruptly ordered to leave camp, taking only what we could carry.

Split into groups of 500, we were led north-eastwards, for the most part using country roads, sleeping in barns when we could find them, but otherwise in the open. After one such exposed night, I suffered frostbite in a foot, and for everyone conditions worsened as we grew weaker. Then, on 5 May 1945, thirty-five days after leaving Fallingbostel, and three days before VE Day and the enemy surrender, the Germans called a halt at a village named Kittlitz. Next morning there were few guards left. And those who remained, handed us their weapons.

When the atrocity of this 'Short Walk' was investigated – there was an arguably yet more heinous three-month 'Long Walk' –, the authorising officer, General Berger, was charged with putting some 80,000 POW's onto the open roads in the coldest winter remembered, so causing 'great privation and death to many thousands of prisoners'. His defence was that the Geneva Convention required him to remove POWs from potential combat zones, that he'd saved them from Soviet savagery ...

We'd been freed, of course, into chaos, but British troops reached us quite quickly, with orders that we should stay put until transport arrived. Soon growing impatient, I set out on a recce, only to run into a mounted German officer leading thirty troops. Before I could raise my hands, the officer asked me where he could surrender. In the next village, I told him, provided his troops were unarmed, and on foot. He promptly had all weapons stacked, and made over to me his horse and revolver, after which I did a laddish-like disappearing act.

After two more frustrating days we commandeered a lorry and drove ourselves to Lunenburg, just become a major Allied base, where our first port of call was the canteen. As we queued, I recall, a piece of white bread filched from a passing tray tasted like sponge cake ...

The following day a Lancaster transport delivered us to Dunsfold, in Surrey. After which our homecoming became dreamlike as we were enfolded into the warm and welcoming care of scores of beaming – and invariably buxom – WAAFs. They kissed us, fed us, escorted us through hot showers and medicals, smilingly delousing and re-kitting us in turn: even sewing on our up-to-date ranks – flight sergeant in my case – and brevets: I put up the new S brevet, for Signaller.

Next, with their farewells musical in our ears, a special train took us to RAF Cosford and an exhaustive debriefing. Told then that we were free to return home, I for one, after my seventeen months of incarceration, found it very hard to believe.

*Flight Sergeant Ted Cathcart, 1945*

Understandably, there was a massive amount of readjustment to be done. Perhaps I misjudged how much, for after a far too rushed courtship I married a former classmate. It has to be remembered that, back then, Bomber Command was in high favour, its aircrews being urged from all quarters, 'Drop one on 'em for me, Son.' But the brought-to-life glamour poster was a doubtful medium through which to view marriage! And sadly, ours was far from an isolated case.

There was too, my Service future to be decided. Although I was on the brink of becoming a warrant officer, I was no long flying, besides which, aircrew ranks were effectively 'wartime only'. Accordingly, having dusted off my Westminster College catering skills, I was posted to RAF Hospital Halton as an AC2 cook: aircraftman class two, the rank I had held on joining! At the same time, however, I was drawing the pay, and wearing the rank of a flight sergeant WOp/AG. As other postings followed I rose to become a joined-at-the-hip sergeant cook and warrant officer WOp/AG: it was a very confusing time for everyone.

Reeling from the personal tragedy of my marriage, I decided to return to flying, taking advantage of a new, three-year service deal. The rules, however, required me to leave the RAF, then reapply, so on 22 July 1946 I got my discharge at the Uxbridge Depot, then five hours later re-enlisted at Kingsway.

'Didn't you like civvy street?' I was asked ...

In January 1947, after several attachments, I was posted to No. 1 Air Signallers School at RAF Swanton Morley, in Norfolk, for aircrew refresher training. That was followed by a spell at RAF Swinderby where the duties included the invidious one of accepting off-the-assembly line Wellingtons, flight testing them to ensure that the makers had fulfilled the contract, then delivering them for scrapping.

A happier posting followed as I passed on to No. 1382 Transport Conversion Unit at RAF Wymeswold, to fly Dakotas. But then I was in the happiest possible frame of mind anyway, for on the leave preceding the move I had met, and begun to become very attached to, the most stunning of girls, Betty Lowrie ...

*Betty Lowrie, 1947*

Once checked out on Dakotas I was detached from my new crew – all ex-Lancaster men – and sent to No. 1333 Transport Support Training Unit at North Luffenham to learn to tow Horsa gliders and drop supplies. I also became a jump master, which qualified me to dispatch paratroops. All very gratifying. Except that on rejoining the crew it was to find we'd been posted to Kabrit, in the Canal Zone. Betty was not best pleased. And nor was I ...

In fact, we ended up in Malta, back on Lancasters, with No. 37 Squadron, carrying out maritime reconnaissance duties. Within days, however, we were moved to RAF Ramat David where Palestinian Arab and Jewish Yishuv – that is, pre-the-Israel-state – forces were hotting up their warring as the British mandate ran out. Our main task was to move equipment to Cyprus but most memorably we were detached to Shallufa, in Egypt, to fly to Kenya and pick up nine Jewish-terrorist detainees for delivery to RAF El Adem, in Libya. It was an extremely bumpy flight, and I still cherish the picture of the terrorists solicitously helping their airsick soldier escorts from the aircraft, hands supportingly outstretched, shoulders draped, not only with their guards' webbing equipment, but their rifles ...

In July 1948 I was posted home, enabling me to see through my divorce, and to spend time with Betty. I was then sent as an instructor to Swinderby, taking the opportunity to give serious thought to signing on. As it was, a new life with Betty proved a greater draw, and in November 1949, after eight years' service, I left the RAF for good.

A year earlier, however, I'd been able to tie a nagging loose end. Flying over the Med, I'd clambered back to the rear turret and triggered off a round from my revolver. After which I'd returned to my wireless set, an air gunner, at long last, who'd actually fired off a shot in the air!

I served six years on the reserve, flying twenty hours annualy and attending training camps during which being paid by both the RAF and my current employer appealed to the laddishness in me. As it was, over the years I became a area sales manager for Hoover; set up my own domestic appliance company; managed multiple departments in a big store; was headhunted by an engineering firm, becoming a director ten years later; and then, aged 53, ran a Youth Training Scheme for Derbyshire County Council.

Betty and I had married in 1952, and had brought up two wonderful children, Jacqueline and Anthony, who in turn had given us families of their own. Family life, we found, was all absorbing.

It was mere chance, then, that got me involved with the RAF once more when, in 1987, I was persuaded to claim my Caterpillar Club badge: the club for those whose life has been saved by a parachute. In the process I was directed to Tom Gatfield, secretary of the No. 49 Squadron Association – the 4(T)9 Association –, early on regaining contact with all my Nancy Pants' crew, bar Len Crossman, who had died in a road accident in 1946.

*Betty Wilcox and Dot Everette, at a No. 49 Squadron Reunion,*
*Petwood Hotel, Woodhall Spa*

In succeeding years Betty and I attended various commemorative events until, as we approached our fortieth wedding anniversary, Betty's health deteriorated. I finally lost her on 18 July 1991, but not before she had declared that her by-then-imminent demise was my laddishly devious plan to avoid buying her a ruby. She was that loving. And that brave!

In my widowhood, involvement with the 4(T)9 Association enriches my life. Not least through my association with John Ward, ex-Parachute Regiment, accomplished artist, and author, for whom I edited *Beware of the Dog at War* (the title derived from the No. 49 Squadron motto) and who gave me so much assistance with my own book, *Ted the Lad*.

I fill my time with numerous activities, my long-term interest in altering houses constantly bemusing my son and daughter. Information technology both intrigues me and keeps my brain from stultifying, so although there has been talk of an aneurism, I make a point of living life to the full.

*Ted Cachart, 2012*

Looking back, I have so much to be thankful for. And just one especial regret. Namely, that I've been unable to determine exactly where Nancy Pants came to earth. For my firm conviction is that somewhere in some German woodland there is a tenderly fashioned, now honourably timeworn, rag doll, gently swinging in a tree, just as it used to swing above Johnny's head in those anguished, flak-torn skies so long ago.

**Flight Sergeant Anthony (Tony) Brindley, air gunner**

We'd been assured that an amnesty had been agreed with the Germans, but it was distinctly eerie to be flying at ultra low level so close to enemy guns; to feel them, in our imagination, tracking us as we swept by at fifty feet, bomb bay open, to free-drop especially strengthened sacks of staples onto, in our case, a racetrack ...

*Aircraftman Two, Trainee Aircrew Cadet Tony Brindley, 1943*

Having been born in 1924 I was fifteen when war was declared. On leaving Derby's Bemrose Grammar School I settled to working where the family farmed, at both Littleover and Markeaton, my labours being extended by evening drills with the Home Guard, in standing sentry over a dump at nearby Findern, and in firing rifles on the range at Burnaston Airfield, now Toyota. In December 1943, however, when my call-up papers arrived, I gave the army a miss by volunteering to fly as RAF aircrew.

I was sent to Birmingham where I underwent a searching medical – including blowing mercury up a tube, and holding it there, breathless, for what seemed like for ever –, sat various tests, and filled in a variety of forms, before being interviewed by a board of three officers who smiled benignly when told I'd like to become a fighter pilot. Having conferred, and shuffled through my papers, they explained that what they were really desperate for were wireless operator/air gunners. Would I agree to volunteer to train for that aircrew category? And smiled widely when I said I would.

In fact, where RAF aircrew selection was concerned, I was to realise over the years that, given that an applicant was in the top grade of fitness, and academically reasonable – and Bemrose had given me far more grounding than would have been required – it was always to be a matter of what the RAF needed at that time. If that was to take a while to sink in, I was to discover far more quickly that I was seeking to become a flier at what was arguably the most critical of times where wartime aircrew recruiting was concerned. Though how critical, even the board would not have realised.

Back in 1939 the RAF's day bombers had suffered grievously when sent against targets in and about Heligoland Bight – or bay. They had then been dispatched at night, only to have the planners realise that, between the crews being unable to find their way to the target, and being unable to hit it when they did find it, the bombing was ineffectual; notwithstanding that it was much vaunted by the press and the BBC. By 1943, though, fundamental lessons had been learnt, and under the control of the commander I was to know as 'Butch' Harris, Bomber Command had become both a powerful and an effective force. In that same year, however, in raiding the Ruhr industries, and Berlin, it had suffered losses rising to as high as 8.9% of the force sent out, when the planners reckoned nearer 5% losses as the most the RAF could suffer and still hope to sustain the offensive. When I applied, therefore, the Service really was desperate for certain aircrew categories.

That notwithstanding, during the year to eighteen months my training as a wireless operator/air gunner might be expected to take, things were to change radically. The bomber effort, for a start, would be switched to support the forthcoming invasion of Europe. And after June 1944, as the Allied armies pushed eastwards, it would become clear that the enemy's defeat was only a matter of time. That being so, the need for replacement aircrew would fall off markedly. My bid to become aircrew, and to do my bit by flying on operations, therefore, was to be played out against a doubly uncertain scenario, the German ability to maintain the struggle, and the speed of the Allies' eastward advance.

Even then dimly aware of this, I fancy, I embarked with high hopes upon a schedule of training that, by then, had become familiar to many thousands, starting off with some weeks in somewhat rarefied St John's Wood – though I didn't know it, the requisitioned luxury flats we lived in were to be the acme of my accommodation in the Service. At that time this was No. 1 Aircrew Reception Centre (ACRC, or 'Arsey Darcey') where, in the course of being kitted out and generally organised, we were buggered about by the most unpleasant set of corporals. If was as if the RAF had followed the lead of London Zoo, where we ate our meals, and bred them for their sarcasm and general obnoxiousness. Whether it was some form of jealousy, or whether they were simply pig ignorant we never could make out.

After St John's Wood, and Lord's, my group of aspirant wireless operator/ air gunners moved on to RAF Bridgnorth, near Shrewsbury, basically for six weeks of square-bashing though we began lectures, not least to learn morse and study aircraft recognition. But altogether a pleasant enough interlude on the River Severn with an upper and lower town holding between them, we maintained, some 57 pubs: pubs in which the distinctive white aircrew-trainee flash in our side-caps made it difficult for us to buy ourselves a beer, 'My round, Lads, and drop one on 'em for me …' for the exploits of Bomber Command were on everyone's lips, not least, ironically enough, Churchill's.

Our subsequent move was to No. 14 Initial Training Wing at Bridlington, on the east coast, some twenty miles north of Hull, where we were accommodated in ice-cold requisitioned seaside flats – shades of luxurious St John's Wood! –, drilled, and began a course of study that included wireless theory, more morse, RAF law, hygiene, current affairs, maths, more aircraft recognition, and armament. The planned schedule was that we would spend six weeks here, rising at what we were learning to call 0600 hours, stopping work at 1800 hours, then getting down to private study. A week or so into the course, however, one of the staff assembled us for a talk.

He started by reminding us that the training for the dual aircrew category we'd embarked upon, that of both wireless operator and air gunner, could take up to eighteen months. And now he called our attention to the way the war seemed to be going. What with Bomber Command about to bring Germany to its knees, and so many Americans crowding to the south coast to assist in what had to be the invasion, we might see that if we carried on with our course we could well miss the war altogether.

On the other hand, if we dropped the wireless-operator part, then the shorter course to qualify us as straight air gunners could have us flying ops within six months, by late 1944 even. It had to be put to us like that, by the by, for all fliers are volunteers, and until they are ops-ready, at least, cannot be coerced. I didn't need to think overlong about it, for having been pondering along those lines anyway, I was already halfway there, and was foremost among the many who snapped up the opportunity offered.

On 27 May 1944, accordingly, having dropped all the wireless work, we were moved to No. 3 Air Gunnery School, at RAF Castle Kennedy, just east of Stranraer, in Scotland, and started gunnery training proper. The course was centred around the Browning machine gun, but to get our eye in we spent a good deal of time shooting at clay pigeons with shotguns, and even with Stens.

In the classroom we learned to recognise stoppages and faults on the Browning, and to cure them, where possible, stripping and reassembling the weapon until we could, literally, do it blindfolded. We also worked through all the niceties of windage, bullet drop under gravity, target leading, deflection shooting, and the 'harmonising' of four machine guns – adjusting the alignment of each – to have them spread an even pattern when the target was in the centre dot of the sight.

Air gunners trained earlier would tell us of sessions firing Brownings from mocked-up turrets which allowed the trainee to fire at models running around a track; also of a sophisticated trainer housed in a dome which had aircraft attacking from all angles. We had none of this, however, firing Brownings off only on the range. Instead, we did all our turret firing in the air.

The aircraft used were Avro Ansons, with each trainee taking turns in its upper-fuselage turret. We duly fired courses at targets on the ground, both land and sea, at drogues towed by Miles Martinets, and took cine-camera shots of co-operating fighters. At the end of the course my logbook summary shows that I'd expended 100 feet of cine-camera footage and fired 1,100 shots on the 25 to 200 yard range; 400 rounds air-to-sea; 300 rounds from the turret, firing abeam; with another 2,500 fired in other abeam, under-tail, and quarter attacks. On one session I scored 15% of hits, which was extraordinarily high, most being very acceptable scores in the 2 and 3% range. So, taken with a good mark in ground work, I was deemed to have made satisfactory progress, and on 15 July 1944, just five weeks or so after D-Day, I received my Air Gunner's brevet, and my sergeant's stripes.

*Miles Martinet*

I was not to realise it for some years, but that timing, post-D-Day, was to preclude all of us not yet operational from the eventual award of the Aircrew Europe Star, and the vast majority of us from having anything to show that we had ever flown on ops at all.

*Sergeant Air Gunner Tony Brindley, 1944*

Off duty the folks at Stranraer had made us very welcome but one of my abiding memories of Castle Kennedy was when I begged a ride in a Sunderland Flying Boat, the massive machine impressing me no end with its spaciousness, which included rest and cooking facilities! Except that flying in it as crew would have meant staring the whole time at so much drab and featureless sea. Though, on reflection, a short while later I might have re-thought the attraction of drabness, when ploughing through skies packed tight with far too many far-from-drab bombers.

On 13 August 1944, those of us who had qualified moved to No. 17 Operational Training Unit (OTU) at RAF Turweston, thirteen miles south-east of Banbury, the satellite of the main unit, at nearby Silverstone. The OTU was operating Vickers Wellington bombers, so we new arrivals, of all aircrew categories, were set loose in a hangar to sort ourselves into crews.

I forget who chose who, but I was pleased to find myself accepted by Sergeant Pilot Phil Marshall. I also teamed up with a fellow gunner, Sergeant John Brown, who promptly bagged the rear turret; a navigator, a wireless operator, and a bomb aimer. Once we got onto heavies we'd also need a flight engineer. I have to confess, though, that names have simply fled. The wireless operator was Scotty, the sergeant-nav's surname was Tipper, but the bomb-aimer's: it's just gone ... And casting ahead, the flight-engineer's remains a blank too.

We did four hours or so with an instructor, then Phil was sent solo; that is, he flew as captain, with his own crew. It was all very interesting. For though a lot of the early exercises concentrated on Phil – circuit flying, and flying on one engine, some sorties with a staff pilot, some with only Phil at the controls –, a fair number included air-gunnery sessions. That was because each category had a screen – a staff instructor – to take us through exercises of our own. So us gunners would have a staff air gunner monitoring us as we practised combat manoeuvres, often enough with a fighter carrying out dummy attacks, and both by day and by night.

On 9 September we moved to Silverstone, the parent unit, progressing to flying cross-countries, primarily for the benefit of the nav and wireless op, but once more including sessions of air firing and bombing, again, by day and by night. A red-marker day in the course came on 27 September 1944 when we were sent out on a near-five-hour night 'Bullseye', the codename, in this case, for flying out towards the enemy coast to divert at least some attention from a real raid setting off from elsewhere. Before any enemy night-fighters could reach our area, however, and as planned, we turned back. And by the start of October 1944, when the course ended, we had flown a total of some fifty-five hours as a crew.

After a fortnight's leave we reassembled and reported to RAF Wigsley, near Newark, a satellite of Swinderby, home of No. 1654 Heavy Conversion Unit

(HCU) where we were to pick up a flight engineer, and learn to operate a four-engined aircraft.

For some time this particular HCU had operated Lancasters. Then, as the demand for Lancasters on first-line squadrons became critical – because of heavy losses – and just before we arrived, it re-equipped with the Short Stirling. This was a massive machine, rearing over twenty feet above the ground, and the bane of many pilots. Shortly after we left Wigsley, the aircraft supply situation changed, and Lancasters came back. Whether our arrival was timely or not, is hard to say. But perhaps some things are predestined.

We flew two details under the supervision of a staff pilot, and after a total of four hours Phil was sent off alone with us. While others found the Stirling unwieldy he seemed to be at ease with it. The next few days saw us busily building up hours and experience. We carried out circuits and landings, practised the technique for high-level bombing, if from only 5,000 feet; carried out the corkscrew evasion tactic and other combat manoeuvres, and moved on to instrument flying. We also practised asymmetric handling – flying on less than four engines – sessions requiring close co-operation between pilot and flight engineer. And just as well, for on 7 November we lost our starboard outer, and had to cut short a night sortie. True, this was during a dual flight, but Phil, at the controls, handled it well.

We turned to cross-countries, combining one with live bombing and fighter affiliation. And on 21 November 1944 we set out solo on a night cross-country. None of us were ever sure what happened. I recorded the flight as 'Boomerang, sick pilot': 'Boomerang' denoting that we had aborted the sortie and returned to base.

As I gathered it, Phil suddenly found trouble focussing on his instruments. With the flight engineer and the navigator helping him we arrived back at Wigsley. But then the trouble really started, for try as he might, Phil couldn't get the approach right. We all did our best to talk him down, with me chipping in from my station in the mid-upper turret, for although, unlike the flight engineer, I'd not been checked out even to fly straight and level, I knew pretty well what things should have looked like just before touchdown. Phil made, I believe, six attempts in all, before finally getting us down on the seventh. I can't remember what the landing was like, but we all walked away from it. Phil, though, was taken into the care of the medics, and his flying days were over.

A great shame, and a personal tragedy to a very pleasant man, and one, who during the course of flying some sixty hours together, we'd grown to know as a very capable captain and pilot.

Three days later the rest of us were in the air once again, carrying out a fighter-affiliation exercise, evading attacks – mock – by a Hurricane, and seeing the practical effect of our corkscrewing technique. The main purpose of this sortie though, I suspect, was to get us back in the saddle, as it were, though it was to be 4 January 1945 before we began flying with our new captain, Sergeant Ralph Taylor.

A delay in my journey to ops, that is, of pretty nearly six weeks!

*Sergeant Ralph Taylor and crew, 1945*

With Ralph at the controls we did another seven or so hours, on one occasion losing an engine and having to overshoot, then land, on three. There were hazards of a different sort too, as on 23 Feb 1945 when, in the course of a night flight that would take us just over six hours, we were warned to delay our return because there were intruders over base; clear proof then that, hard pressed though it was, the Luftwaffe had lost none of its offensive spirit.

Then, on 3 March 1945, with all of us having done enough to complete our conversion, we moved to RAF Feltwell, ten miles west of Thetford, in Norfolk, to undergo a course on a new electronic bombing aid called Gee-H.

Among other things, Feltwell had recently become the home for a Lancaster flight from the Bomber Command Development Unit who were pedalling such electronic aids as Gee, H2S, Oboe, and now, Gee-H. What we did not know was that the RAF was already planning ahead for the time when the priority would be for crews trained for long-range operational sorties in the Far East, hence the Gee-H course, primarily for navigators.

During our Stirling conversion we'd become familiar with Gee, the very accurate, electronic, all-weather-night-or-day navigational aid – the nav twiddled knobs to move markers on his radar screen, then plotted our exact position on a chart: he could even lead us into a near-blind landing with it!

We'd also been introduced to H2S, a ground-mapping radar that could be used for bombing but was most useful for navigating from the North Sea onwards, as the enemy jammed Gee beyond that (The letter 'G', by the way, had become a code for grid navigation, 'H' denoting a bombing system).

As for Oboe, we knew this to be the most accurate bombing aid ever. Two ground stations did all the work of guiding a master-bomber crew to the target, then telling them when to drop their markers so that main force, aiming and releasing on the descending flares, would hit the target. All the master-bomber crew had to do was press the release button: and that could just as well have been done by the ground station too! And even though it wasn't done by the ground station, it effectively put the crew – as some might note wryly not that many years later – in the same category as the whiz-kid astronaut who opened his instructions to read, 'Feed the monkey'.

Gee-H, though was a step up, we now learnt, in which the Oboe equipment was carried on board, and operated by the navigator, a black box on the aircraft interrogating the two ground stations. All very complex, but though fractionally less accurate than Oboe, up to 80 bombers at a time could use it, nor was it so readily jammed.

I did not log any flights during the Gee-H course, but I presume the nav, the bomb aimer, and Ralph, possibly even the wireless operator and the flight engineer, would have spent some time in the air actually operating the equipment, or fiddling with the boxes. I can only suppose us gunners would have been in the gunnery section brushing up on our aircraft recognition. And when the course finished, on 20 March 1945, we took a long-drawn communal crew breath, for after all those months of training – indeed, those years for Ralph and the nav –, it was finally time for us to be formally introduced to the machine we were take on ops, the Avro Lancaster.

Our posting was to No. 138 Squadron, a No. 3 Group formation, stationed at RAF Tuddenham, near Bury St Edmunds, Suffolk. For much of the war No. 138, as a special-duties squadron, had operated from the hush-hush airfield at Tempsford, clandestinely dropping and landing agents and supplies in occupied Europe. Just three weeks before, though, on 9 March 1945, it had dropped the cloak and dagger stuff and become a regular Bomber Command squadron, giving up its Halifaxes and Stirlings and converting to the Lancaster.

The wartime-traditional home for training crews on the Lancaster had been RAF Syerston, though during our Gee-H attachment Feltwell had received No. 3 Lancaster Finishing School. In a departure from the norm, however, we were to convert on the squadron, almost certainly because, having converted en-masse themselves just weeks before, they were all geared up to training.

As an airfield Tuddenham was pretty basic. We were used to Nissen huts by now, with the St John's Wood luxury flats a distant memory. Far more importantly we all settled well on the Lancaster. But then it would have been hard to find fault with the already celebrated machine. Even so, our conversion was not without incident. On one occasion we had to land on three engines for real, and on another a coolant leak forced us to cut short a detail: we took it for granted, of course, that when first-line squadrons were directed to give up aircraft to training units they donated their most worn specimens. Then again we had to foreshorten two other sorties because of weather, one because cloud precluded a bombing practice, the other due to a thunderstorm over the runway: but that was how weather affected any stage of flying training, and was the prime reason why so many pilots and navigators had trained in the settled-weather skies of the States and the Commonwealth.

In the next week or so we flew sorties using Gee-H to bomb the range from 15,000 to 18,000 feet, also a night cross-country using H2S, and carrying a war load for the first time – surely we weren't going to miss out on ops now! And we flew on fighter affiliation, during which, again for the first time, I used a gyroscopic gunsight to track a clipped-wing Spitfire.

With this sophisticated aid we gunners'd set in the target aircraft's wingspan – in studying aircraft recognition we'd committed all such detail to memory –, after which the device itself worked out how much we should lead the target by, and how much up-elevation to employ to allow for bullet drop. Basically we'd centre two points, the fixed aiming point, and a moving one generated by the magic-gyroscope's wizardry that gave the corrected aiming point.

On switching aircrew categories back at Bridlington I'd hoped to be operational in late 1944, but with odd days tagged on here and there through training blockages, and with the to-be-critical six-week setback after losing Phil, to be ops-ready in early 1945 wasn't a bad second. As I told myself, had I insisted on additionally qualifying as a wireless operator I'd still have nearly eight months of the training syllabus to go! And with the Allied armies – not least the Russians – pressing the enemy ever closer, my waning chances of ever seeing ops had begun to seriously concern me. Now, though, things were definitely looking hopeful. What with carrying actual war loads, and having the facility of a gyro gunsight, it seemed ever more likely that I'd be in time even yet.

The norm of squadron acceptance would have been that at some time during our settling-in period, in our case a mix of settling in and converting, Ralph would have flown as second dickie to a more experienced pilot in order to see how an operation was conducted. And the rest of us would have waited with baited breath until he got back: far too many pilots failed to return from such second-dickie sorties. In our case, however, on 29 March 1945, when we finally appeared on No. 138's Battle Order, we flew as a complete crew, though with a squadron pilot acting as nominal captain.

Hard, of course, to recreate the atmosphere of those far off days, now so many years ago. And yet there must have been nervous anticipation. We knew the statistics, as far as they could be known then. But we knew too, that being shot down wasn't necessarily the end. Accordingly we'd been lectured on evasion after, perish the thought, coming down in the Reich. As for baling out, I'd even swung to earth from a parachute-training tower at Ringway; and each of us wore a whistle on our battledress collar to help us rendezvous after landing.

*Escape and evasion equipment: whistle, worn on battledress collar, to rendezvous, or to summon assistance*

Yet what comes back to me is the anticipation, with any fear being that, even at this late stage, Hitler would call it off: that despite my change-of-horses to straight air gunner I might yet miss out on the war. Not that I was any war lover, still less a glory hunter. But I did want to do my bit. And there was that thing Dr Johnson said – I can't remember what squadron he was on – about men thinking meanly of themselves for not having been a soldier ... or at sea. Or presumably, Bomber-Command aircrew. Fortunately we didn't have long to stew on that score, for take-off time was set for 1230 hours. A daylight raid, then; and yet another sign of radically changed times.

The destination was Salzglitter (Hallendorf), to the south-west of Brunswick, beyond the Ruhr, an unthinkable daylight penetration just short months before, and indeed, destined to be the RAF's longest daylight penetration of the war. The actual target was the Hermann Goering Benzole (effectively, petrol) Plant and steel mill with No. 138 Squadron forming part of a main force of 130 No. 3 Group Lancasters that actually got airborne – 150 had been the planned number but the weather was not that good and there were unserviceabilities. As an experience, I wouldn't have missed it, though nearly seven hours of sky-searching for fighters that never came – not least our escort – was wearing in the extreme.

That we were to be escorted by the long-range Mustangs of No. 611 Squadron, from RAF Hunsdon, in Hertfordshire, was among several factors that permitted such an audacious penetration. Another was that, by this time, the Germans had few fighters, certainly too few to scramble against a formation which, as their radars could see, were shortly to be joined by Mustangs. What nobody anticipated was that the Mustang leader, being unable to break clear of cloud, would abort them some fifteen minutes short of joining us. And even then one of their number failed to return to base, though whether from malfunction, enemy action, or from becoming disoriented, is not known.

*RAF Mustang*

We too found that the skies near the target were cloudy up to 22,000 feet, and with total cover in some areas. Even so we were able to bomb successfully, and our bomb-camera results attracted no specific criticism. As for the opposition, comparing it with descriptions given by experienced crews, I judged the flak to be weak. I was still fascinated, however, to see a faint dot in the sky ahead rapidly flower as the charge expanded to leave a hanging smudge of benign-looking smoke, but I got the impression that Hallendorf had few guns. Which was a good thing, for it only needed one shrapnel fragment in the wrong place ... After all, weak as the opposition might have been, that op still took the measure of the unfortunate Mustang pilot, Warrant Officer Henry Standrin.

No Lancasters were lost, but the results overall were disappointing, photo-reconnaissance showing that the bombing had been widely scattered, with little damage being done.

Reflecting on that disappointing raid summary, it occurs that, for the first time in at least a year, squadrons accustomed to the by-now highly sophisticated way night bombing had developed, found themselves in an alien environment. Each crew had always been aware that they were part of a huge, unlit force heading towards a single point. They had been protected from this awareness, however, by the darkness. Now, though, during daylight, there would hardly have been a moment when they weren't forcibly reminded that they were not alone. Indeed, a gunner from another squadron maintained that – never having had the opportunity to fire a shot – he had finally earned his keep in warning his skipper to break away as another Lancaster emerged from cloud on a heading converging with their own.

In fact, unlike the Americans, who always flew in formation, nobody in our main force would have been able to relax, for now, flying in their accustomed gaggles, they could actually see the variations in the flight paths as Lancasters closed, and re-closed, all heading for the same initial point, but each navigating independently, and each with its own variation of height, heading, and speed. Even on the run-in the same would have applied, only this time with aircraft only too obviously visible, looming overhead, and with laden bomb bays gaping ...

Then again, while most of the nine squadrons involved must have been unsettled by this suddenly visible lack of cohesion, for our squadron the whole operation was daunting, having so recently transferred both to Bomber Command and to Lancasters.

Even so, as a crew, we'd done an op, so all the months of training had paid off. And I, in particular, had achieved my goal! It was with especial zest, therefore, that we boarded the buses that were laid on to take us to the various pubs and dancehalls in Newmarket and Bury St Edmonds where we were always made so welcome. One down. And just twenty-nine to go. Hitler willing ...

It was the best part of two weeks before we were called upon for our second op, but at 2015 hours on 13 April 1945 we got airborne to raid shipping and dock installations at Kiel, the raid centring on the U-boat yards. Flak was rated by some crews as heavy, while others noted how well the target had been marked by our Pathfinders, lending accuracy to the bombing, and leading to massive fires springing up. Even so, the raid wash-up read 'poor attack with scattered bombing'.

The sortie took us six hours, and we dropped twelve five-hundred pounders and a single four-thousand pounder: a standard load. The force comprised 377 Lancs and 105 Halifaxes from Nos. 3, 6, and 8 Groups, of which two Lancasters were lost,

The very next afternoon we were on the Battle Order again, taking off at 1515 hours to raid Potsdam, effectively a suburb of Berlin, where we once more dropped a standard load, the sortie lasting nearly nine hours. The main force comprised 500 Lancasters and twelve Mosquitoes, the sky was clear, and experienced crews were gratified to find that so much of the previously thorny territory we had to overfly was now in Allied hands. For my part, I noted that, even as we ran in, the whole place seemed to be on fire.

Although Mosquitoes were, even then, in the process of visiting Berlin on thirty-six successive nights, it had been just over a year since a major force had tested the city's defences. I judged the flak to be weak, and indeed, bursting below the stream. But night-fighters were abroad, and while we saw none, they killed the flight engineer aboard a New Zealand squadron Lancaster, with two Lancs failing to return.

The target was a railway installation and a barracks, but photo-reconnaissance showed that, as the aiming point had been the centre of Potsdam, substantial damage had also been caused to the town itself, with other bombs widespread over Berlin. The summation, therefore, was that the raid had been 'moderately successful'. In fact, it would transpire that this was to be the last major Bomber Command raid on a German city.

On 18 April, at 1030 hours we got airborne to raid the twin isles of Heligoland. These, we learnt at briefing, had become British after they had menaced our shipping during the Napoleonic wars, and had remained so for 83 years, up to 1890. In the First World War again, they had caused similar problems to our shipping. Then, in the interwar period, Nazi Germany had built U-boat facilities and installed anti-aircraft defences in direct contravention of the Versailles Treaty. The isles had also been the arena for the disastrous daylight attacks RAF planners had sent Hampdens on in the early weeks of the war.

There was little comparison between the Hampden debacle and our raid. In all, our bombing force consisted of 969 aircraft; 617 Lancasters, 332 Halifaxes, and twenty Mosquitoes. The leading wave reported hundreds of vessels scattering seawards as they approached. Indeed, after a second raid next day both isles were evacuated.

Three Halifaxes were lost, but the attack was recorded as 'successful', with the airfield, the naval base, and indeed the town, being left like 'a moonscape'. For our part we dropped ten one-thousand pounders and four five-hundred pounders, the sortie lasting just over five hours.

The question might be asked why so much ordnance – and three Halifaxes, twenty-one aircrew at least – should have been expended on two islets whose facilities could no longer affect the outcome of the war. Indeed, the contemporary press, clearly pondering that very question, could only hazard that it was 'in all probability an anti-submarine measure', with cross-Channel supply traffic in mind. One has to wonder, though: in planning the 1939 series of Heligoland-Bight raids, the RAF planners got it wrong. Is it just conceivable that the twin 1945 raids were payback? Conceivably even, a chance seized upon to once and for all reduce islets that had for so long posed a threat to British interests.

Two days later, on 20 April 1945, we took off at 0950 as part of one hundred No. 3 Group Lancasters, with RAF Mustang escort, to attack the fuel storage depot at Regensburg, on the Danube, in Bavaria, a follow-up to earlier raids directed against its Messerschmitt works and ball-bearing factory. It took us seven and a half hours, and not for the first time I was intrigued to hear English-speaking German operators attempting to counteract the calm, unruffled instructions of the master bomber. It was, in fact, the final raid in the campaign against oil targets that had lasted since June 1944, and was rated 'successful'. One Lancaster was lost.

Ops undoubtedly stirred the blood as the most realistic of exercises never could. Even so, a few days later we might have expected some measure of excitement from a fighter affiliation exercise, except that we landed after ten minutes on being advised that there was nobody to play with us. The following day we got airborne on another such exercise, this time carrying as passenger a fighter pilot, recorded in my log book as Flight Lieutenant O'Bern who, once the exercise was over and he was given control by Ralph, threw the Lanc around as if it too was a fighter. I had become accustomed to corkscrewing, but this put an entirely different strain on my stomach. Though, compared with ops, even such gyrations did not really stir the blood.

Just as well, undoubtedly, that I did not know that my operational days were over. Had I done so, the sense of letdown might have been extreme. Later, I would have to become reconciled to the fact that, after all the months of training and anticipation, there were to be no more ops. I would, of course, be able to tell myself that, having got well established on my tour, I had not been disappointed; that having deliberately pitted myself against the odds, I had not been found wanting.

What was undeniably a little bitter, was the reflection that although we had become ops-ready in time to spend three profitable weeks raiding the enemy, Sod's law meant that, setting aside the delays due to training blockages, we had missed out on six more weeks of ops due to the hiatus when we lost Phil.

As it was, having to accommodate this was to be cushioned by a series of flights that were both gratifying and bizarre. For starting on 30 April 1945 we got airborne to drop supplies to the starving populace of Amsterdam, returning the next day to drop at The Hague. We'd been assured that an amnesty had been agreed with the Germans, but it was distinctly eerie to be flying at ultra low level so close to enemy guns; to feel them, in our imagination, tracking us as we swept by at fifty feet, bomb bay open, to free-drop especially strengthened sacks of staples onto, in our case, a racetrack. At the same time it was a highly emotional experience, for we were flying so low that the Dutch people gathered on buildings were waving down at us, and I can see them yet, clearly overcome with joy, flags waving, and obviously cheering us. Perhaps seeing the joyous side of war like this helped in my near-instant transition from warrior to humanitarian.

*Gratitude for Operation Manna, 1995*

There was a lot more cheering and flag waving a week later, on the 8 May 1945, when the news came through that it was all over. In Europe, at least. For many of us, however, the jollifications were cut short as Lanc crews were recalled from the pubs to our various stations, to be warned for a high priority task, codenamed Exodus, to start first thing next day.

Exodus turned out to be the repatriation of Allied prisoners of war, with No. 138's part being to position to Juvencourt, near Reims, in France, and take former POWs, up to twenty-four at a time, seated on the floor, back to Dunsfold in Surrey. This occupied us until the 22 May, with another one-off trip on 30 May. It was a duty that gave us many a heart-rending moment, especially when the lads arrived back in Britain ...

The war in Europe was over, but in view of what we'd heard of Japanese fanaticism, the Far-Eastern campaign seemed set to drag on for years. The RAF was working flat out to assemble a task group – Tiger Force – to send to the Far-Eastern theatre, therefore bombing, air firing and fighter affiliation sorties continued unabated, though with greater emphasis now on formation flying.

On the other hand, there had already been evidence that some things were running down, for as early as 25 May we'd been sent to jettison bombs in the North Sea. A little later we would repeat the exercise, dropping canisters of incendiaries into Cardigan Bay.

Domestically, most of the crew had become flight sergeants. Ralph had been one for some months. Now he was commissioned as a pilot officer. Basically, however, we carried on with training sorties, and waited to see what would happen.

What did happen, was that on 19 June 1945 I was handed an aerial camera, given a quick briefing on how to use it, then sent to try out my artistic prowess in the sky. One hour and forty minutes I was given. After that, the camera was taken away, and as the weeks passed I began to think that would be the last of it. Whatever *it* was.

On 5 July 1945, however, the squadrons to be involved were briefed for what we came to know as Operation Revue. The purpose of Revue was to provide a mosaic of photographs from which maps could be made. Accordingly, crews were assigned areas. The navs worked out the grids, the pilots flew them, and crew members who had been trained in air photography – like me – took the snaps. All through July, accordingly, our crew flogged its way up and down our assigned sectors.

We started in the Brunswick area (flying an eight-hour sortie), flew forwards and back across an area of France (eight hours), Denmark (six hours), France and Italy (ten hours), to France again (nine hours), and then, after a break until September 1945, to France and Germany (seven hours), and finally, North Wales (three hours) ...

On the face of it the whole thing seemed straightforward. Yet at the same time we were aware of pressure being applied. In fact, the rumour was that the government wanted to get the maps made before the various war-shocked sovereign states recovered enough to complain. As for Wales, presumably they were simply due a new map.

On 15 August 1945, however, while we were busy on Revue, the atomic bombs had been dropped, Japan had surrendered, and Tiger Force had been put on hold. And on 31 October, the units earmarked for it were taken off stand by.

After Revue finished we resumed the round of training flights, which inevitably meant encountering snags. For the most part these were merely frustrating, so that on a cross-country when the main navigation aid was to be the mapping radar H2S, it broke down, leaving us nothing to do but return to base. Then again, we were just running in on the bombing range when our bombsight gave up. More critical was to have our airspeed indicator stop reading in flight, when Ralph, needing to keep the speed up to avoid stalling on the approach, landed us at Woodbridge, one of the long, wide, purpose-built crash strips.

And on 18 November 1945, two days after carrying out a final cross country flight, the crew parted company with No. 138 Squadron, being transferred on posting to No. 35 Squadron, at RAF Gravely, five miles south of Huntingdon.

No. 35 Squadron, we found, had an illustrious history. As such, it had been one of the original five squadrons selected for the Pathfinder Force, the force which, in turn, had been so instrumental in reducing the German defences to the level I had experienced during my operational flights. It had then played a major part in bombing operations following on from some tellingly significant raids on D-Day. More latterly it had been earmarked for

Tiger Force, and had only been stood down a little over a fortnight before we joined.

Our main task was to repatriate British troops from the Eighth Army who were presently cooped up in holding camps in Italy, an undertaking codenamed Operation Dodge. For our crew Dodge started on 25 November 1945 when we flew from Gravely to Tibbenham, north of Diss, in Norfolk, followed by an eight hour leg to Ciampino, Rome. On 1 December 1945, we went on to one of the holding camps at Bari, way down on the south-east coast, and then, on 12 December, to the other at Pomigliano, Naples, touching down with a rough-running engine. And there we stayed, doubtfully eyeing a smoking Vesuvius, for two and a half weeks, awaiting spares. As Christmas came, and went.

The spares eventually arrived. But on 29 December 1945 when, with our engine allegedly made good, we carried out an air test, it failed on us, necessitating yet another landing on three. There was then a further delay, until 3 January 1946, when we finally made it back to base, via Tibbenham once again. I can only presume that the troops we were to ferry home – priority having been given to those who had been away for four and five years – had been repatriated by other aircraft. Or indeed, by ship ...

On arriving back at base it was the end of the road for the crew. Demob numbers were coming up, and with the others having signed on before me – and spent longer in training – they were soon on their way. We'd been through a lot together, what with one thing and another. But as it was back then, there was little time for reflection, once your number came up you couldn't wait to clear the station.

With the others gone, I remained with No. 35, flying on training sorties with various captains, at times now, in the rear turret. So that, by the time I did my final flight, in mid May 1946, when my own demob number came up, I had logged a total of 304 hours in the air. I was finally discharged in Blackpool, on 15 June 1946, after some three years in the Service.

Just three years: so infinitesimal a part of my life. And so long ago now. I rather think, at the time, I left the RAF without regrets. Certainly, I cannot remember giving much thought to staying in: and anyway there would have been little enough call for an air gunner ...

On being demobbed, however, I might well have returned to farming. Except that another opportunity had arisen in the interim, in another family business set up at the turn of the twentieth century in Derby, that of Brindley's Ladieswear. With the lack of silk stockings rivalling that of bananas as measures of austerity there was a lot of leeway to be made up. Starting in the office, I made Brindley's my career until I retired in 1990. Instrumental in all my decisions throughout my post-war life, of course, was my wife, whom I met in 1947 and was eventually to lose in 1992. What with my family, and the business, I gave little thought to those three fleeting year of wartime service. Indeed, it is only since I have been, in that sense, alone that I have made contact again, largely in company with other veterans.

Early on I joined the recently defunct Aircrew Association, and became a regular participant in events held at such venues as the Yorkshire Air Museum and East Kirkby. Along with my friend and British Legion associate Nevil Mottershead, I even supped NAAFI tea served by Victoria Wood on television! A daunting undertaking, I can tell you. But then it could be that in our youthful dicing in hostile skies we became inured to all life's challenges.

Or, perhaps, to all but one. For what could have armoured us against the opprobrium with which our efforts – sacrifices, for so many Bomber-Command aircrew – were to be regarded, almost before the ink was dry on the unconditional-surrender document? In 2013, sixty-eight years after the event, a Bomber Command Clasp was made available. How much less grudging we were, all those years ago!

*Tony Brindley, 2013*

# 6. The Jammy Beggar

## Warrant Officer George Reginald Hutton, air gunner

What annoyed us throughout the Schweinfurt op was the intermittent bleeping from a rearward-pointing radar gear named Monica. Its function was to detect fighters closing from the rear, but it cheesed us off so much that on all subsequent trips we kept it switched off. Only months later, and only after many bomber losses, did the boffins discover that it was the Monica signal the enemy fighters were homing in on.

*Sergeant George Hutton, 1943*

In 1941, when my call-up papers arrived, I was helping to build the 'Wooden Wonder' Mosquito fighter-bomber at the de Havilland Plant at Leavesden. I'd hoped to break free of my reserved occupation by applying to fly as RAF aircrew, but it was not until 11 April 1942 that I was actually attested into the Service. Even then there was a never-to-be-explained-muddle, for after a runaround that lasted until 12 June 1942, I was discharged, and resumed work at de Havillands.

For the next eight months I was both busily and usefully engaged with the Mosquito, but things eventually got sorted out and on 5 February 1943 I began training as an air gunner.

After being kitted out at St John's Wood, it was up to Blackpool for squarebashing, then to No. 1 Elementary Air Gunnery School at Bridlington followed, on 1 May 1943, by No. 1 Air Gunners School, at RAF Pembrey, in Carmarthenshire.

Here, using a mocked-up Browning turret, we fired an initial course on the twenty-five-yard range, expending some 1,300 rounds of ball and tracer; that is, live bullets and trail-leaving bullets. After that we graduated to Bristol Blenheim bombers and during fourteen hours in the air fired off 2,800 rounds in exercises embracing air-to-ground – loosing off at targets on the beach; air-to-air – firing at drogues towed behind other aircraft; and learning deflection shooting, that is, 'leading' fast-flying fighters by aiming at the point where they would be when our bullets arrived; we also learnt to use tracers to bring our bullet stream onto target.

The scores achieved can seem absurdly low: my overall average of hits to rounds fired, for example, being just 6.2%. This, though, was deemed creditable, my logbook being annotated, 'Hard, keen worker who will make a very useful air crew member.' And on 12 June 1943, now a qualified sergeant air gunner, I sewed up my AG brevet – the air gunner's half wing.

*The Air Gunner's brevet*

We resumed training at No. 1483 (Bomber) Gunnery Flight, at RAF Newmarket Heath, in Suffolk, a unit whose purpose was to give pre-operational training to bomb aimers and air gunners who, like me, came directly from training schools rather than from operational training units. Here, we broadened our experience by flying thirteen hours on Vickers Wellingtons, during which I shot off another 2,000 rounds, but also used the cine-camera gun, completing the course on 17 June 1943.

On 8 July, after a few days' leave, we made the short hop to RAF Waterbeach, near Cambridge, to No. 1651 Heavy Conversion Unit, where we were to become acquainted with the Short Stirling heavy bomber; and even more significantly, with the crews we were to fly with on operations. Until now the five of them – a first and second pilot, a navigator/bomb aimer, a front gunner/wireless operator and a tail gunner – had been gaining experience on twin-engined types. To operate the Stirling, however, they needed an upper gunner and a flight engineer.

As it transpired, I was posted in three days after the rest, so as the others had already formed themselves into crews I found myself detailed to one that had ended up short of a mid-upper gunner.

Although all seven of us gelled well, a process to be cemented during much of a first tour of thirty operations, and by many a night spent bevying in the Cambridgeshire pubs, we ended up chopping and changing so much that any crew list could only be representative. On my twenty-ninth operation, for example, a Lancaster raid on D-Day, 6 June 1944, my crew comprised:

Flight Sergeant Duncliffe, pilot, from Rugby (aged 21, with 23 ops),
Flight Sergeant Jock Lewis, navigator, from Aberdeen,
Flight Sergeant Harry Bourne, bomb aimer, from Faversham,
Sergeant Hollis, flight engineer, from Burnley,
Sergeant Baker, wireless operator/air gunner, from Amersham,
Flight Sergeant George Hutton, mid-upper gunner (a Watford lad), and
Sergeant Guy, rear gunner, from Glasgow.

*The Short Stirling*

For us gunners the conversion was straightforward enough, although I must confess to spending most of the first Stirling sortie trying to discover where to plug in my oxygen tube! The machine's technical complexities, certainly, gave many a headache to our flight engineers, while the majority of pilots found it a real beast to handle on the ground, particularly in a crosswind. Even having been checked out for operations one pilot swung on take-off, got airborne with a section of the bomb-dump fence dangling behind him, and touched down several hours later having taken it to Germany and back.

The conversion began with exercises designed to familiarise the pilots and flight engineers with handling the machine: circuits and landings, steep turns, and flying with various engines stopped. In all we did just under twenty hours, three hours by day, and fifteen by night.

We then moved on to cross-country flying, the exercises culminating, on 8 July 1943, in a near six-hour exercise designated as a 'Bullseye', that is, a flight which aimed to be as near as possible to a real operational sortie. And on landing, with our crew rated as fully operational, my log book showed that I had flown a total of fifty-seven hours.

On 25 July 1943 we reported to No. 199 Squadron, at RAF Lakenheath, near Mildenhall, in Suffolk, where we did another twenty-odd hours of acclimatisation. The day before we appeared on the operations board for the first time, however, the new gunners were called before the squadron gunnery officer.

'Hutton, isn't it?' he opened, singling me out. 'Tell us what your training's taught you.'

Though taken aback, I spoke about firing ahead of fast-closing fighters, about using tracer to bring home a stream of bullets, and, of course, about aircraft recognition. My theme, throughout, was aggressiveness.

He nodded. Then looked around. 'All agree?' I was glad to hear a chorus of assent.

'Right,' he said. 'Then here and now forget all that. Here, we ask just two things of you. First, never stop searching the sky. Second, the instant you see something that appears threatening, shout, "Port, go!" or "Starboard, go!" as you think fit. Your pilot will instantly push into a spiral until you're in the clear.' Again he paused. 'The very last thing we want is for you to spew tracer and give away your position.' He paused yet again. 'Any questions?'

But he knew there wouldn't be. Each of us had got the message. Loud, clear, and lasting.

We flew our first operation on 1 August 1943, carrying out a night sea-mining operation off Bordeaux in which we sowed Mk. 1 mines weighing 1,500 pounds and containing some 750 pounds of explosive. This first op, lasting nearly seven and a half hours, held its own tensions, but was essentially uneventful. What a relief though, to finally log an operational flight!

We were back on ops just days later, raiding Nuremburg, our first German target, and after that, on two successive occasions, Turin, across the Alps, each trip taking over eight hours. It was during the Turin sorties that we first became truly aware of the altitude limitations of the Stirling, for we had to thread our way past moonlit Alpine peaks rising to nearly 16,000 feet while our service ceiling – effectively, the best altitude we could hope for – was only 16,500 feet.

On 23 August it was back to Germany again, this time to the Big One, Berlin. I suppose this should have been significant, but we all realised that any target was fraught, that there was no such thing as an 'easy' op.

On approaching Berlin, however, the defences couldn't fail to impress. They were said to spread twenty to thirty miles wide, with the flak controllers continually varying the bursting height so that the glare of explosions rose and fell like the tide of some baleful sea. I have to say, though, that I found the display fascinating, rather than daunting. Clearly I had the right nature for the job; it didn't pay to be too imaginative.

I remember we carried two American fliers, newly arrived from the States, to give them a taste of what 'missions' – as they called ops – were like. As we neared the flak they eyed it appreciatively.

'Wa-all,' drawled one of them finally, 'very impressive. But when do you start grabbing some altitood?'

'Altitude?' our pilot told him, 'I'm afraid this is it, Old Boy.'

There was a brief silence. And then a heartfelt, '*Jesus Christ!*'

On any American type they would have been flying at nearer 30,000 feet, way above virtually all the flak.

Terrain clearance, rather than altitude, proved a major problem when we were tasked to block the Fréjus Rail Tunnel, at Modane, on 16 September 1943. The tunnel allowed the enemy to move materiel from France to Italy, but the rails ran in a steep gorge, so even had the marking been good, hitting the tunnel's mouth would have been difficult. 127 Stirlings were committed, and those, like our section, detailed to go in low, had to form a procession. Having dropped, therefore, there was no question of turning back towards flat ground, all the pilots could do was haul back on the stick and hope to zoom-climb clear. Fortunately the Stirling was surprisingly manoeuvrable at low level, but even after avoiding the terrain we had to plough through the 170 Halifaxes and 43 Lancasters who were attacking the main rail installation, 340 bombers in total. An absorbing way, if not a comfortable one, in which to pass some eight hours. Two Halifaxes and one Stirling were lost.

At Modane we dropped four 1,000 pound high-explosive bombs. More commonly we released a mix of high explosives and incendiaries, as when, early in September, we raided the Dunlop rubber factory at Montluçon. On one occasion, though, our crew took no ordnance at all, but only the metallic strips called 'Window', which were dropped to clutter up the enemy radars and confuse the defences. And at Hanover, on 27 September, our load was all incendiaries, eleven canisters of thirty pounders and eleven of four pounders.

What was to be my last op on No. 199 Squadron, and also on Stirlings, I flew on 4 October 1943 when we raided Frankfurt. On landing I had completed eleven ops, and flown 61 day and 104 night hours, 82 of these operational. By the time I flew my next op, on 6 December 1943, I had moved to No. 514 Squadron at RAF Waterbeach, Cambridge, and onto everyone's favourite, the Avro Lancaster.

There was simply no comparison between the Stirling and the Lancaster. To a gunner one turret was much the same as another, but from the moment you climbed aboard the Lanc, the difference was palpable. And once you felt the acceleration on the runway you knew you were aboard something special!

The pilot and the flight engineer had learnt to handle the new machine during a conversion course, but my first Lancaster flight was my twelfth op, and to Berlin once more, a destination we reprised the very next night. Whereas in the Stirling Berlin took us over nine hours, the Lanc got us back to base in something over seven.

Even so we did some muttering on 14 January 1944 when, ninety minutes out towards Brunswick, an intercom failure forced us to turn back. This meant that we'd been through the pre-op nerving up, and even crossed the enemy coastal defences, and all for nothing, for an aborted trip – a 'Boomerang' – didn't count against the thirty ops required. Yet on 24 February we had to abort a Leipzig op, and on 8 June, one near Paris.

Another non-op, though, was most welcome. We were actually lined up ready to go when the trip was scrubbed because of bad weather. The rest of the squadron were as cast down as they would have been at a boomerang, whereas the cancellation enabled our crew to get away a day early on a week's leave. 'Jammy sods,' the others barracked.

Not all pilots inspired equal degrees of confidence, and mid January, when we assigned to fly with a newly-arrived pilot, ushered in a particularly uncomfortable period for our crew. We flew with him for some eleven hours, among other things on navigational exercises and a four-hour weight-and-load exercise – on the Lancaster, of course, we could carry 14,000 pounds of bombs up to just over 21,000 feet. Although by now we were all relatively competent, our new pilot was continually chivvying us. As for his own performance, he not only taxied the aircraft into a loaded bomb trolley but attempted to land with his wheels up.

Even so we were hoping for the best when, on 24 February 1944, he got us airborne for Leipzig. An hour out, however, two engines began to run so rough that one had to be stopped and feathered. This meant that we slowed, and fell back, lost our place in the bomber stream, and even lagged behind the radar-blanking effect of Window.

'We'll carry on,' our pilot declared.

The silence on the intercom was deafening. What he was proposing was that for a full five or so hours we were to be a lame duck, and the prey, therefore, of every anti-aircraft gun and night-fighter the Germans had.

'Then you'll have to do it on your own,' the flight engineer said bluntly, 'I'll have no part in it.'

There was another silence . 'Give us a course to base, Nav,' the pilot said finally. And we all relaxed. Only to find that a little premature.

At a late stage he became dissatisfied with his landing approach, perhaps he was a little high. Anyway, he pushed forward the throttles, but evidently forgot to compensate for the lack of power from the dead engine, for the aircraft skidded off to one side, passing between two hangars before he regained control. I distinctly recall gazing down into the terrified face of a cyclist only feet below me.

After sleeping it off, another gunner and I sought an interview with the wing commander and said we didn't want to fly with this pilot any more.

The wing co eyed the tasking board, taking in the number of ops we'd done. 'You both know what you're talking about. Right, I'll see to it, but –' he turned to us appealingly, 'Don't spread it about, otherwise we'll never get anyone to fly with the bugger.'

Others did fly with him, of course, so he probably settled, but on 30 June 1944 he and his crew failed to return from an op near Caen.

Our next outing was to Schweinfurt, and despite it being a dicey flog of seven hours plus, we found it a refreshing change, with any harrying coming from outside, and not inside.

What annoyed us throughout, though, was the intermittent bleeping from a rearward-pointing radar gear named Monica. Its function was to detect fighters closing from the rear, but it cheesed us off so much that on all subsequent trips we kept it switched off. Only months later, and only after many bomber losses, did the boffins discover that it was the Monica signal the enemy fighters were homing in on.

Nobody doubted that the Germans were technically able, but there was one encounter I've never been able to satisfactorily reconcile. We were just about to run in when I saw two streaks of light closing with us. I called an evading turn, *only to see the streaks follow suit*: most definitely so! I was about to call a reverse turn when, like burnt-out fireworks, they faltered, and fell away.

At de-briefing my report was noted, but that was that. It would be very many years before I learnt that the Germans had indeed been experimenting with air-to-air homing missiles.

Another encounter we had with a night-fighter was very nearly as bizarre. We were running in on the target when the nav called for a relatively marked heading change to starboard. The aircraft banked over slightly and I found myself gazing down at a German night-fighter just feet below us. It too was in a right-hand bank but against the ground fires I could see that its pilot was craning downwards. He had no idea we were there, while I had not the slightest notion of trying to bring my guns to bear. The skipper levelled the wings, and moments later we dropped our bombs. And turned for home ...

There was one pilot we flew with, Warrant Officer McGown, who had all our confidence. On 30 March 1944 we'd done an op to Nuremburg, but unexpected headwinds ran us short of fuel. Then, on coasting in, we learnt that Waterbeach was experiencing dense fog. Mac made several approaches but was never able to line up satisfactorily. In the end – we logged the flight as lasting nine hours and twenty-five minutes –, he climbed away, giving us the option of staying with the aircraft while he and the flight engineer put it down blind, or of baling out.

After a brief discussion, the rest of us decided to take to our parachutes. For my part I knelt at the exit to avoid hitting my head, and tumbled out. Moments later, I pulled the ripcord, and found myself floating earthwards through the blackness.

McGown got the aircraft onto the ground safely enough and although it had to be written off after a wheel ran into a ditch, he and the flight engineer were OK. As were us parachutists. Even the wireless operator, who landed on a roof and with his canopy draped on one side of its ridge and him on the other, found himself dangling near a skylight. Moments later this flew open as the startled resident demanded, 'What the hell are you doing up here?'

'Bird-nesting,' our w/op told him brightly. At which he was dragged in, affably nodding to the wife, abed still with a sheet pulled up around her.

Quite a character, our sparks. After his first op, having decided that his legs were vulnerable, he flew squatting on his seat. And just as well, for when a projectile transited his compartment low down, passing beneath the seat, it left him unscathed.

For my part I landed sedately in a field, then followed a line of telegraph poles until I reached a sizeable house, where the door was opened by a trimly turned-out maid. She squealed at the sight of me and ran off upstairs, returning shortly afterwards to advise, 'Madam says, won't you please come in?'

Madam – a doctor – insisted on having breakfast prepared while the authorities were phoned. Halfway through the meal a soldier was ushered in, 'So this is where you got to,' he acknowledged, 'we've been searching all over.'

Prompted by our hostess, he joined me, with gusto. As, a little later, did a search party of policemen. Eventually, well nourished and cosseted, I was delivered to Saffron Waldon police station and thence to base, some seventeen miles away.

And so it was that I became a member of the celebrated Caterpillar Club, having had a parachute save my life!

*Caterpillar Club certificate, and brooch*

One of my closest calls afforded the whole crew considerable amusement. Our practice was to go onto oxygen as we settled into the climb. On one high-altitude training sortie, however, our resident Gremlins decided to sabotage my oxygen regulator. As a result, with my brain starved of oxygen, I became dopey and began to babble on the intercom. All very amusing, and the rest had a great time of it until the pilot cut the throttles and brought us down to an altitude where I came to my senses. I had to suffer a considerable amount of ribbing, of course, and pay for several rounds.

Rounds, because as I indicated earlier, we spent a considerable amount of our free time 'bevying' in the local pubs. Indeed, I might even say that we focused more upon drinking than we did upon wenching. Strange that, for we were all young, with very normal drives, and there were scuds of attractive girls around.

Though there were a few girls we tended to steer clear of. Like the stunner we grew to know as 'Flak Annie' – most stations had one. Delightful though she was, every lad she dated got the chop ...

This though, probably tickled our, arguably, far too ready sense of black humour. Black humour typified by the squadron starting a 'GH chop board', and betting on who would get the chop first, me (GH, George Hutton) or my best friend, a gunner on another crew, named George Henry, again GH. Our crews had joined the squadron on the same day and were within one op of each other, the order swapping after each tasking change or boomerang. As it happened, both of us survived the war.

Our friendship, however, revealed a lot about our inner feelings back then. I still maintain that once we'd landed I never felt nervous, a few beers, and I could sleep like a babe. Nothing to do with courage. It was just my temperament. And my youth.

It was gradually borne upon me, however, that if George was airborne on an op while my crew were stood down, I was quite unable to sleep. I'd toss and turn until the lads began making their approaches. And even then it was only when I heard George's boots clumping along the passage that I could drop off. And George, I eventually discovered, had the same experience!

There was nervousness enough in the air, of course, even when we settled with the trusty Flight Sergeant Joe Duncliffe as our pilot. On one notable occasion we'd been damaged by both fighters and flak in the target area and were just beginning to relax as we approached the Dutch coast; only to be coned by what seemed like scores of searchlights and to become the focus of the most furious concentration of flak. Spiralling did us no good, it was as if the glare had us pinned to the sky. Only when we got far enough out to sea did they lose us, and allow us to begin breathing once more.

Joe showed his calibre that night, for having coasted in he set about having every system checked, putting down flaps and undercarriage, and in particular having us use our hand torches to ensure that the tyres were undamaged. Only then did he descend from parachuting height and make an approach.

With Joe at the helm we continued to raid industrial centres, successively visiting Cologne, Stuttgart, Essen, and Fredrickshaven. From April 1944 onwards, however, we began to be tasked against rail installations, notably at Aachen, only just over the Belgian border, where the defences were fierce and night-fighters abounded. Our squadron lost one aircraft, but the force as a whole, 162 Lancasters, lost 12, or 7.4%. At less cost we also raided rail centres at Rouen, Nantes, Laon, Courtrai, Angers, and Trappes, and bombed artillery concentrations at Cap Griz Nez.

It was clear that the intention was to disrupt communications networks in advance of the invasion: at this stage only the date remained to be settled, for the build up could hardly be missed.

On 6 June 1944, D-Day, we were airborne just before dawn, our target a strongpoint of six-inch coastal guns at Ouistreham, near Caen. Earlier, there had been a definite buzz at briefing, a sense of impending events.

'Special orders from Group,' the station commander had announced on closing the briefing. 'Take no notice of anything you see in the Channel. Under no circumstances jettison bombs to the west of your route. Above all, don't overshoot your target.' He'd allowed a moment for comment, then held up his hand. 'I've not been told that this is the Second Front, but if you knock out these batteries you'll have done a grand job.'

The whole thing had been unusual. Not least being called for briefing an hour or so after midnight when we were normally under way long before then. And the weather had turned kind. For some days it had been rough and stormy, indeed, later we'd learn that it had caused General Eisenhower to put the invasion back a day. Now though, although there was low cloud, the upper sky was moonlit. Not an unmixed blessing, for the scores of bombers were only too easy to see, a sight that kept the intercom busy with soft advisories, 'Kite dead ahead, above, Skip,' and moments later, 'Kite on your port bow, Skip, same height.'

The bomber stream aside, what really set our nerves tingling was the scene that greeted us over the Channel. There were two vast convoys, each comprising thousands of vessels, all heading for France. Around them were scuds of other ships, escort destroyers we thought, wheeling about and fretting the surface with their washes.

The naval bombardment began when we were some fifteen miles from the Normandy coast, fuelling great splashes of colour that lit up the low cloud. There were corresponding flashes from inland, and once a massive explosion that actually burst through the cloud canopy. A few minutes more, and just off to the right, three flak ships opened up, their tracer streaking skywards towards something – not us, thank goodness! – that had caught their attention.

At the same time the composition of the fleets below changed, the warships giving way to innumerable landing craft, each under its own power, each leading its own wake as it headed for its assigned spot on the beach.

There was so much to take in. So much too, though, to ignore. For vigilance was always the gunners' first priority. Yet though our eyes were ceaselessly sweeping the skies, we were still aware of bomb-aimer Harry's monologue, 'Bomb doors open, Skip,' and moments later, 'Keep her steady ...' Then, 'Bombs gone,' and the upward surge.

There followed the necessary holding of heading until the photo flash went off, then the acceleration as Joe throttled up and banked over onto the homebound course. Another fraught time, with immediate warnings on the intercom, 'Kite to port, Skip,' as others turned homebound too. And the first signs of opposition.

'Look out, Skip. Right ahead of us. Flak coming up.'

And Joe's laconic response, 'Ever seen it going down, Harry?'

The exchange brought to mind one from an earlier sortie when the flak on the run up had been particularly bad. With bombs gone the nav had called, virtually pleading, 'Skip, get us out of here, and I'll give you a course for home.' 'Get us out of here?' Joe-the-driver protested, 'you were the one got us in here in the first place.'

Now on D-Day, heading home, the cloud cleared for a moment or two, just long enough to give us a final glimpse of the vast armada still closing with the French coast – I'd hear later that there had been over 6,000 vessels!

At which juncture the ever paler skies above us became full of American aircraft, Fortresses and Liberators, with scuds of escort fighters all, like us, with wings and fuselages bearing black and white stripes, painted overnight for instant identification, all hell-bent on furthering the good work. In truth, few three-hour five minute periods in my life have been quite so full of incident!

The next day was intended to be equally special. For me, if not for Eisenhower. The op was to take us to a target near Paris. And it was to be my thirtieth, the last of my tour. Just over an hour out, however, our compasses went wild, leaving us no option but to abort. Yet another boomerang!

I didn't have long to wait, though, for we were on the tasking board just a day later, 8 June 1944, and back to Northern France again, this time to the rail yards of Fougères. The weather was not that good, but at least it held off the German fighters, and with the target lying south and west of the new fighting front we saw plenty going on below. As for our target, having steadied on course for home we could see smoke towering through thousands of feet.

The sortie took four hours and forty minutes, and when we touched down I had completed my first tour. Thirty reckonable operations, a total of 179 operational hours flown (81 plus on the Stirling, 98 on the Lancaster), and a grand total of 298 hours, 89 by day and 209 by night. Two aircraft of the stream did not return. And one of them was Warrant Officer McGown's.

When crews finished their thirty ops there were a few who opted to continue, when another fifteen sorties with a crew they knew and trusted would count as the second tour, and the limit of their commitment. This was not an option for me as I was the only one completing my tour. As it was I accepted the wing commander's thanks, 'cleared' the station, shouldered my kitbags, and hurried off on leave.

At that time the expectation for tour-ex aircrew was that they would be 'screened' for six months or so: that is, they would be otherwise employed before being recalled for a second, and final, tour. In my case, I became a gunnery instructor with No. 11 Air Gunnery School at RAF Andreas, one of two adjacent airfields (the other being Jurby) near Ramsey, Isle of Man.

I arrived in mid-August 1944 and was given a full briefing. The pupils, I discovered, were put through a very comprehensive ten-week course that covered gunnery theory and familiarised them with every gun and turret they were likely to encounter on a squadron. The flying was done in Ansons and Wellingtons, with Martinets to tow drogues, while air-to-ground and air-to-sea firing was carried out on the doorstep, at the Point of Ayre, the island's northernmost extremity. Certainly, it looked as if my rest tour was going to be both a busy one and an interesting one. I was not to know that it was to be even more interesting than I could have supposed.

The briefing over, I found myself at a loose end. The mess would be empty until classes finished, so on a whim I hitched a ride into Ramsey. At first sight the resort didn't seem to have much to offer.

'There's a Local Aid canteen, Chiefy,' the driver suggested – by now I was a flight sergeant, with a crown above my three stripes, and so, a 'chiefy' in the parlance. Churlish of me to say it, but obliging as he was, I have to say

that the driver was a most unlikely Cupid!

The canteen, a tin-roofed affair, was almost empty apart from the staff, although it did contain two dogs who had evidently made it their home. It also contained the most attractive young WAAF wireless operator, Leading Aircraftwoman Barbara Wood (forevermore, Babs to me ...)

### Leading Aircraftwoman Barbara Wood, 1944

Barbara was stationed at Ramsey, in what had been designed as a new wing of the ancient grammar school, where her job was to monitor transmissions from aircraft using the extensive training area bounded by Liverpool, Glasgow, and Belfast.

In Barbara's part of the operation – there were also radar stations involved –, aircraft position reports received by her and her colleagues would be presented as moveable counters on a table map set beneath the controller's balcony. This enabled the controller to keep the various bombing and firing ranges efficiently occupied while minimising the risk of participating aircraft bumping into each other. In fact, the system was the forerunner of Britain's modern air traffic control system.

I have to confess, however, that job descriptions took back-burner space for quite some time. Suffice to say that this serendipitous meeting led to a happy marriage of coming up to seventy years' standing.

From then on I spent as much time as possible with Barbara. Work, though kept me busy, for although the overriding need for air gunners had passed, the number of trainees in the system had yet to reflect this.

I started my instructional duties on 21 August 1944 flying in a single-engined Miles Martinet, warily eyeing an Anson aboard which pupil air gunners were carrying out beam attacks on a drogue that suddenly seemed all too close to our tail.

Most days, though, I flew in the Anson myself, monitoring pupils firing from its turret. We spent time on firing air-to-ground, and employed both live ammunition and cine-camera guns as pupils dealt with beam, quarter, and cross-over attacks from participating fighters. Additionally, pupils flew in our sadly aged Wellingtons, not least learning to use tracer as an aiming tool. The hour-long sessions lacked the tension of ops but were never dull.

On 31 December 1944, however, I was recalled to operations. Naturally the posting caused something of a hiatus in the relationship between me and Barbara, except that we were realists: there was, after all, a war on ...

I was sent to the No. 2 Group Support Unit at RAF Fersfield, near Diss, in Norfolk, a unit that maintained a pool of aircrew from which No. 2 Group could replace casualties or people completing their operational tours. The aircraft it flew was the North American Mitchell, the B-25 twin-engined tactical bomber operated by the Group's squadrons in Europe.

*North American B-25 Mitchell*

Our Mitchells carried four crew, a pilot, a navigator, a wireless operator/ air gunner, and an air gunner. For the greater part of February 1945 I flew with our commanding officer, Wing Commander Cyril Carpenter, variously filling the mid-upper, waist, and rear gunner positions. The wing co was great to fly with, though his easy approachability led to a tragicomic mix-up.

On 22 February 1945 we'd just landed when an ops clerk told me that Barbara had phoned from Rochdale, asking if I could get a few days leave to support her as her father had become seriously ill. The wing co glanced at the clock. 'Double off now,' he said, 'and you'll get a train. We'll sort the paperwork out when you get back.'

Having stayed at Rochdale for three days, I arrived back at Fersfield after dark and, finding our section of the Nissen hut empty, concluded that the rest of the crew had landed away, the weather not having been that special.

Next morning, halfway through shaving, I was mystified when someone did a double-take on seeing me, muttered, 'Jammy beggar!' and disappeared. Only to be yet more mystified, at breakfast, by similar reactions. It then transpired that the day before, 25 February 1945, the wing co's Mitchell, being flown at low level, in bad visibility, had hit some trees and crashed in Clumber Park, near Worksop. None of my crew had survived, so with no paperwork on file, those not immediately involved with the flight had assumed I'd been aboard ...

Throughout March 1945 I flew with a Flight Lieutenant Barlow, increasingly concentrating on map-reading sorties, for as the primary task of the squadrons in Europe was close support to the army, accurate map reading was essential to avoid bombing our own forces.

For Barlow's crew the awaited call to ops came at the end of March, and in early April 1945 we joined No. 180 Squadron, Second Tactical Air Force, at Melsbroek (Brussels), in Belgium. Altogether, my rest tour had lasted nearly eight months: I was certainly jammier than many.

As Melsbroek we were billeted in a convent which was so bitterly cold that I thought back fondly to the over-warm environment of de Havillands where I'd dreamed up the competition couplet, 'Turn off the heaters, and build more Moskeeters'. *Well,* it won me a ten-pound prize!

Beyond the convent, there was much evidence of the previous tenants, not least one of the hangars which the Germans had disguised as a row of cottages.

*Luftwaffe hangar disguised as a row of cottages*

I began my second tour of operations on 6 April 1945 with a two and a half hour daytime bombing sortie to Sögel, in Lower Saxony, following this with one of similar length on 11 April when we were summoned to bomb troops concentrated at Cloppenburg, a little further into Saxony.

In quick succession we then bombed rail yards at Saltau on Germany's Lüneburg Heath, gun positions near Voorst, in Holland, a factory near Arnhem, troop billets at Oldenburg, raided Dunkirk twice, then returned to Oldenburg to pulverise its rail yards.

These ops were quite unlike those on my first tour. All were daylight sorties – and therefore, by convention, logged in green, as apposed to red – and the longest was under four hours. Most called for a medium- or low-level approach to the target which brought us under fire from weapons of all calibres. Zestful flights, but hardly comfortable. I did, however, fly as mid-upper gunner, the position in which I felt most at home. We flew some twenty operational hours before, on 30 April, the squadron upped sticks and moved into Germany itself, to Achmer, near Osnabrück.

On 1 May 1945 we bombed an airfield near Lübeck, just an hour away. It was the tenth op of my second tour, my fortieth in total. And my last. For on 4 May 1945 Field Marshal Montgomery accepted the unconditional surrender of all German forces in our area.

With the war effectively over, it was time for taking stock. So on 4 June I started a series of flights, taking Canadian Army personnel on 'Cook's sightseeing tours of the Ruhr. In like vein I went avisiting and had a photo of me taken with Cologne Cathedral rising above the rubble.

***Warrant Officer George Hutton in Cologne***

On 7 June we returned to Fersfield for a week's training. After which we did a fair amount of shuttling between Europe and England until, on 24 August 1945, I did my last Service flight, closing my flying logbook on 279 day and 213 night hours, a total of 492 hours, including 202 on operations.

And five days later, on 30 August 1945, Barbara and I were married in Rochdale. It was to be 4 November 1946, however, before my demob number came up, and I left the RAF.

My wartime service had given me many memories, both pleasant, and unpleasant. One aspect of the experience, however, that of recognition, was to rankle.

Although I never bothered to claim my medals, my Service and Release Book shows my award entitlement to be the 1939/45 Star, the France and Germany Star, and the award specifically for fliers, the Aircrew Europe Star. Yet those who began their operational flying with me on No. 180 Squadron, starting after 5 June 1944, were ineligible for the Aircrew Europe, so got nothing to show that they'd flown on operations.

Then, of course, once the war was over Bomber Command became a national pariah. True, the outcasts seized their chance to react at the Bomber Command Reunion at the Albert Hall on 12 March 1949 when the official order of events was disrupted by a 7,000 voice chant of 'We want Butch'. At which juncture a cable was read out from the former C.-in-C. Bomber Command who was then living in Cape Town. This was Marshal of the Royal Air Force Sir Arthur Travers Harris – His posh nickname was 'Bomber', but to us he was always 'Butch', for butcher – more black humour!

Having praised the ground personnel who kept us all flying, Butch went on, 'But, above all, my admiration to those too few survivors of our devoted air crews who knocked the enemy flat ... and whose sons, if need be, will knock him yet flatter, after the long-haired gentry get through picking him up, dusting him off and kissing him better – yet once again ...'. He even gave us instructors a mention, 'My salaams to the instructors who kept their necks stuck out to lessen odds on other necks.'

It is with wryness, therefore, that I view the issue of a Bomber Command Clasp in 2013, nearly seventy years after the event.

*Bomber Command Clasp, 2013*

Having left the service, I followed a career in de Havillands at Broughton, near Chester, remaining after 1960 when they became Hawker Siddeley, and working in engineering design until I retired. Initially I not only had a reserve commitment to the RAF, but also a promise that, if remobilized because the present conflict had started up again, I was to be paid five shillings!

Rather better remuneration was offered when I was approached to train air gunners for the Argentinean air force. But Barbara and I decided that forty air-gunnery ops was more than enough neck-sticking-out for anyone, no matter how jammy an individual.

*George Hutton, 2013*

# 7. All Is Destiny

## Warrant Officer Ronald Hubert (Squiggle) Eeles. air gunner (rear turret)

I banged at the turret's doors with my elbows, reached up and rearwards for the handholds, then half-swung, half-backed into the tail section. Staggering onto cramped legs I grabbed my 'chute from its stowage, looked forward, registered Speedy, the mid-upper, but beyond him, saw nothing but red-tinged smoke. Then there was only the open door, and the night.

*So was this was how Destiny played the game ...*

*Sergeant Ron Eeles, 1943, air gunner*

When war broke out I was fifteen and had left school to work in a Smethwick firm making metal-framed windows: under government pressure everyone wanted Nissen-type huts so business was booming. I worked in the office by day but swelled my ten shillings a week pay by welding frames in the factory at night. Good wages, but I was harbouring a long-held ambition to join the RAF, although my mother was dead set against the notion. As a stopgap, therefore, I joined the newly-instituted Air Training Corps, and bided my time.

It came in late 1942 when I heard of the RAF's Pilot-Navigator-Bomb-Aimer (PNB) recruiting drive and got permission from work to apply. After medicals and a battery of tests and interviews I found myself before a board of three officers who seemed taken aback when I told them I wanted to become an air gunner.

'You're not interested in PNB, then?' the senior member asked.

'No, sir.' I'd done my homework and thought I could see the way the war was going.

The board conferred once more over my paperwork. I'd always thought myself a duffer at grammar school, and had left when it had been evacuated after the Birmingham Blitz. They, though, seemed satisfied.

'Then what about wireless operator/air gunner?'

Again, I'd done my homework. The wireless training would take months. Months which would lessen my chances of doing some payback.

'Air gunner, Sir,' I insisted.

Finally, they indicated a puzzled acceptance, but warned me I'd still have to wait until I was eighteen and a half.

### The Birmingham Blitz, 1940 – 1943

Duly attested as a trainee air gunner, but obliged to wait, I resumed work. And on the very morning I turned the stipulated age, call-up papers formally summoned me to Lord's Cricket Ground for kitting up and the like. After that, it was full steam ahead, seven weeks at No. 20 Initial Training Wing at Bridlington ... Except that, sunning myself on the beach, I came out in a rash, and was in trepidation, the RAF counting sunburn as a self-inflicted injury. All that happened, though, was that I was put back for a week.

In late May 1943 I arrived at the Elementary Gunnery School at Bridgnorth, Shropshire. Having taken my arrival chit around the station in the morning, however, and fired off a few rounds from a Browning machine gun after lunch, I was told that the course was cancelled. What they needed, though, were volunteers for immediate transfer to No. 11 Air Gunnery School, at Andreas, on the Isle of Man. Nothing loth to get some overseas service in, I put up my hand.

I arrived at the far shore – Douglas – without having disgraced myself on the choppy voyage over, and began training in earnest, four of us at a time flying hour-long sorties in 'Annie' Ansons. A very friendly aircraft, except that its undercarriage had to be wound up and down: some 130 turns before two green indicators showed. This would not have been so bad had the chief gunnery officer not insisted that we fly in Sidcot flying suits: still stifling, though we wore nothing beneath them.

Many flights were spent firing from the Anson's dorsal – back-mounted – turret at canvas drogues towed by Miles Martinet trainers. When we used live ammunition the Martinets would hold the drogue level 300 yards off our beam, but when we used camera guns they would attack from 400 yards, close to 150 yards – using either a curve of pursuit, or a shallow dive –, and break off at 150 yards. Progress was not helped by guns jamming, or firing slow, or being badly aligned, by turrets jerking, or even fusing altogether. Nor did it help to have a drogue lose its back half, with any shots scored disappearing.

Perhaps too, things were made more difficult by having some Czech and Polish pilots who always gave the impression of being drunk. I particularly remember a Sergeant Glowgowski persisting with the sortie despite low cloud forcing the Martinet down to 300 feet with bad visibility below. Even so, I scored a very decent 12 hits out of 200, so maybe, 'resting' from ops as Glowgowski was, he knew what he was about.

Anyway, defects and mad Poles notwithstanding, we made the most of every sortie, and on 17 July 1943, having flown 21 hours; obtained 83.6% in the ground-school exams; and scored two exceptional 11% hits in air-firing to produce an overall 'very acceptable' average of 2.5% hits, my log book was annotated 'Sound knowledge: a good, practical worker,' and I was awarded my air-gunner brevet and sergeant's stripes. If 'award' is the right word for being told to draw them from stores.

At the end of July 1943 our group of newly-qualified air gunners arrived at No. 29 Operational Training Unit, RAF Bruntingthorpe, to the south of Leicester, then equipped with Wellingtons. That first afternoon all new course members were assembled in the sun behind one of the hangars to sort themselves into crews. Perhaps I was too shy to push myself forward, but I was leaning against a fence when a scruffy-looking pilot strolled up.

'Would you like to fly with me?' he asked in a public school accent.

This was Sergeant Pilot George Edward (Ted) Ball – he'd call me 'Squiggle', or Sergeant; I'd call him Skipper, Ted, or Sir, as the Service occasion demanded. He had already gathered the rest of the five-man crew the Wellington required. Listing them now, they were,

Sergeant George Millar, navigator

Sergeant G.A. (Ray) Rae, Royal Canadian Air Force, bomb aimer

Sergeant (later Pilot Officer) John (Ian) Kernahan, wireless operator

And me, Sergeant Ronald H. (Squiggle) Eeles, air gunner (rear turret).

The first part of the course was spent on lectures, so although the five of us got to know each other to a certain extent it was only when we began flying that we started to gell as a crew.

We began the flying phase on 10 March 1943, moving to Bruntingthorpe's satellite, RAF Bitteswell, where we started on circuits and landings, not least single-engined landings, then took in high-level bombing, and some air-firing, including fighter affiliation. After that, on 6 September we returned to Bruntingthorpe for the advanced exercises, mainly increasingly ambitious navigational cross-countries. These included a 'Bullseye', the code name for a cross-country designed to come as close to an operational sortie as possible, in this case a long-ranging, six-and-a-half-hour flight across southern England and Wales in the course of which we were intercepted by a Beaufighter. Having got airborne on a second Bullseye we were recalled when bad weather closed in.

One trip I found particularly intriguing included an air-firing session for which, once we got over the sea, I had to reel out a drogue, loose off 400 shots as it trailed behind my turret, then reel it back in for subsequent checking. In fact, that sortie too was curtailed by bad weather, forcing us to divert into Woodhall Spa.

We were to finish the course by carrying out a 'Nickel', that is, a leaflet drop over enemy territory, except that the oxygen supply failed and we had to turn back after an hour in the air. And what a palaver that caused! We were individually interviewed to determine whether the fault had been genuine. Most of us found the suspicion that we might be lily-livered laughable. Only months later would we fully appreciate that it had been no laughing matter to Skipper Ted.

Two days later, however, we duly dropped our leaflets over Orleans, the sortie taking us nearly five hours. Strangely, thinking of it in retrospect, such an extended flight over far-from-benign territory did not count as an operation ...

That aside, the successful flight marked the end of the course, during which we had flown some 85 hours, bringing my logbook total to 106 hours.

At this stage, the start of November 1943, we ran up against a training blockage and were sent to mark time at RAF Scampton. On 28 November, however, I was detached to RAF Syerston, near Newark, to No. 1485 Gunnery Course, where I sat through a half-dozen short flights on a Wellington during which I practised with a camera gun as various pilots put me through the corkscrew evasion manoeuvre: a spiralling, tight-turning descent designed to throw off fighters. I rather think rear gunners were put through this to see how they coped: if their stomachs were upset by the forces generated at the rear end of the Wellington, they'd be of little use to a crew if their somewhat-longer heavy bomber had to evade. Possibly my overseas ferry trip paid off, for although I had to fight off 'blackout' as 'g' drained the blood from my brain, I did not become sick or otherwise incapacitated.

In early December 1943, the reassembled crew reported to RAF Swinderby, to No. 1660 Heavy Conversion Unit, to learn to fly a heavy four-engined bomber, in this case the Short Stirling. To this end the crew was swelled by a flight engineer and a gunner to man the mid-upper turret. And so we gained, I list them:

Sergeant Eric (Ricky) Wardman, flight engineer,

Sergeant E. E. (Speedy) Quick, air gunner (mid-upper).

To most fliers the Stirling was both a beast and a disappointment, but I liked it from the start. Its cockpit was miles up in the air, which meant that on take off the tail came clear of the runway long before the main wheels lifted off: accordingly I proposed that I should log ten minutes extra on every flight.

Conversion started by getting the pilot and flight engineer used to the aircraft – and to each other –, by flying circuits and landings. After that we spent a while flying on three engines, approaching to land, then going around again as if we'd been balked. After that we moved away from Swinderby to carry out fighter affiliation, high-level bombing, and increasingly, tactical exercises, finishing with a quite modest 'Bullseye': in this case a two-and-a-bit-hour decoy flight towards the enemy coast to distract their radars from a real penetration.

We finished the course on 10 January 1944, having flown 39 hours, 16 by night, bringing my total to 148 hours, 56 by night. They then moved us to Syerston – in my case, back to Syerston –, and I took my first real look at the Avro Lancaster!

Syerston's main unit was No. 5 Lancaster Finishing School: the Stirling interlude having been necessitated because Lancasters, at that time, were scarcer than gold dust. As I say, I found the Stirling fine. Now, though, I'm talking of the Lancaster. All these years later, yet I still thrill to the memory of it bellowing to full power down the runway!

Once more we started by pounding the circuit, and flying with various engines stopped; though none of us was that happy with an instructor who persisted in having Ted do overshoots with not just one, but two, engines stopped.

Such perversions aside, the run of exercises followed what had now become the normal pattern. With each of us being allocated time to practise his own specialisation, I was able to hone my skills with the camera gun. I took most pleasure, though, in becoming familiar with the Frazer Nash FN20 hydraulically-operated turret. The FN20's four Brownings each pumped out 600 belt-fed rounds a minute from a total supply of 10,000 rounds to provide a formidable tail defence. Admittedly, the rounds we used were only 0.303 inch calibre, and not the 0.79 inch calibre of the enemy fighters. But one can't have everything.

As a crew we were interacting well, for by now we were thoroughly at home with each other – though I did find my fellow gunner, Speedy Quick, something of a sharp dealer. We were also far more than merely at-home with the Lancaster. On 29 January 1944, we flew another two-and-a-bit hour 'Bullseye', following which we were signed up as operations-ready, having done 19 hours on the Lancaster, 10 at night. My total was then 168 hours.

Our posting was to No. 49 Squadron, of No. 5 Group, Bomber Command, then stationed at RAF Fiskerton, to the east of Lincoln. And just two days later, on 3 February 1944, Ted took us on a training cross-country which marked the start of a settling-in period. This allowed us to practise air-firing, but also high-level and radar bombing using both the Gee navigational aid and the H2S ground-mapping radar. We also navigated by wireless aids that were 'emergency only' on ops because the enemy could home onto them. Then too, we practised landing off beam-approaches.

And on 15 February 1944 Ted appeared on the Battle Order,

programmed to fly at another pilot's shoulder to see how it was done. Then he'd come back and show the rest how ops were conducted. The *rest*, though, because I too was to bomb Berlin! A departure from the norm, but I was to fill in for a Pilot Officer Meggeson's rear gunner. I viewed the board avidly, feasting on my name, yet seeing too the rubble-filled streets of central Birmingham ...

Ted and I both being tasked meant that, at tour's end, we would be an op ahead of the rest of the crew. And though it wasn't to happen, I've frequently pondered on what I'd have done as they embarked on that final op. But I know in my heart that I would have gone with them.

As it was, the Berlin trip took 6 hours and 40 minutes, and with never a boring moment. I found the defences thoroughly alive to their task, and the effects as we neared the city, and for a good hundred miles as we departed it, just as spectacular as I'd anticipated. I even exchanged fire with a Messerschmitt Bf109!

In truth, the encounter was so fleeting that I could do nothing but open up, though the standard drill was that I'd shout for the pilot to corkscrew. However, caution was called for, because while it was easy to spiral down, it took a lot of lone flying to clamber back to the herd protection afforded by the bomber stream. In fact, I was to find that the most important service I could render to a crew was to keep a good lookout going.

A regular occurrence was to advise Ted when a condensation trail began to form behind us, for it not only blotted out my rearward vision but showed the enemy defences exactly where we were. The meteorological chaps did their best to forecast the 'minimum trailing' level, but when they got it wrong Ted would climb or descend, hoping for air of a different humidity, until I advised him that the trail had stopped.

Vigilance also helped minimise the collision risk. As when we ran up to the target and a Halifax, silhouetted against the fires and only feet below us, began to lift, imperceptibly at first, then far too swiftly.

'Skip, turn port –' was as far as I got in warning Ted. Even so he'd begun to heel left when flak caught the Halifax square on – I was looking directly down onto it now. One wing immediately broke off, the two motors bringing it soaring towards us. Then the whole thing was a tangle of blazing wreckage falling away. Destiny, most surely. For had the Halibag not been there we'd have collected that flak ourselves ...

Our first operation as a crew, with the skipper promoted to pilot officer! was to Schweinfurt, on the River Main, in northern Bavaria. The target was the roller- and ball-bearing works to the west of the town, with 734 aircraft engaged. We took off at 1830 hours, and landed just over eight wearying hours later. Unnoticed at the time, I dare say, this clocked up 200 hours for me.

By then I was well practised in getting into the turret. Reaching up for two hand holds overhead, one swung in feet first. After that, there was the electrically illuminated ring sight to be switched on, then the guns to be exercised, using controls like bicycle-handle grips both to elevate and traverse them, the hydraulics giving pretty nearly a one-eighty-degree coverage.

An electrically-heated flying suit helped make long hours in the turret bearable. But on one interminable flight the heating to my feet went awry, so that I ended up with one frozen and the other badly blistered. Heating aside, though, it was always a long time to be cramped up into a turret, especially as I made it a point of pride not to leave my station during an op.

Pride, but using the Elsan toilet was pretty near impossible. Fine for most crew members, who flew in battledress and roll-necked sweaters, and particularly the wireless operator whose station got the full blast of the engine-heated air and who often landed par-roasted. Not only was the rear turret unheated, however, but most of the perspex had been taken out to improve the visibility, so exposing the gunner to the Arctic temperatures encountered at high altitudes: a peculiar side-effect to removing the perspex was that gunners could actually smell flak bursts!

*Gunners having their Taylor flying suits fastened. Other crew are wearing battledress and mae wests*

*Sergeant Ron Eeles and 'Speedy' Quick, in Taylor flying suits*

Attempting to alleviate the intense cold meant kitting up with an electrically-heated suit, then donning a Taylor flying suit, a long, bright-yellow – dinghy-coloured – garment made even bulkier by buoyancy chambers: so obviating the need for a mae-west lifejacket. The turret could be separated from the fuselage by two swing-doors, but these were difficult to close, bundled up as we were, so mostly we left them open. Vacating the turret, therefore, was a case of pushing back until we popped out like a cork from a bottle. Better by far, then, to pee on the tailwheel before take-off, then bottle it up until landing ...

Another regular problem was to have the rear-turret's oxygen supply ice up. This was remedied by disconnecting the tube and sucking it. Except that the metal connector tended to adhere painfully to lips and tongue.

Then too, it was a constant battle to keep the guns from freezing: the least trace of oil, and you had a stoppage on your hands. Not good if night-fighters came a-calling!

A new, radar-controlled set-up was in the offing, Village Inn, it was to be called. The first thing to be done, we understood, was to set in the attacker's wingspan. But what would the Jerry be doing meanwhile, we asked?

On 25 February 1944 we got airborne for Augsburg carrying one 4,000 pounder high-explosive bomb and a load of incendiaries, ninety-two 30-pounders and six-hundred 4-pounders. This was a follow-up to an American raid on Augsberg's Messerschmitt factory earlier that day. 594 RAF bombers were employed, of which twenty-one were lost, at least four in collisions. The bombing, though, photo-recce showed, had been accurate. We landed after 7 hours and 40 minutes.

On 1 March, and again two weeks later, we raided Stuttgart, on the second occasion with the loss of forty-four bombers; both trips, for us, took over eight hours. Then we paid two visits to Frankfurt, taking something over six hours each. And on 24 March it was back to Berlin again. Unknown to us at the time, this was to be the final raid in the long-running Battle of Berlin, and what with flak and night-fighters seventy-two bombers failed to return. On the return we diverted into Waddington, having been airborne for 7 hours 45 minutes.

Later that month we raided Essen, bombing through ten-tenths cloud. And on 30 March 1944 we raided Nuremburg in what proved to be the RAF's costliest ever foray with some 96 Lancasters and Halifaxes being lost of the 795 engaged. To spell it out, a loss of at least 672 aircrew.

In April 1944 the general focus of raiding switched from German industries to targets bearing in some way on the anticipated invasion. Accordingly, on 5 April we were part of a force of 114 No. 5 Group Lancasters attacking the German night-fighter factory at Toulouse. And on 9 April the squadron carried out a solo op laying mines in Danzig Bay. Our crew laid five 1,500 pounders, the op taking 8 hours 20 minutes.

We were back on the Battle Order the very next day, raiding the marshalling yards at Tours. Problems with the marking meant delays before some aircraft could bomb, but the defences were light, although one aircraft was lost. Our crew was able to bomb promptly, landing after 5 hours 50 minutes.

The return had not been without incident, however, for an unexpected outbreak of flak showed us to be off track. George, our nav, then remembered that, doubting the magnetic compass, he had turned to the master compass: now shown to be faulty!

On 26 April we raided Schweinfurt again, an op made singular by both a weird occurrence, and a visitation from the past.

Having done the pre-op night flying test, we were alerted by the sound of a shot, and found that Speedy, messing about in some cack-handed way in his mid-upper turret, had managed to put a round through his palm. The doc saw to him swiftly enough, but as he wouldn't allow Speedy to fly, his place was taken by Peter Valescu who, aeons later, would write of that op from his home in Santiago.

Peter reminded me – as if I needed reminding! – that on the way out we'd lost our starboard engine and as a result, probably being a little overladen with bombs, we'd drifted down to 16,000 feet. After a crew discussion, we'd decided to carry on – how young we were! Consequently, we arrived over this hotly-contested target thirty minutes late, having every flak gun, searchlight, and night-fighter solely to ourselves.

Increasingly aware of how alone we were, we ran in. Only to have Ray, our bomb aimer, ask Ted to go around as he couldn't see the yellow marker we were to bomb on. This was a most unwelcome request at any time, yet Ted said nothing, merely began the repositioning racetrack. Not only that, unlike the rest of us, he made no comment when Ray called for a second go-around. In truth, the marker had probably long burnt out, we were so late. Indeed, even after our third run-in, when we'd dropped, and held heading until the photo-flash had gone off – proving where we'd been – Ted merely said, 'Let's go home, Nav.'

To a man we'd been braced up, indeed Peter wrote of the trip as the 'most dicey I've experienced'. And almost certainly he was recalling the tension. For as weird as Speedy shooting himself, though we dwelt over the target for a good fifteen minutes, there was not the slightest sign of opposition! No flak, no searching beams, no night-fighters, no near collision, no nothing … Nor did anything happen on the return. Though as Peter also remembered, it was a 'long, lonely trip home, the main stream having returned long before.'

In retrospect it was clear that Ted's experience after aborting our initial 'Nickel' had made him determined never to open himself to even the suspicion of timidity again. A wearying 8 hours 50 minutes that op took us.

Two days later we spent just under eight hours raiding an aircraft factory in Oslo, and on 1 May 1944 returned to Toulouse, this time to attack the tank repair facility on the airfield. The master bomber held us off to give the French workers time to get clear, but what hadn't been anticipated was an influx of flak units. Even so we landed safely after an eight-hour flight.

By now we'd completed sixteen ops, or Ted and I had – but let's not quibble. Despite having over half the required thirty ops under my belt, however, I had no illusions about experience being a shield, fully aware, as I was, that Destiny alone called the shots.

On 3 May 1944 my name appeared on the Bombing Order for the seventeenth time when we were tasked to raid Mailly Le Camp, to the east of Paris, the target being a Panzer base well situated to cover the Normandy area. In addition to our own crew we carried Flying Officer Martin, DFM, a staff air gunner who was to observe anti-aircraft activity. We got airborne exactly on schedule at 2157 hours, heart-warmingly waved off, as ever, by well-wishing station personnel.

My contention that all is Destiny came to me with unwonted force even as we roared down the runway when, for the first time ever, I felt no surge of exhilaration. And then the wheels thumped up, and whimsy left me.

The flight out was uneventful and as our assigned bombing height was to be just 7,100 feet, I kept myself at a comfortable temperature by periodically switching off my electrically-heated suit. On arrival in the Mailly area we were sent to orbit a yellow marker, except that as we circled, the night sky was so clear that we could see scores of other aircraft doing the same. Not only that, but any instructions that might have released us were blotted out by an American Forces Broadcasting Station playing 'Deep in the heart of Texas', with the requisite hand clapping. As it was, we spent a good thirty minutes orbiting like that!

Though we were not aware of the entire picture, we knew that 346 Lancasters and 14 Mosquitoes were involved, making the risk of collision enormous. What we didn't know was that the raid leader, the deservedly celebrated Leonard Cheshire, felt obliged to be more than normally meticulous in marking the target. His diligence paid off in that the only French casualties were caused by a Lancaster crashing onto their house. Holding main force off that long, however, enabled the night-fighters to reassemble, leading to the loss of forty-two Lancasters.

As we'd been held remote from Mailly, I saw little of the opposition until Ted began the run in. Then, scanning the sky about me, I realised that I was looking at five Lancasters falling, each with flame licking along its leading edges. Additionally, there were fireballs, as others hit the ground. Suddenly, though, our airframe shuddered, there was a huge explosion, and a pink flash along our port side, a pause, then Ted's voice saying levelly, 'Christ!' And a moment later, 'Put on 'chutes, Chaps.'

Within a second of this the aircraft shuddered again, and as more flak hit home there was a sizzling in my earphones before the intercom went dead.

I'd just pulled off my helmet when – and I must insist upon this – I distinctly saw my mother's face. 'Jump, Son,' she was saying. 'Jump'. It is a phenomenon that mystified me then, as it does to this day. I fully believe it happened, yet it remains alien to my pragmatic nature. I can rationalise, of course, that I was a state of intense mental excitement, and making preparations to jump anyway, and yet ...

Squeezing out of the turret and grabbing my parachute from its stowage, I saw Speedy, who had come back from his mid-upper position to our drop-away rear-door emergency exit. Always two steps ahead, he had guarded against the hatch being jammed by equipping himself with the fire axe. Then he was gone. Snapping the parachute pack to my harness's chest hooks, I looked forward, and seeing nothing but smoke and the persistent red glare, I rolled – as recommended – into the night. Even so my feet brushed along the tailplane, fortunately, without dislodging my flying boots.

Baling out was like falling into a raging river. I'd located and taken hold of the parachute's 'D' ring before leaving, but had no recollection of pulling it. Suddenly, though, I felt the tug on my harness as the unseen canopy above me billowed out. As we'd been flying so low the descent did not take long, but I remember it was a reasonably pleasant sensation – in itself – while it lasted.

At the time, of course, I had many more things on my mind. Above all, relief that I was coming down in France, and not in Germany, where the populace were known to deal out rough justice to downed aircrew.

Taking stock, I wondered at the lack of noise, only later discovering that I was, in fact, some forty miles from Mailly, and nearer Reims. Looking down, I saw that I was heading towards a small lake surrounded by woodland, but before I could work out which lift webs to pull to guide me clear, I landed heavily, and utterly unexpectedly. Because I'd been drifting backwards my skull thumped into ground, though the impact was cushioned by a buoyancy panel of my Taylor suit. And now, in the moment before I scrambled to my feet, I did begin hearing sounds: distant crumpings, that may have been bombs, but definitely shouts, and the barking of dogs.

Hurriedly now, banging the release buckle of my parachute harness, and eying the canopy as it ghosted off to collapse against some trees, I struggled out of both my flying suits. Next, I ripped off my brevet and sergeant's stripes, and stuffed them in my battledress pocket, but wasted no time in even thinking about concealing the flying suits, let alone the parachute, before leaving what I'd realised was a clearing at the best pace I could muster. As I did so, however, there was an almighty roar as a Mosquito passed overhead at treetop height, presumably on its way home after dropping the last of its markers. Nor did that pragmatic bent of mine allow me to spend even a second envying him. Destiny was in control.

The task before me was to find succour before the Germans picked me up. For what remained of the night, therefore, I kept walking, at one time actually hearing voices from the direction of a sizeable fire-glow. Concluding that this was a crashed aircraft, I slanted away, knowing that it would draw troops. Then again, as dawn broke, so an approaching engine note gave me timely warning of an observation aircraft which proceeded to quarter the woods. At length, however, it cleared off, and I resumed my tramp.

Just before it became truly light I came to a village, and from a vantage point saw a group of Jerry motor-cycle troops. Backing into the trees again, I made my way to the far end of the village, and choosing the nearest house, and seeing the door standing open, pushed inside. This alarmed both the elderly Frenchman I came upon, and his dog, and as the dog let out a fusillade of barks and the man a series of shrill 'Allemandes!' I turned tail and hurriedly rushed back into the woods.

I felt not a little aggrieved, I recall, because I had my silk escape-map, and all I wanted was to orientate myself. Tiring now, as reaction began to catch up with me, I stumbled on. Vaguely, I remember coming upon a large house ... And suddenly, all went blank. I rather fancy it was about 0900 hours ...

I was brought to my senses by a blow in the ribs, and looked up to see a German soldier withdrawing his foot for another kick. Then I saw an officer with his pistol pointing at my head, and beyond him, several other soldiers. Nobody said it, but I gathered that for me, the war was over.

Having ensured that I was fit to walk, they took me back to the village, and then to an army headquarters where I was searched and put in a cell. They held me there for two days before moving me to a nearby town where I was joined by a navigator from, it turned out, No. 50 Squadron. We were separated next morning, however, and I was sent, under guard, to the Luftwaffe's Dulag Luft interrogation centre near Frankfurt.

Coming into Frankfurt on the train I cast surreptitious glances at the widespread destruction I'd helped create during my two visits, yet although I was obviously a downed flier nobody seemed outraged by my presence. Our wait to change trains coincided with an air raid, but again, when I was ushered into a shelter, none of the Germans there took umbrage.

On arrival at Dulag Luft I was put into solitary confinement, seeing nobody for the next twelve days apart from two occasions when I was interrogated. Both sessions were relatively innocuous, and even the charge that having stripped off my insignia I could be treated as a spy was only mildly pressed, and then let drop. I must have been small beer to them, of course, for as a gunner I knew nothing about radar or radio countermeasures. Even had they brought it up, I daresay they could have told me more about the proposed Village-Inn radar gunsight than I knew.

Accordingly, on the thirteenth day I was released into the transit camp to await allocation to a prisoner of war camp. I remember how glad I was to be among people again. I was not even that surprised to come upon Speedy, who having leapt into the night, had seemingly fallen into a staff job distributing red-cross parcels and clothing, and eating well in the kitchens.

Speedy too, believed that the rest of the crew must have died. So although we now knew, from our interrogators, that forty-two Lancasters had come down, it would not be until we were repatriated that I heard any more.

It then transpired that, despite a night-fighter inflicting further damage, Ted had managed to get the aircraft home, his tenacity being recognised by the immediate award of a Distinguished Flying Cross. He and the crew, supplemented by two replacement gunners, had subsequently carried on with their operational tours, only to be killed on 7 July 1944 during an attack on the V1 Flying Bomb site at Saint-Leu-d'Esserent, just west of Creil. I never saw official confirmation, but it was widely held that their aircraft had been shot down by another Lancaster.

Parting with Speedy once more, I was entrained for Silesia, and Stalag Luft Three, at Sagan where, on 24 May 1944, I became POW No. 4912.

Sagan was an officers' camp housing some 750 RAF personnel, but with a dozen or so senior-NCO aircrew to carry out administrative tasks. I won't attempt a description of life in a POW camp, who can possibly compete with Steve McQueen! although I cannot recall having the use of a motor cycle. I do remember though, that one American arrival bore the legend 'Murder Inc' across the back of his flying jacket.

In stark contrast, in October 1944 we were joined by some aircrew who had been incarcerated in Buchenwald concentration camp. Luckily, the Luftwaffe had got wind of their plight and insisted upon their transfer to a POW facility. Shaven-headed and skeletal, they were given a double issue of red-cross parcels to help build them up. The experience, though, had sunk deep, so that, at the twice-daily roll calls, whenever a guard chopped down a hand to mark the count, they would flinch.

On a lighter note I might mention that, in becoming a member of the Caterpillar Club – by baling out and having my life preserved by a parachute – I aroused a certain wry envy in another POW, Flight Sergeant Nik Alkemade, a fellow Lancaster rear gunner. On 24 March 1944 Nik had survived jumping out from 18,000 feet. Except that, because his parachute pack had been engulfed in flames, and he had jumped without it, plummeting from a pine tree into a snowdrift and walking away little the worse for wear, he was disbarred from becoming a member of the Club.

Enough said about Sagan, however, and yet I have to concede that even now there are times when, on awakening, I dread opening my eyes for fear of finding myself back there.

In January 1945, in what was a ferociously severe winter, the camp was evacuated in the face of the Russian advance. Generalleutnant Gottlob Berger, the general officer responsible for POWs, would subsequently claim that he was fulfilling his obligations under the Geneva Convention by removing prisoners from a potential combat area.

Over the next three months we were kept on the move, first westwards, to avoid the Russians, then eastwards, as the British and Americans pushed ever deeper into the Reich. We would march by day and be turned into the fields at night to find what shelter we could. On occasion, however, we were moved in cattle wagons, once to a German naval camp between Hamburg and Bremen. From there, though, we began a north-easterly march in a bid to avoid both our pincering allies.

Tragically, our column, and others like it, became the target for low-flying, quick-triggering Typhoons who inflicted many casualties: the American term coined so much later, 'blue on blue' – or 'friendly fire' –, was a phenomenon we became only too familiar with.

Eventually we were directed into a farm where we were left for three days. Our odyssey having become a way of life, we fully expected to be driven out onto the roads once more. But on the fourth morning the grinding of motors and squeal of caterpillar tracks heralded the arrival of British Comet tanks, and with them, our liberation.

A very smooth organisation then swept us up, ultimately taking us to airfields where we were flown home, in my case, by Lancaster! Our next stop, feted all the way, was the RAF Hospital at Cosford, in Shropshire, to No. 106 Personnel Reception Centre, where we underwent exhaustive medicals, were re-kitted, judiciously fattened up, and sent home on leave.

Arriving at the railway station, I bounded up the stairs to the end of the queue, to find immediately ahead of me – by only one space, but ahead of me nonetheless – who else, but Speedy Quick!

Reporting for duty after leave I had to choose what I was to do until my demob number came up. One complication was that nobody seemed sure whether I was a warrant officer or an aircraftman class two. Would training as a cook suit me? The RAF police, then? Then how about a driving course? The full thing, run by the British School of Motoring, progressing from cars through to lorries and buses. That suited fine. And so I moved to RAF Buntingsdale Hall, near Ternhill. Meanwhile, as my health improved, I vainly pressed for a flying job. But finally my number came up and, not without regret, I was demobilised in late 1946.

I was fortunate in securing civilian employment almost at once, starting with a brewery company that was eventually taken over by Bass. Though I just might have returned to the RAF, for within a week of starting work, Air Ministry wrote asking me to rejoin. By then, however, I'd been singled out by a beautiful young girl in a ladies' excuse me. Rita, her name was, and although she proved to have as long-lasting an interest in aircraft as I have, we decided that enough was enough. Instead then, I made a career with Bass, managing their estates until I retired in 1985.

Until then I was rather too busy to do much looking back. After that, however, I spent quite some time interacting with the Air Training Corps. And much later still, I made contact with the flourishing No. 49 Squadron Association.

I have frequently been asked what I feel about Bomber Command's post-war descent into opprobrium. All I can offer is that, having seen the savagery meted out to Birmingham, I welcomed the chance to repay the perpetrators in their own coin.

Then again I was spared one aspect of the resentment engendered among so many Bomber Command veterans, for in starting ops long before

D Day, I became entitled to the Aircrew Europe Star, an award which shows anyone in the know that I did, in fact, fly as aircrew. As the rules fell out, those who began ops later had nothing to show that they had volunteered to put their lives on the line. Possibly, the institution of the 2013 Bomber Command clasp may do something to alleviate the overall slur, but it might well be felt to be too little, and a lot too late.

All I can do is give thanks to Destiny that I was in a position to do my bit, at a time when Britain's need was so desperate that everyone's bit was wanted.

*Ron Eeles, 2013*

# 8. To The Playground Of The Gods

## Warrant Officer Graham White, pilot

And then a treetop stopped the good engine. I recall the tailplane folding across in front of the windscreen, at which point my seat must have broken free for I came to several feet from what was now a pile of debris. There was an all-pervading smell of petrol, and having seen crashed Mosquitoes catch fire, I banged my quick-release box, and struggled clear ...

*Aircrew cadet Graham White, 1943*

Having demonstrated my propensity to draw cartoons even before I joined the sixth form of Derby's Bemrose Grammar School – I'd actually sold one to *Men Only*! – wielding a pencil in a drawing office might have seemed a natural progression. In fact, the work called for so little imagination that I soon grew bored. Fortunately, by July 1941, as I approached seventeen,

I had discovered that I could get a release from this 'reserved occupation' by volunteering to fly. Arguably even then I might have harboured doubts about volunteering, but as fliers couldn't be directed in the way that soldiers, and coalminers, could, volunteering was the only way in.

The day after signing forms in the recruiting office I was sent to the Aircrew Assessment Centre at Birmingham where, having passed an exacting medical, I was subjected to a battery of tests designed to show whether I was suitable to be a flier. Until recently, I was to learn, such selection had been made solely according to the interviewer's notion of whether the applicant was the 'right type'. However, as the RAF found itself with a fifty per cent failure rate after selection, the psychologists had been brought in.

One innovation was an electro-mechanical co-ordination tester. Another was a series of fifteen-minute tests formulated by a Professor Bartlett covering English, basic arithmetic, and 'general intelligence', the latter often enough requiring 'lateral thinking'.

The final step was to appear before a group captain, a squadron leader, and a flight lieutenant who were pleased to inform me that I was deemed 'suitable PNB': suitable to be trained as pilot, navigator, or bomb aimer – and, therefore, as wireless operator or air gunner. At which stage they were ready to smilingly dismiss me. Except that I told them I wanted to become a pilot, nothing less. The smiles disappeared, the wing commander telling me sternly that he was most disappointed with me, that a good type would have been willing to serve his country in any capacity ... Even so, I emerged as the only one of my cadre to have been accepted.

My immediate problem lay in persuading my mother to give her permission. Fortunately, she did so, accordingly I amicably disengaged myself from my Home Guard unit but not so amicably from my boss, earning instead his lasting displeasure.

The new assessment process, by the by, did not change overmuch throughout the war, but its inception dropped pilot-in-training failures from forty-eight to twenty-five per cent.

In November 1941 I was summoned to the Aircrew Reception Centre at St John's Wood, in London, where we lived in high-rise flats, ate in London Zoo, and received our pay, £1/17/6d (£1.87.5p) a fortnight. We also drilled and, marching between venues, were kitted out and jabbed. With the process complete, however, I was volunteered – RAF style – to give blood, my blood group being the newly-desirable Rhesus positive, only to have my circulation refuse to play.

After a holding spell at Brighton we were sent to the Initial Training Wing at Stratford-upon-Avon where we continued to drill but also got down to studying aircraft recognition, theory of flight, morse code, navigation and meteorology. With the exams behind us we were sent to kill time again, on this occasion to No. 2 Elementary Gliding School at Weston-on-the-Green, near Bicester. I got myself a flight in an Audax, a variant of the Hawker Hart light bomber, though for the most part we were used to haul gliders back to the take-off point.

Once the training blockage cleared we moved to No. 9 Elementary Flying Training – and grading – School at Anstey, near Leicester, where each aspirant was given twelve hours on Tiger Moths to show that he had the aptitude to be a pilot, with those who failed being offered, initially, navigator's courses. With the assistance of a very competent sergeant flying instructor, However, I went through with no problems. And I have to say that although, even this early in our journey, there had been a fair amount of frustration, the experience of going solo really did make me feel that I was sharing the playground of the Gods.

At that time the majority of flying training for pilots and navigators was done overseas, where settled weather afforded continuity. Aspirants were held at the Aircrew Despatch Centre at Heaton Park, in Manchester, until a passage became available, when they were entrained to the Clyde, in our case to be jammed aboard a converted freighter for what turned out to be a most miserable Atlantic crossing. With little to do to pass the time but play poker and eye the waves, food loomed large, except that along with a daily issue of four loaves to every twelve men, the main meals were slopped into a single mess tin, savoury and sweet alike.

Having eaten, the 'heads' were simply an unscreened row of holes constantly flushed by sea water, while sleeping accommodation was a mass of hammocks. Crouching beneath them after a nocturnal visit to the heads we held that yours was the one that didn't curse you.

After some twelve days of wallowing we disembarked at Halifax, Nova Scotia, to face a full day's train journey to No. 31 Personnel Disposal Unit at Royal Canadian Air Force Station Monckton, in New Brunswick. We were not held long, however, before being entrained once more, this time for a five-day journey south through the States, to Arizona.

Food on the train was of the hamburgers and coke variety, eaten in our carriages. Beyond that we were expected to sleep feet up on the opposite seat, though this proved so uncomfortable that we dismantled the seats and made up mattresses with the cushions. Except that this led to a confrontation with the conductor who took petty revenge by locking us in. Eventually, however, we were deposited in the Sonora Desert and transported on to sweltering hot Falcon Field, near Mesa.

We now learnt the significance of the letters BATTS which had been stencilled on our kitbags back at Heaton Park. The wartime flying training scheme in the States had been set up under the auspices of General 'Hap' Arnold, a celebrated aviation pioneer and the American equivalent of Britain's 'Father of the Royal Air Force', Lord Trenchard. Under the 1941 'Arnold Scheme' it was expected that RAF and United States Army Air Corps (USAAC) pupils would train alongside each other, except that domestic problems arose.

The root cause was that, being a branch of the American army, the Air Corps regarded the instilling of discipline as the fundamental purpose of the training. This resulted in RAF pupils being returned to the UK for such military misdemeanours as displaying an untidy kit layout. What the RAF wanted, conversely, was not blind obedience, but aircrew with the ability to think, and act, for themselves when the occasion demanded.

There was another factor, which actually saw one of my own course being shipped home. The Air Corps espoused an 'honour' code under which it was the bounden duty of cadets to report disciplinary infringements. So when one of our lads beat up an American airfield, an Air Corps cadet took his number, and reported him.

And 'our' lads, because by this time the major differences had been overcome by setting up six 'British All-Through Training Schools': the 'BATTS' of our kitbags.

Not that the RAF system was without blemishes. Anyone from a public school was viewed as officer material, those from grammars as definitely lower-deck. This was evidenced on our course where the 'man most likely' spoke beautifully but despite the desert heat, never showered. Until the rest of us forced him into one fully dressed.

The training was organised so that half a group did ground lectures in the morning and flew during the afternoon, alternating daily with the other half. As we enjoyed near-perfect weather conditions, flying training progressed smoothly. The basic 1941 scheme had three phases, Primary, a 60 hour – some ten weeks – period in which pupils flew Boeing Stearman PT-17 biplanes; then Basic, and finally Advanced, flying the AT-6A low-wing monoplane – with flaps and retractable undercarriage –, the RAF knew as the Harvard. Our course, in 1942, happened to be the first to drop the Basic phase.

We progressed through the standard flying training syllabus, graduating after a series of long-ranging navigational cross-countries, although with virtually unlimited visibility and any road, railway, or settlement being singular, I never found these that onerous.

On graduation we were presented with RAF pilot's wings and sergeant's stripes, together with an invitation to declare the sort of aircraft we'd like to go to war on. Most put Spitfires, but for some unaccountable reason I put down 'twin-engined fighter-bombers'. Not really volunteering, but volunteering of a sort, I suppose.

Notwithstanding the bad feeling engendered by the exercise of the honour system, and perhaps because of a degree of different thinking now that the USAAC had become the USAAF – the United States Army Air Force –, we got on well with some American cadets who joined us for the night-flying phase of the course. This liaison came about after the Americans had become somewhat unhappy about their own results in that field, and following an investigative visit by Hap Arnold himself. Certainly the cadets responded happily to the more relaxed attitude of the RAF.

We also got on well with the local people who, in their turn, went out of their way to make us welcome. So it was that when a fellow pupil, Jack Harrow, had elected to give a talk and asked me to join him –'There'll be loads of girls' –, I jumped at the chance. The venue, however, turned out to be a Sunday School and the girls eleven years old. Further, having done little more than introduce me as the very chap to tell them what life was like for children in wartime Britain, Jack smugly sat down.

On another occasion a lady giving us a lift went some miles out of the way to exhibit us to her cousin. 'Well,' the cousin observed wonderingly, 'they sure picked up the language quickly.'

Despite the friendliness, however, we were bucked up when, having left Arizona's sweltering heat, we arrived back at Monckton in a snowstorm, for we were going home. In fact, we sailed from New York, joining 5,000 American troops aboard the *Queen Elizabeth* as she made a solo dash for Gourock.

Our first posting after disembarkation leave was to No. 19 Pilot's Advanced Flying Unit at Dalcross, near Inverness, to train on twin-engined Oxfords. Not only did we have to learn to manage two engines but to operate in temperate weather conditions and to navigate over a landscape that was an absolute tangle of features. One, moreover, that was blacked out at night and where both our own defences and enemy intruders had to be taken into account. Fortunately, flying a twin came easily to me, even on instruments, at night, and in bad weather. Dealing with an asymmetric condition, as if flak had taken out an engine, was harder, but the procedure, once learnt, was to stand me in good stead.

Our next move was to No. 1536 Beam Approach Training Flight, at Spitalgate, near Grantham, where we learnt to navigate and carry out bad weather approaches using radio beams. And having completed the course everyone else was shipped off to various operational training units to fly heavies, next step for them being the war. No war for me, however, but a niche as a staff pilot at RAF Ouston, near Newcastle, where my task was to fly an Anson while a navigator/radar instructor and four pupils practised radar interceptions turn and turn about with another Anson.

At the time I was incensed at being moved aside from the main stream. Only much later did I reflect that two thirds of all those who had departed for heavies failed to survive. Further, even after recalling the preference I'd expressed for 'for twin-engined fighter-bombers', it took a while to dawn on me that I'd been admitted, by the back door, as it were, to the exclusive world of the night-fighter.

This only crystallised when I was posted up to the Borders, to No. 54 Operational Training Unit at RAF Charterhall: 'Slaughter Hall', to those in the know. There, I had to master the unpredictable and innately malevolent Beaufighter Mk. 2. My first priority, though, was to find a navigator/radar to fly with. I'd settled on one, and relaxed for a few days, only to have

him change his mind and suit himself elsewhere. Disconsolate, I came upon another nav/rad sitting on a bench, equally downcast. His pilot had proved unsuitable. And so I came together with John David Wooding – 'Dagwood', after the cartoon character – destined to be my nav/radar in the war and my friend for sixty-seven years after it.

*Sergeant Navigator John David (Dagwood) Wooding, 1944*

And 'Slaughter Hall'? Of the unit's eighty-four Merlin-engined Beaufighter Mk. 2s, thirty-nine crashed. Among these was one we should have flown except that I developed a stye. Another trainee crew took it, and did not return. Indeed, since Jack Harrow – the Sunday-School man – had flown into an Arizonian mountain, the toll of training accidents had been ongoing.

Before going solo we were given two sessions in a Beaufort, then a trip standing looking over the instructor's shoulder on a Beaufighter. A fraught time for us pilots, but arguably more so for our prospective crew mates, gathered near the runway watching our efforts. There was a second solo flight, after which we flew as a crew.

One feature of the night-flying syllabus was to fly 'Duskers', that is, to start a detail of circuits and landings in the very late afternoon and fly through until it was pitch dark, particularly through the uncertain gloom of twilight.

We returned to the Beaufort to hone our instrument flying skills, wearing sodium glasses to blot out the daylight as we carried out all the normal evolutions but also blind landings, faithfully following the directions of the instructor until the wheels rumbled on the ground: a great confidence booster.

Our next move was to nearby RAF Winfield to fly the Beaufighter Mk. 6, a variant with far more powerful engines and very happy on just one, as I discovered when I lost one. It also had an advanced Airborne Interception Radar (AI), the Mk. 8, with a single screen rather than two.

On 23 February 1944, following a period of leave, we were posted to No. 515 (Special Duties) Squadron at RAF Little Snoring, in Norfolk. On arrival, however, we found, to our horror, Beaufighter Mk. 2s! We also discovered that many of the navigators were not radar trained. Equally concerning, it was clear that No. 515 was not a happy unit. Evidencing this, when I came top on a test on the Merlin engine, the CO berated the officers for letting a sergeant beat them. Within days, both irritated and confused, I asked for a squadron change, arguing that our radar training would be wasted. The CO's reaction was to assemble all crews, tell them he wanted no bad apples, and send us packing.

As we left, my former flight commander at Ouston, an officer who had gained my respect, told me sadly, 'Chalky, you don't know what you're missing.' And had things not panned out as they did he would have been right. For although I knew, in joining No. 515 we'd become part of No. 100 (Special Duties) Group, I had no notion of the task planned for the group, nor of the enormous influence it was to have on bomber operations. All I'd seen was its inception, equipped, as it was, with the dregs other units were prepared to release to it. In the event, John and I found ourselves transferred to Fighter Command, or as it was nonsensically called at that stage of the war, Air Defence of Great Britain Command.

*Bristol Beaufighter*

*de Havilland Mosquito, night-fighter variant*

We duly reported to No. 85 Squadron at West Malling, in Kent, to find, to our delight, that they were equipped with the night-fighter variant of the de Havilland Mosquito. Though bulbous nosed due to its being packed with specialist radar equipment, this version of the 'Wooden Wonder' performed magnificently.

Even so, while awaiting take-off clearance on my first solo I came close to blotting my copy book when my engines began overheating. I swung onto the runway – a strip with now-powder-dry earth on top of Somerfeldt mesh –, and powered off. The CO, fast approaching in his Spitfire, was met with a cloud of dust and forced to overshoot.

The air was suddenly filled with his blue-tinged demands that I land and report myself. Instead, I cleared the circuit and politically changed radio channels until, trapped on the last one, I pulled the jack plug and sucked it, causing my transmissions to howl.

On landing after half an hour I was approached by the air control officer. The CO, fed up with waiting, had deputised him to tell me off.

'That was your first Mossie take-off, wasn't it?' he asked. Told it was, he looked towards the headquarters office. 'Silly bugger.'

But as I turned away he commented, 'Don't pull that wet jack-plug trick too often, will you ...'

John and I were now operations ready, only there was no trade for us, particularly as we were not allowed to take our Mk. 10 radar over the continent for fear that its core component, the cavity magnetron, would fall into enemy hands. And two weeks later, on 1 May 1944, the squadron was transferred – back to No. 100 Group!

This time around we learnt that the Special Duties Group had been formed in November 1943 to help minimise the savage losses Bomber Command was suffering; on 30 March 1944, raiding Nüremberg, they had lost ninety-six bombers! Ultimately the Group's various activities were to cut losses by a full eighty per cent!

Among other measures to help achieve this its Fortresses and Halifaxes used the 'Mandrel' jamming radar to clutter the enemy's long-range radar displays, effectively creating an electronic blackout – the Mandrel Screen – across the North Sea to shield the assembling main force. Its aircraft also had equipment to jam, and otherwise confuse, communications to and from enemy defence-control centres.

*Flying Fortress B-17*

Then there were the long-range Mosquitoes patrolling above, below, and alongside the bomber stream, one shepherd every fifteen minutes. At low level its intruder Mosquitoes dwelled around German night-fighter bases and fighter assembly beacons. There were also free-ranging Mosquitoes, hunter-killers, once cleared to do so, using the latest American radars.

We were assigned to low-level night-intrusion, flying so low that radar was valueless, the ground returns blotting out target echoes. In fact, we became so much part of the scene that a Luftwaffe corporal would describe how, uncertain of the road back to base, he had 'walked towards the sound of the enemy intruder plane'.

Among equipments the Group employed was 'Serrate', which allowed us to home onto the radar pulses the German night-fighters sent out in detecting our bomber stream. Serrate though, gave direction but no range, which meant many a frustrating chase. 'Perfectos' was a gear which allowed us to home onto the enemy's equivalent of our Identification-Friend-or-Foe auto-interrogation radar: until they switched it off. The same applied to their backward-looking radar, the 'Naxos', initially we'd home onto it, then they caught on.

The boffins had solved one outstanding problem, though, that of closing the gap between homing onto a target using Airborne Interception Radar (AI) and getting close enough visually confirm that it was, indeed, a hostile; they'd given us a telescope-like infra-red device which showed the quarry's engine heat. Even so, our main AI sets had their shortcomings, for at low levels, with ground returns swamping targets, the enemy only had to dive for us to lose them. The Mk. 10 AI, however, had a good twenty-mile range and once we were cleared to take it on deep penetration sorties we no longer needed either Serrate or Perfectos.

Then, for navigation, there was Gee. The Germans were able to jam this lattice-radar system mid-way over the North Sea, but before we lost the signal we could fix our position and so update the wind. But all these equipments had to be packed into the never-overgenerous Mosquito cockpit, leaving scant room for a bulkily clad pilot and navigator.

*Mosquito cockpit, with central H2S, mapping radar*

There was a hiatus in the main task when some Mosquito squadrons were assigned to counter the V1 Flying-Bomb threat. But then John and I had our own hiatus when, as No. 85 moved north to West Raynham, our CO somewhat coldly offered us to No. 239 Squadron, a Serrate unit who found themselves shorthanded.

In fact, it turned out to be great move, for although No. 239 Squadron still had only the Mk.4 radar and relatively tired Mosquito Mark 2s, they had a tremendous spirit. A spirit which sustained us when we moved to neighbouring Massingham to get Serrate experience on Beaufighter Mk 6s and an engine exploded during my first take-off just after we overflew an Irish labourer who happened to be cycling down the runway at the time. A great shock for all concerned, but one that gave me useful experience in actual asymmetric handling.

After all our training we finally flew our first operational sortie on 11 July 1944 when we were dispatched to carry out an anti-intruder night patrol of the eastern side of the invasion beaches. Though no intruders appeared we savoured that extra edge given by flying over enemy territory. And having started we visited, in quick succession, Orleans, Kiel, Heligoland, and Darmstadt.

Between times, of course, we continued to exercise our skills. And, as always, training took its toll. In the course of a 'Haystack' exercise – finding another aircraft in the vastness of the night sky was much akin to the proverbial needle search – a pair carried out the interception at 25,000 feet, then dived to sea level to coast in. When one of them simply vanished, my contention was that they had misread their altimeter by ten thousand feet, something it was only too easy to do with the mark of instrument we had.

On another training sortie one of our aircraft, liaising with a heavy bomber, flew at low speed into its propwash, spun, and crashed. Not only were both crew members killed but also the bomber's flight engineer, who had begged a ride. Who had volunteered ...

In contrast to our training losses our operational losses were minimal, free-roving rangers having whittled down the German night-fighters.

Our tour settled into a pattern. Each day we'd check the Operations Board, eyeing the crews listed, together with the ops completed. The requirement was thirty, although when this was temporarily increased to thirty-five we viewed it with equanimity, for a 'rest' tour spent instructing raw crews was fraught.

Those appearing on the list would carry out a night-flying test. Those not listed would be detailed for sessions on the Link instrument-flying trainer or for lectures on aircraft recognition.

At the prescribed time the crews would assemble in the lecture room in headquarters where the curtain would be drawn back to reveal each crew's designated route. Typically, the operation might call for a diversion towards the Ruhr followed by an actual attack on Bremen, with various No. 100 Group stations across East Anglia tasked to provide the component parts. No. 141 Squadron, sharing the airfield with us, might provide the low-level intruders, leaving us to fly as bomber-escorts.

The met man would do his best to tell us what weather to expect, and the Intelligence officer would issue us with the recognition colours of the day, both Allied and enemy. The navs would huddle for their own briefing. while pilots would collect the minimum-detail 'Captain of Aircraft Map'.

There might even be a boffin with a new offering from the Telecommunications Research Establishment at Malvern, the source of the technological gear with which our radio-countermeasures war was fought.

*Crews discuss briefed op before take-off. Graham White on left*

Briefing over, we'd try to relax until a typically 2300 hours take-off time, writing letters, playing snooker, listening to the wireless ... And finally, as time drew near, we'd slip battledress tunics over white sweaters and repair to the crew room to kit up. Once at the aircraft there'd be the ritual wetting of a tyre, despite notices from high up that urine rotted the rubber.

Settled in the cockpit, the check list was lengthy. The nav would select the outer fuel tanks – it was handier for him to do it –, I'd open the throttles slightly, beckon for clearance, and start the port engine. With both engines running there'd be the check that the ignition circuits were functioning, with only the acceptable drop in revs when a magneto was switched off.

On taxying out we'd check the flight instruments, and work through the pre-take off checks, and at last, in night-fighter style, the clearance would come, 'Two Three, clear to scramble'.

Take-off, as always on the Mossie, meant opening the throttle swiftly and smoothly to the stop: twelve pounds boost. We'd get the tail up as soon as possible to get directional control from the rudder: it didn't pay to let a swing develop! At 125 mph we'd come unstuck, and some part of our nerves would relax a little as we passed the safety speed of 170 mph: only above that could one rely upon being able to contain the yaw from a failed engine.

The climb would be marked by our periodical oxygen checks, and the sudden surge as the air pressure decreased and the supercharger, sensing that the fuel charge needed more air, changed gear. Soon, though, John would begin picking up the green blips indicating that we were approaching the bomber stream. At which we'd take up position, though remaining well clear of their guns ...

Ostend was a typical coasting-in spot, by which time we'd be level at around 20,000 feet. It would then take us some twenty-five minutes to edge into the Ruhr at Münster, on our diversion leg, encountering the orange flashes of a box barrage. Every instinct would tell you to duck and weave, but logic, and experience, dictated that you kept the speed up and didn't deviate from course.

An hour later, John might call, 'Contact! At twelve thousand feet. Ten degrees, at three o'clock.' Only too typically this would lead to a protracted chase. Only to have the target detect our approach and dive, when we'd lose him in the ground echoes, and bewail anew, 'If only we had the Mk. 10!'

On one occasion, however, we chased a bogey at our top speed, only for it to leave us standing. I jammed the throttles through the wire to emergency boost and still found myself outstripped. Indeed, I exceeded the emergency boost limitation by a good few minutes, for which I was soundly berated when we got back. In fact, they never allowed those two engines to be sent on ops again, although a Rolls Royce friend told me he'd seen a Merlin run at emergency boost for 72 hours! As for the mystery target, it could only have been one of the German's jets, a Messerschmitt Me 262 would be my guess.

Having given up the chase we'd be back shadowing the stream as it steadied over Bremen, scanning both a night sky alive with flak and searchlights and a surface become a mass of fires, bomb bursts, and coloured markers. We'd note too, blazing bombers going down ...

The duty completed, we'd turn for home, initially employing 'Starboard wing on the Pole Star' until we were clear of jamming and could get a Gee fix once more. And a final bit of airmanship, declaring 'overhead' a good fifteen minutes out and being allocated a reasonable joining height. Smilingly ignoring the calls of 'bloody liar' as, with full flaps, down, we flared over the threshold having stolen a ten-minute march on other arrivals.

After that it was a case of throwing off tiredness and concentrating on getting the speed just right: the Mosquito was such a clean aircraft that it demanded spot-on speed control. Then a touch of rudder to ensure that there was no sideways drift on touchdown: the undercarriage didn't like that.

And having handed over to the groundcrew, 'What did you get, Chalky?' 'Back.' Followed by the walk towards de-briefing, seemingly unseen by the blue-uniformed figures making their way to work, as if, as I have said elsewhere, we were yesterday's ghosts.

And after de-briefing, the breakfast silence, broken only by Chiefy coming to tell me that we'd collected twenty-four pieces of shrapnel, one of which had expended itself on the cannon running just beneath my thighs ...

For a while, engine problems began to enliven ops. On the first occasion my starboard propeller suddenly sped up and began to rotate far beyond limits. Fortunately we'd been lectured not long before on the fault in the constant speed unit which led to this 'overspeeding': while the drag caused by a windmilling prop is extreme, that of an out-of-control prop is stupendous. Ready with the correct procedure, then, I was gratified to see the revs die down until I was able to feather the blades: turning them edge on to the airflow to create a minimum of drag.

On the next occasion we'd just crossed the Dutch coast at 20,000 feet when I began to feel unaccountably uncomfortable. A quick scan showed nothing untoward. And then Dagwood said, almost conversationally, 'I think the starboard engine's on fire.'

Within moments what I first saw as a trail of black smoke was joined by a flicker of flame from the exhaust. Fire in the air requires prompt action. And a fair degree of luck. Fortunately the engine stopped and the prop feathered just as it should. But after discharging the single-shot extinguisher, the flame came back to life. All that was left to me was to side-slip, trusting to the airflow to choke out the fire. As it did. After which, always turning into the live engine, never against the dead one – the contemporary maxim –, we headed for home.

In such circumstances things are rarely straightforward, and late into the approach we were warned that base had a blocked runway. At which an emergency system kicked in to provide a succession of searchlights which arced towards the ground in the direction of Woodbridge, one of the dedicated crash-landing airstrips, so guiding us to a safe haven. Investigation showed that the flame traps – mesh-like devices which prevent fuel-air mixtures catching fire where they shouldn't – had burnt out, allowing the exhaust gases to ignite our fuel lines. We were only too glad to be back, but the RAF were equally glad to have their bomber returned, and awarded my efforts with a green commendation.

The third occasion began similarly when, having crossed the enemy coast, I detected the initial signs of yet another overspeed; a sudden faltering in rpm, then a surge. This time I had the prop stopped and feathered and my starboard wingtip on the Pole Star before Dagwood could say a word.

In due course I began planning for yet another night asymmetric landing.

'I can hardly believe,' I muttered. 'Two overspeeds ...'

'Oh,' returned Dagwood, 'I wondered why you turned back. I was just a little slow in switching tanks, but it seemed to be catching OK ...'

And so I restarted the dead engine, and touched down moments later on two.

The 100 Group strategy was paying off, but new tactics were always under consideration, one being 'The Net' in which we sent Mosquitoes in line astern to fly down both the eastern and western borders of Germany. At a given time both groups turned inwards, the idea being that we'd scoop up any night-fighters encountered. The trouble was that group's activities overall had been too successful, and there was nobody to scoop up.

Indeed, Dagwood and I had been caught by one of our own rangers just weeks back, and shortly after I'd clocked up my thirtieth op. My headphones suddenly erupted with the imperative, 'Bogey! Bogey! Turn starboard.' This was for identification. Except that, shocked, I pulled left, the 'natural' way. To be told, 'I said starboard, Clot.'

By this time our operational zone was shrinking rapidly, especially as we were barred from the area allotted to the Second Tactical Air Force as they cleared the way for the advancing Allied armies. We continued to do intruder sorties, but rarely with any result. On occasion, though, we flew in support of Lancaster raids aiding the Russians, our final operational sortie, in April 1945, being to Prauen, in Czechoslovakia, a 1,200 mile round trip which took us five hours.

And suddenly, it was, effectively, all over. No. 100 Group's pioneering work on long-range, all-weather, night-fighting and electronic warfare was researched on Operation Post Mortem, a combined exercise with German air controllers. And a new squadron commander dickered for our transfer to the Far East, only to be forestalled by the atomic bombs.

Then it really was all over. Within weeks No. 100 Group ceased to exist. Other Groups, long jealous of the equipment our higher priority had robbed them of, grabbed it away. As with Group, so with the squadron, which disbanded without a whimper, leaving only a dull sense of disillusionment.

Before we lost our aircraft, however, we were allowed to fly a Cook's tour of the areas we'd operated over. We also took part in several celebratory fly-pasts. And at a personal level two of us on a home pass celebrated by entering Nottingham City Hall through a back window and joining the bigwigs on the balcony to take the plaudits of the crowd gathered below.

*Nottingham City Hall, VE Night; with aircrew on balcony*

Many airmen had no trades to return to, and were offered educational and vocational training to teach them the required skills. Dagwood began instructing on this scheme, ultimately becoming a teacher, and we remained firm friends until his death in 2012. For my part I had no wish to put myself back under my old manager, and having decided that BOAC would be swamped by heavy-bomber boys, I decided to stay in the Service.

I was posted back to No. 85 Squadron, at Tangmere, on the South Coast, but it soon became obvious that the Service was changing radically. Most noticeably, the easy relationship between officer and senior-NCO aircrew became only too evident by its absence. Even some jobs depressed, like flying newly-checked-over Mosquitoes to West Freugh, in Scotland, only to see them bulldozed for scrap.

We flew high-level met sorties for the weather boffins, taking temperature and air pressure readings up to 40,000 feet. We also flew air-gunnery sorties on the Northumberland coast. More hearteningly, in 1946 we did the first of what were to be regular detachments to Lübeck, to supplement the day-fighter squadrons of Second Tactical Air Force in deterring the Soviets. Most significantly I met and married my wife, Phyl, a Canadian born nurse, which gave me more to think of than flying.

Abruptly, though, having realised that I'd never taken a rest, the RAF sent me to Central Flying School at Little Rissington to become an instructor. This, though, palled from the start, so I managed to get withdrawn from the course, although instead of being returned to the squadron, and to the married quarter I had my eye on, I was sent to No. 1 Ferry Unit at Pershore, in Worcestershire.

They were engaged in ferrying Mosquitoes out to Australia and New Zealand, and along a fantastic route. Except that, finding myself barred from taking part because I was a non-swimmer! I applied for a transfer, and was reassigned to my old squadron, now stationed at West Malling.

Some time later a weather diversion into Tangmere gave me the opportunity to spend a weekend at home with Phyl. And as my nav wanted to get up to

London it was agreed that I'd fly the sixty miles back to West Malling solo. It was, I suppose, a form of volunteering, so I should have known better ...

On the Monday, having got airborne, I held a thousand feet and had just glimpsed a misty West Malling runway when my starboard engine lost all power and began shedding petrol into the slipstream. Lowering the nose to maintain speed, I stabbed at the red feathering button, and was relieved when the propeller blades began to slow, and turn edge-on. Only, to my dismay, to begin to rotate once again.

Eying the trees rising towards me I reached out and jabbed at the button again. I was still hoping to reach the runway, except that I was sinking ever more rapidly. And then a treetop stopped the good engine. I recall the tailplane folding across in front of the windscreen, at which point my seat must have broken free for I came to several feet from what was now a pile of debris. There was an all-pervading smell of petrol, and having seen crashed Mosquitoes catch fire, I banged my quick-release box, and struggled clear, not yet aware that apart from numerous cuts and bruises I had suffered a broken leg, and a broken wrist. First to reach me were a farmer, a land girl, and a German POW, but with the runway only yards off I was soon in the hands of an RAF doctor.

In the aftermath of the crash I was to spend ten, often agonising, months in Orpington Hospital. Early on, the court of inquiry determined that the cause of the starboard engine failure had been a blocked filter. When they came to interview me, therefore, their professional interest was on the wider aspects of the crash. Having reflected so long on the incident, I was able to proffer that, with my attention fixed ahead of me, that second stab I'd made at the feathering button just might have hit the port one: that is, the wrong one, so causing that engine too, to falter. There was no proof that this had been the case but in the interests of flight safety the two feathering buttons were moved further apart.

After my discharge from hospital I rejoined a squadron that was eagerly awaiting the exchange their Mosquitoes for NF.2 Meteor jets. Much else had changed too, so that I found the Service an even sadder place. My enlistment was up, except that on my release medical any compensation for my still gimpy leg was turned down flat. It was to be fifty years before I re-applied and finally began to receive a pension, but there was never any question of having it backdated.

I left the RAF in November 1950 after nine years, departing in possession of many memories, with quite a few regrets, and convinced that on returning to the family firm, a sheet-metal concern, my flying days were over. At that time I had flown thirty-three operational sorties – Dagwood had flown thirty-five – and flown a fair old total of operational hours, and a fair few more non-operational, the latter often just as hazardous.

Even at the time I was often asked how I handled fear, and it is a question I've pondered since. A small measure, of course, sharpens the senses. On occasion, the sound of my heavier breathing on take-off made me aware of some inherent stress. But where operational flying was concerned I still have to insist that I was always too busy planning ahead to be actually afraid.

I did, however, come across a crew who seemed to suffer beyond the norm. Successive observations made by a home-based night-fighter crew using the advanced Mk. 10 radar, strongly suggested that the crew in question would depart on an operation but merely circle out at sea. Unlike bomber lads whose target photo-flashes showed where they'd been, there was no such method of checking on lone rangers like us. But if guilty, that crew would have been the exception.

Another topic that often arises is the post-war treatment of Bomber Command. There can be no doubt that the crews, lionised when they were the country's only way of striking back, became political pariahs. Even now the recent award of a Bomber Command Clasp is viewed by many as derisory. But hopefully that is still an unfinished campaign.

*Graham White, 2014*

As I say, I thought I'd put a flying life behind me. In 1951, however, when I still had reserve service to complete, a chilling of the political climate led the RAF to call me to the colours once again. I had become rather bored with civvy street, and as well as a rekindled desire to fly, there was the blandishment of a handsome bounty.

In July 1951, therefore, I began refreshing on Harvard trainers at No. 1 Flying Training School, RAF Oakington, in Cambridge. Then I was checked out on the de Havilland Vampire, a single-engined, single-seater jet. As some sort of introduction I was sent solo in the unwieldy Griffon-engined Spitfire Mk. 12, and though my only flight on that was full of drama, the transition to the tricycle-undercarriaged jet was satisfyingly smooth, as jet flight itself was to prove.

Having finished the course, however, the niggles began. Most notably I was told that the bonus did not apply to those with a reserve commitment

… In the end I got some paid leave and what they called termination benefit, but only about half my expectation.

Now, so many years on, much of the resentment such slights engendered has gone, for I balance it, as I say towards the end of my autobiographical book (*Night Fighter over Germany*, Pen & Sword, see Selective References), 'Once you have flown in the small hours of the night, you can never be quite the same person again. Because you can never forget that tremendous feeling of freedom, and awe at the immensity of the universe. It stays with you for the remainder of your life.'

Certainly it has for me.

# 9. 'If We Send Parkin's Crew Direct ...'

## Warrant Officer Bill Cooke, air gunner

As we drove past the airfield on the main road, there was a massive great Stirling which had skidded off the runway and run headlong into a hangar. Now, crumpled and tail high, it was looking very forlorn.

'That's what you'll be on,' the driver said chattily.

*Sergeant Bill Cooke, 1943*

When war broke out in 1939, I was fourteen and had just left school. I'd got a job in Mansfield as a delivery lad which involved acting as driver's mate and, on occasion, getting behind the wheel. Later, when the driver was off sick, a wartime relaxation of the rules meant that provided I displayed 'L' plates I was able to drive alone. It was an interesting job, but in 1943, with my call-up imminent, I began making preparations. I'd got a brother and sister in the RAF – the brother a rigger with No. 106 Squadron, Bomber Command – and I'd long decided I wanted to be a pilot.

Having looked into it, I'd found that I was academically suitable, having attended what was then known as a Central School, such schools filling a gap between grammars and technical or trade schools. I felt pretty fit too, so I seemed to be in with a good chance. To that end I began buying *Aeroplane*, and *Aircraft Recognition*, and to teach myself the morse code.

My call-up papers duly arrived, and at the medical I cleared the first hurdles – conscription into the army, or consignment to the mines – by declaring that I wanted to fly. Some weeks later, accordingly, I attended an aircrew selection centre in Birmingham where I underwent a far more intensive medical, which went well, and worked through two days of aptitude tests and interviews, emerging rather dazed by all the detail, but holding the top grading of 'Fit PNB' (Pilot, navigator, bomb aimer), that is, suitable for all categories of aircrew. Which, though, the board wanted to know, did I want to be trained as. No hesitation, 'As an air gunner, sirs.' Which brought nods of knowing approval all round. 'Want to get into the war, eh!'

And that was the case. This change of aspiration, from pilot to air gunner, had been no snap decision but had been turned over for months past. It was now mid 1943, and the writing was on the wall for the Germans. With Bomber Command pounding them by night and the Americans by day, and with everyone talking of a Second Front, it was clearly just a matter of time before they packed it in. Pilot training, and indeed navigator and wireless-operator training, took the best part of two years, which would mean the whole thing would be over by the time I got my wings. The swiftest way in, then, was as an air gunner. Indeed, without any undue hold-ups, I might even be operational within six months: by early 1944!

The brown buff OHMS (on His Majesty's Service) envelope duly arrived, with rail warrant, and instructions directing me to report to St John's Wood, effectively, Lord's Cricket Ground. We were accommodated in nearby flats, and in the two weeks we spent there we were injected, learnt to stand to attention and march a bit, did physical training, and were kitted out.

Having got us fully equipped, they then carried out an inspection. We were paraded at just gone midday in greatcoats and full webbing equipment, with gas capes neatly rolled on our packs. During the procedure, we had to show we knew how to use these, unshipping our packs, spreading out the poncho capes and draping ourselves with them from head to toe. Only then, of course, we had to roll them up again. And to the corporal drill instructor's satisfaction. And under dire threat of extra PT ...

It was all very well, but this was time consuming, and dragged out even longer as the directing staff walked behind us, using a rod to measure the length of our greatcoats: 'Two inches up on this one, sergeant.' Then again, it was midsummer and the heat was atrocious. Hardly surprising, then, when there was a sudden commotion as one of our number collapsed in a faint. At which, they hurriedly dismissed us and, a day or so later, our mutual business done, sent us off on leave.

Our real square-bashing was carried out at No 15 Initial Training Wing, Bridlington, where we spent four weeks. Being a 'titch' I best remember the sizing manoeuvre, in which the flight was nattily formed with me in the very centre of a column with tall chaps both to front and rear. What this meant was that whichever way we were progressing I had to move at a near run to avoid getting left behind or alternatively, being trampled underboot from the rear. Indeed, I was heartily glad to pass to the next phase.

This was to No 18 Initial Training Wing, at Bridgnorth in Shropshire. Here, it was more of the same; drill, physical training, but with Service lectures, aircraft recognition, and, for all aircrew aspirants, morse, with both key and Aldis (signalling) lamp.

This time our end-of-course leave was a little more extended while we waited for a training blockage to clear. Finally though, in late October 1943, we were called forward for our aircrew training proper, to No. 12 Air Gunnery School at RAF Bishop's Court, in Northern Ireland. Here we became best friends with the Browning 0.303 inch calibre machine gun, learning to strip and reassemble it until we could do it blindfolded, or in the dark. Alongside this, lectures intensified in aircraft recognition. We fired off shotguns at clay pigeons, and Brownings at targets on the butts, taking turns in a rigged-up turret. Then we progressed to air exercises in Avro Ansons, firing air to ground, and at drogue targets tugged behind other aircraft, each pupil firing off 200 colour-coded bullets in turn: colour coded so that scores could be apportioned. We also flew sorties using camera guns against co-operating fighters.

I had deliberately chosen the air-gunner role for its shorter training period. Yet air gunnery proved to be no sinecure, although we swiftly grew adept at fixing the target in our ring-and-bead sights, and duly allowing for leading or deflection, bullet drop, and windage. In fact, my end-of-course summary records that I scored an overall average of 2.7% of hits. That is, of course, a miss percentage of 97.3%! Yet that was deemed fine, indeed, with an 87% exam result, I was top of the course.

*Flying logbook summary of my air gunnery course*

I have to confess that I'd found it reasonably straightforward, though I well remember another course member, a Corporal Keen, probably an ex-Boy, and certainly a serving regular with quite a lot of experience, who ruefully congratulated me, 'I'd strained myself to be top, Titch, but you pipped me at the post.'

We finished the course on 31 December 1943 with a formal parade, for which we'd prepared overnight, sewing sergeant's stripes and air-gunner brevets onto our battledresses – the brevet being a half-wing centred by the letters AG. After that, we'd packed, ready for the off. Now, on the big day, with it raining like the clappers, we paraded in our greatcoats as aircraftmen class one, to be ceremoniously handed a set of stripes and a brevet each. Once dismissed, now sergeants, we rushed off to the billets, sewed the stripes onto our greatcoats, and jumped aboard the transport for Larne Harbour.

The day had gone well, and leave beckoned. But the always temperamental Irish Sea proved so rough that the ferry itself was unable to dock at Stranraer. Instead, we had to transfer to a bobbing little launch, and having reached the dock, to gingerly judge the upward surge, then grab at and ascend a vertical iron ladder. No mean trick while encumbered with greatcoats, with full webbing surmounted by steel helmets, and shouldering both an ordinary kit bag and one with flying kit, all in the pitch darkness. Nor were we helped by having two service policemen (SPs) brusquely call down, 'Have your leave passes ready.' An order which led one of the lads to tell the unseen SP what he could do with his pass, faithfully promising to supply a stamp for the transaction. It broke the tension, and, of course, it gratified us to see the momentary confusion as the white-capped corporals found themselves confronting an ever growing crowd of brand-new, already provenly bolshy sergeants.

We had quite a lengthy leave, before reporting to No. 16 Operational Training Unit, at Upper Heyford, on 8 February 1944. Here we were to fly Wellingtons, which would require a six-man crew. Accordingly, we were assembled in the sergeant's mess, officers and all, and left to our own devices. Throughout training I'd palled up with a lad called Stan Humble (he answered to 'Butch'), so we decided to stay together. We approached a couple of likely-looking pilots, colonials, as I recall, Australians or New Zealanders, but they'd got themselves gunners. Then we struck lucky in finding Jack Parkin. Having spent a while flying in some training capacity he was already a flight sergeant. After that, the three of us soon gathered the others we needed. At the end of the session, therefore, our crew list read:

Flight Sergeant (later Flying Officer) Jack Parkin, pilot

Sergeant Nickson, navigator (anno domini: his first name escapes me: Nick, surely?)

Sergeant Edward Thompson (Dickie) Durtnal, bomb aimer

Sergeant John Kean, wireless operator/air gunner

Sergeant Bill (Titch) Cooke, air gunner (mid-upper)

Sergeant Stan (Butch) Humble, air gunner (rear gunner).

Once we moved on to heavies, this would be supplemented by a flight engineer, in our case, Sergeant Lesley S (Sticky) Glue. Les had been working for Airwork Services but had decided he wanted to get into the war.

We spent the best part of three months at Heyford, flying all manner of exercises, from circuits to wide-ranging navigational sorties. The latter would often include bombing sessions, using eleven-pound practice bombs, and air-firing, either live against ground targets and towed drogues, or with camera guns if we were doing fighter-affiliation. Each of the three gunners aboard would take turns firing from the rear turret. And three gunners, for although John Kean would invariably fly in the wireless-operator's station, he also had a gunnery role.

We completed the course on 30 April 1944, by which time I'd flown a total of just over a hundred hours, sixty by day, forty-two by night. Now it was time for us to convert to heavy bombers. Except that the system was jammed again. To mark time, as it were, we were shunted off to RAF Scampton, near Lincoln, for a three week aircrew commando course. In truth, all they did was keep us running about, probably to tire us out and prevent us from becoming fractious. For by this time we all felt that we'd been training for ever: even I'd been in the system for something like nine months!

On 21 May 1944, however, we were moved on. This time to Winthorpe, near Newark, where No. 1661 Conversion Unit prepared No. 5 Group's crews for heavy bombers. Our introduction was hardly encouraging. As we drove past the airfield on the main road, there was a massive great Stirling which had skidded off the runway and run headlong into a hangar. Now, crumpled and tail high, it was looking very forlorn.

'That's what you'll be on,' the driver said chattily.

In fact, although the Stirling could be a handful, standing so high off the ground – the cockpit was twenty-two feet nine inches from the tarmac: how trivia sticks! – and both looking and being unwieldy, Jack, now aided by Les Glue, settled to it very well.

We flew more circuits, did a lot of flying on less than four engines, and extended our cross-country exercises using the radar navigational aids Gee and Loran which made the nav's task easier. For us gunners, it was, to a large extent, more of the same, but by the time we finished, on 5 July 1944, I'd done a total of 150-plus hours, a hundred by day and fifty-three by night.

Now, though, came a real treat, when we moved down the road to RAF Syerston, to No. 5 Lancaster Finishing School, to convert to the Avro Lancaster. Oh! what a pleasant aircraft. Just everything about it pleased. Certainly, all of us fell for it, and I gravitated to the mid-upper turret.

Getting into my station was quite an athletic procedure, although I hardly thought of it that way, back then. You grabbed a secure hold on the starboard side, and stepping up from the bomb-bay floor, hoisted yourself skywards. Then you brought a wide band of rubberised canvas across beneath your backside and hooked it to a strongpoint to form a secure, if never particularly comfortable, seat.

To do the job, you switched on the gunsight, illuminating the ring and ball. Then you grasped the controls, like bicycle handlebar grips. Depressing them slightly, powered the turret's hydraulics. After that, twisting the hands, brought the turret around laterally, while rolling the hands forwards or backwards moved the twin guns in elevation. We'd get the target in the ring and ball gunsight, make the normal corrections, and let fly.

How effective we'd have been in fighting off a Messerschmitt Bf110 night-fighter, or a Focke-Wulf FW190 with our relatively puny 0.303 inch calibre bullets, I cannot say from personal experience, for during our entire first tour neither Stan nor I ever had to fire off our guns in anger, although I once had a two-second glimpse of a Bf110!

We didn't spend long at Syerston, flying only another fourteen hours, equally split between night and day, but it was a happy stay. Not only did we have the Lancaster, but the long-awaited goal was in plain sight.

On 23 July 1944, an operations-ready crew at last, we reported to RAF Fiskerton, just east of Lincoln, to join No. 49 Squadron. During a brief settling-in period we were formally accepted after a night-flying test with one of the squadron pilots.

'They're OK,' we pictured him saying to himself. 'They should last five ops ...' The requirement, of course, being thirty.

Jack was the first to fly on an operation, following the normal custom of a new captain flying as a supernumerary with an experienced crew to see how it was done.

'What was it like?' we asked eagerly. He probably said something like, 'Interesting,' But even had he gone into detail it would have meant little until we'd experienced it for ourselves. Which we were to do, on 26 July 1944, when 'Parkin's crew' appeared on the Battle Order for the first time. For my part, I'd hoped to be operational by early 1944, but after the training delays, mid 1944 was pretty fair going!

That first night we raided railway installations on the Givors-Lyon line, way down in France, taking nearly nine hours. It was all very strange, and not quite as we'd expected, after hearing so many accounts from crews who had spent the previous year targeting the Ruhr. Now, however, after the invasion, the initial priority was to help the ground forces to push eastwards through

France, towards Germany. Putting railways temporarily out of commission, therefore, was vital to hindering enemy reinforcements.

Even so, I was duly impressed by the flak and the bomb flashes, though, in truth, my main occupation was to keep warm. A turret is always a draughty place, but the weather that night was poor, with cloud and severe icing hampering everything. Apart from wearing full flying clothing and a sweater, I was helped by electrically heated gloves, topped by multi-layered silk gloves, then forearm-length leather gauntlets; yet still my fingers froze. At least my neck was not encumbered by collar and tie, for we'd been warned not to wear these in case we ditched, and they shrank, and throttled us. As it happened, my sister had embroidered me a very nice white scarf which I treasure still. But the one I actually chose to wear on ops was of blue silk with white polka dots and was even kinder on my neck as I screwed it around, constantly searching the sky. I treasure that equally.

*The white scarf embroidered by my sister, with my initials, and No. 49 Squadron*

The first problem had been that of getting to the actual target, and I must confess that I was never to be all that sure of Nick the Nav. Mind you, navigators had so little to go on, with winds guessed hours before by some met man in Britain, and often enough nothing but deduced reckoning to go on in flight. True, Gee would take us to some targets, and the ground-mapping radar, H2S, when it worked, would be of enormous help in getting en-route pinpoints, although we never used it for target finding as such, for throughout our tour of operations we were led in by Mosquito pathfinders dropping markers.

Conversely, I felt from that first op that bomb-aimer Dickie Durtnal had got it about right. At Givors, despite the weather, our photo-flood shot showed that he had dropped squarely on the markers. Fortunately, it would be many years before accurate assessments of our efforts emerged; at the time we trusted that employing the techniques evolved through so many sacrifices would get our bombs onto the target.

After Givors we flew pretty well every other night. As with all flying, each trip was an experience in itself, but all merge into the anonymous entries of a logbook; green for daylight ops, red for night. Even so, some stand out.

Among those I count the first of the daylight raids we carried out against mobile V1 sites. From the start, I have to say, it was pretty chaotic. Each crew had been left to fly its own course out so that, on arrival at the running-in point, the bomber stream had little cohesion. As we neared the target I watched in horror as a Lanc strayed beneath another one just as it let its load go. The lower Lanc simply ceased to exist. Nor did I see a single parachute come out. After that, though, things got more organised, and we flew a series of squadron formation flights, so that the next such raid saw squadrons stepped up at different altitudes.

Targets that prevented the enemy from firing his 'reprisal weapons' at Holland and Britain were afforded at least equal priority to those disrupting his communications. Accordingly we raided Trossy St Maximin, Secqueville, and the caves at St Leu D'Esserent, all of which were storage areas for V1 Flying Bombs.

We also visited Châtellerault, so striking at both railway and V weapons. After which we returned to Givors once again: German forced-labour gangs carried out repairs remarkably quickly.

We switched then to Germany itself, raiding Brunswick, Darmstadt, and Stuttgart, experiencing now the incredible defence-in-depth other crews had told us about. And as they had said, it was pretty appalling. In fact, John Kean, our wireless op, came out of his cubbyhole as we began our first Ruhr run in, looked out, said an uncouth word, then returned to his wireless set, pulled his curtain and, we swore, never again left his station during any of our ops.

On 15 August 1944 we raided Deelen Airfield, in Holland, deducing a month later that this had been the start of softening-up operations for the airborne landings at Arnhem. After that we returned to German targets, to Mönchengladbach and Handorf (Münster).

Just after this the squadron was stood down from operations while the automatic gun-laying turret known as Village Inn was fitted. Training took from 29 August to 10 September, but once our Lancasters were so equipped our defensive capability increased markedly.

Basically, the whole set-up was radar controlled. We'd feed in the range, and the wingspan of the enemy fighter – we had such details at our fingertips –, the radar 'blip' grew wings, then we'd drive the turret until the winged blip was in the centre of the gunsight, and the radar did the rest. Having seen the results using camera guns, I was very impressed: indeed, the boffins claimed it would score 60% hits. As with everything technical, though, it had to be watched. As we found on our first op with it fitted, raiding Darmstadt.

Keen to use it in action, we were elated to pick up a contact, and more so to find that it wasn't giving the correct recognition signal. I had Jack go into a corkscrew. Only to have Butch, in the rear turret, advise that the contact had not only followed us through the evolution, but was still closing.

'I can't see it yet,' Butch added tersely. I was peering hard. But what with the darkness, and being in and out of broken cloud, I was pushed to give any useful guidance. What I hoped to see was that day's identification code from a largely blacked-out headlight.

Then, with sudden decision, Butch decided, 'I'll give it a few more moments, then have a go.'

I waited, but then a fragment of cloud must have parted.

'Don't shoot.' I yelled. 'It's a Mosquito.' And then, 'The bloody idiot hasn't switched his Z transmitter on.'

Fortunately Butch didn't fire, and equally fortunately the Mosquito crews' aircraft recognition must have been on a par with mine, for promptly parting company we both went about our own business.

On 27 September 1944, back on the Battle Order, we again extended ourselves, this time to bomb Kaiserslautern, a round trip of nearly seven hours. Then, on 19 October, we did an even longer flog to Nuremburg, taking seven and a half hours, exceeding this, on 28 October, by raiding the U-boat pens at Bergen, in Norway. On this op we were part of a force of 237 Lancs but, having encountered thick, lowering cloud, the master bomber called off the raid before our section could release. On the return, having our load still aboard, and having eyed the fuel, we were forced to put in at Burn, in North Yorkshire, after nearly eight hours in the air.

But sortie length meant little, as we were reminded on 2 November when we once more got the full Ruhr treatment over Düsseldorf, a trip that is recorded in my log book as taking just five and a half hours. We were part of a 992 aircraft force, including 561 Lancasters, 400 Halifaxes, and 31 Mosquitoes. The opposition was severe, accounting for nineteen aircraft, eight Lancasters and eleven Halifaxes, but the bombing was rated as accurate with significant damage being done to the designated targets: chemical, steel, and machinery-manufacturing facilities. As it happened, this was the last raid Bomber Command was to carry out on Düsseldorf.

The Dortmund-Ems Canal, connecting the Ruhr with the North Sea, and so forming a lifeline for much of Germany's industry, had long been a primary target for Bomber Command. On 4 November 1944, in a near five-hour trip, our crew attacked its aqueduct at Ladbergen, returning twice the same month to Gravenhorst, its junction with the Mettelland Canal.

One wonders at how many bombs were expended, and how many lives lost, in trying to put these canals out of commission. And certainly damage was caused on occasion, indeed, after our third attack, on 21 November 1944, photo-interpreters counted fifty-nine barges left high and dry. But though reconnaissance photos soon showed a veritable moonscape of bomb craters, the canal still functioned. Even so, we were assured that the complex really was a telling target, and this claim, at least, was borne out by German sources after the war.

We did have some light relief on the return from one such trip when, after a five-hour flight, a weather diversion put us into the American base at Horsham St Faith, near Norwich. Bad weather had once more prevented us from dropping and we'd had to jettison four bombs to get down to a safe landing weight.

The Americans welcomed us with their customary warmth. Then, 'Any bombs on board?' their groundcrew queried. 'We jettisoned four,' we told them, adding, straightfaced, 'so we've only got ten one-thousand pounders left.' They were gratifyingly astounded. Their B-24 Liberators, what with the vast number of crew they carried, and so many big – 0.5 inch calibre – machine guns, could only lift about five one thousand-pounders. To rub it in, just before we departed, one of our chaps opened his bomb doors, when they were totally floored by the Lanc's thirty-three foot long bomb bay.

On 4 December 1944, we took part in what proved to be a devastating attack on a rail target at Heilbronn. We were, I believe, part of a force of 280 or so Lancs, led by pathfinder Mosquitoes. The weather was good, and again our own photo-flood showed a spot-on drop. It would seem, however, that successive crews releasing too soon spread the damage well short of the designated target.

Our penultimate op, on 11 December 1944, was against a dam on the River Urft. We were told at briefing that General Eisenhower had given its destruction highest priority. I seem to remember that 230 Lancs did their best, except that it wasn't good enough. Possibly the staff had misjudged the structure of the dam, for although damaged, it didn't break.

On 17 December 1944 we got airborne on the final op of our tour. This one to Munich. A flog that, on landing, had taken us nine hours and twenty minutes. All those hours, perched on my bum-numbing seat strap! And at that, we hurried. For among our contingent, was G for George, being flown by Squadron Leader George Lace, DFC, DFM, finishing not his first, but his second tour.

A real gent. Before coming to No. 49 Squadron he'd been with No. 106, where my brother was serving as an airman and, on arriving, had made a point of looking me out, a mere sprog air gunner, and passing on my brother's best wishes. A nice touch, which made it particularly heinous when, as we both roared in, and the tower advised, 'E for Easy' – that was us – 'cleared to land. G-George, you are number two,' Jack chirped blithely, 'Up your gorge, George!'

We were now tour-ex. We'd completed our thirty reckonable ops, and could look forward to a good spell of leave followed by at least three months off ops. Further, with units so flush with crews, and the armies now fairly pelting eastwards, it seemed doubtful that we'd be recalled for a second tour. Besides, we'd done all there was to be done. We'd done our thirty ops, and Jack, now commissioned, had honoured the crew by being awarded a Distinguished Flying Cross. Where I was concerned I'd flown a total of 419 hours, 201 by day and 218 by night.

We'd cleared from the station, and were gathered at the squadron office to be given details of the postings to follow our leaves, when Jack, having been called in first, came out looking whiter than white, clearly in a state of shock. 'I've been posted to bloody India,' he told us.

We were all taken aback. But after a moment or two, we began to take stock. What lay in store for most of us had to be dicing with death on some operational training unit, training new crews. Whereas the mystic Far East was beckoning ...

'When I told them I planned to get married,' Jack was saying, 'they simply said they'd give me an extra forty-eight whenever I needed it.'

Nick-the-Nav had recently become a proud father, while Sticky had a wife, so home postings suited them. The rest of us, however, were of one mind.

'We'll come with you,' we chorused.

I have to admit that the voyage outbound, effectively travelling steerage on what was then the troopship *Capetown Castle*, took some of the gloss off the mystique. Or perhaps that was the effect of the nights I spent on a pointless guard duty. Unless the idea was that senior NCOs mounting guard would keep the passengering aircrew and WAAFs apart, or stop someone from pinching the anchor.

On disembarking, we travelled to Kolar, in Southern India, home of No. 1673 Heavy Conversion Unit, where we were checked-out on long-range Liberators, an American aircraft from the same stable as those we'd seen at Horsham St Faith, and one that, despite being a Lancaster man, I have to concede wasn't too bad at all.

South East Asia Command assigned us to No. 99 Squadron, whom we found at Dhubalia airstrip, some sixty miles east of Calcutta, where they were tasked with bombing targets in Burma. We hardly had time to settle in before, on 12 June 1945, we found ourselves raiding bridges – one rail, two road – at Bilin, the aim being to prevent the Japs trying to re-take Rangoon. And this was an altogether new game, on a vast new pitch, the flight taking us a full eleven and a half hours.

*No. 99 Squadron Liberators at Dhubalia*

*Bilin river bridge destroyed*

Nor were we that well looked after. Back on Lancs we'd had our flasks and sandwiches, and caffeine tablets enough to keep us awake. Here, despite such enormous distances to cover, and the facilities the Americans had put into their own Liberators, we got just a K-ration – the American combat-meal-in-a-box – and the advice, 'Fill up your water bottles.' No doubt we'd have settled happily enough, however, except that just three days later, on 15 June 1945, seven of the squadron's aircraft were sent to attack shipping off the Siamese coast.

We'd been briefed that a Japanese tanker was on its way to deliver to their forces a much needed re-supply of aviation fuel. Our crew was among those detailed to attack this target; other crews were told off to deal with the destroyer escort. All very well, except that the weather was too foul to fly in even loose formation. Accordingly, we pressed on by ourselves, and eventually sighted the flotilla. Only three others did so, we'd discover, and each of them sustained damage. In fact, as we closed, we actually saw another Liberator launch an attack on the destroyer. Then we became busy with our own affairs.

Jack turned in with bomb doors open, while I began firing from the front turret to keep the tanker's gunners occupied. Conditions were so rough, though, that Jack could not drop, only before he could reposition for a second run, the destroyer caught us with a burst of ack-ack. There was a great bang, and I lost consciousness. When I came to, I pushed open the turret's doors, expecting to find the nav and bomb aimer facing me. Instead, I saw that the nosewheel doors – their escape exit – were open, and their stations empty!

Much later I would learn that they had baled out, the nav being killed when his chute failed to open, the bomb aimer being fished from the sea by the Japs and finishing the war as a POW. Fearing that I'd been left alone, I went dazedly further aft, and was gratified to see both pilots in their seats.

We seemed to be flying all right, but the aircraft was clearly in a sorry state. The bomb doors were still open, so I could see that our two extra fuel tanks, normally suspended within the bomb bay, had fallen away. Also, although we'd been unable to drop our bombs, some had fallen free, while another, jerked loose, was hanging in a way that prevented us from jettisoning the rest.

Getting rid of it proved to be a job and a half. Eventually, having made use of one of the flight engineer's spanners, Butch and I managed to unbolt its carrier, allowing the problem bomb to fall away. After that, ridding ourselves of the rest was straightforward. Or as straightforward as it could be, bouncing around above a wind-lashed sea with both pilots struggling to hold the plane in level flight.

With the bomb doors closed, things began to return to normal. Jack and the second pilot, Peter Miles – it was his first op –, conferred between them, and reckoned that we had some two or three hundred miles to go to reach the friendly strip at Mingladon, Rangoon. Fuel, without the lost auxiliary tanks, would be touch and go. But all seemed fair enough.

Except that at this juncture Butch decided to show me what the rest had assimilated during the period when I'd been out of things. Namely, that a shell from the destroyer had taken away our entire starboard fin and rudder! So how the two pilots were keeping us even relatively straight and level was anyone's guess. Certainly the revelation set me doing a rapid assimilation for myself ...

Time crawled. But eventually we located the strip, to the north of the city. The weather had improved, but the pilots still had their work cut out, and after some fourteen hours in the air, must have been exhausted. Jack commenced a turning approach, his concentration not helped by red Very flares from the caravan – meaning, do not land – and a stream of advice on the radio that the strip wasn't suitable for a bomber. Unknown to us at the time, we were also being tracked by heavy anti-aircraft guns who, suspicious of anything coming from the Jap-held south-east, had also been slow to recognise our sadly modified silhouette.

Jack threw away the first approach, and turned for another, getting lower every moment. Unable to do anything to help, Butch and I, positioned in the mid section, clutched hands. Perhaps it was the requirement to put down the undercarriage or the flaps, whatever the two of them up front chose to do, but suddenly, as if the poor old Lib had finally had enough, everything went topsy-turvy as it plunged heavily into a paddy field.

Wits shaken, Butch and I, finding that the aircraft had broken apart, simply blundered our way out, then splashed briefly across the paddy until we fell, to be taken in care only moments later by the anti-aircraft gunners who had sped to the crash in their jeep. The flight engineer also emerged unscathed, and the second pilot was not too badly injured. John Kean, on the other hand, suffered harrowingly. The turret had collapsed onto his calf, holding him trapped. Hopefully, as the hours dragged by with the struggle to extricate him continuing, he remained unaware of a member of the crash crew, rifle in hand, hovering against the chance of the wreck going up in flames. John survived. Jack, though, had been killed instantly.

On 1 July 1945, back at Dhubalia, with Jack interred in Rangoon cemetery, our squadron commander, Wing Commander Webster, DSO, DFC, placed a handwritten commendation in every survivor's log book: 'This aircraft only reached a home base because of the excellent crew discipline and co-operation.' I suppose it was a fitting enough epitaph for Jack. And one that makes this survivor very proud to have been so singled out.

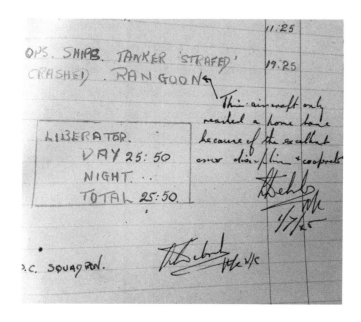

*Handwritten commendation*

It was to be an epitaph too, to my operational flying. When I closed my logbook I had flown thirty-two operational sorties, and recorded 454 hours flying, 240 by day, including 26 hours on the Liberator, and 224 hours by night.

It was the last of my operational flying, then, and the last too of my reckonable flying as aircrew, for as there were no crews short of gunners Butch and I were surplus to requirement. The squadron couldn't use us, so we were posted away, to Group Headquarters, in Calcutta.

Within days, however, I was hospitalized with mosquito-derived dengue fever, sinking so deep during the most critical two weeks that I lost all track of time. Fortunately, the medics knew their stuff and once I began to come out of it they sent me to recuperate at Nainital Hill Station, nearly 7,000 feet up in the Himalayan foothills.

On returning to duty I was sent to a personnel transit camp where I supervised the delivery of welfare parcels to troops on outlying units. I also became responsible for accounting for spirits and beer stocks to sergeant's and officer's messes in the area, an involvement which, on one occasion, took me to Delhi. By Avro York there, Douglas Dakota back. I might indeed, have carried on home, for although my father had just died I'd been unable to get a compassionate release as my sister and brother were available to take care of things. Even so, it was a close-run thing, 'I thought you were coming all the way to Blighty with us,' the York's air quartermaster observed. I was tempted, but prudence won out, and it was back to Calcutta on the Dak.

*Avro York*

Having spent a year in Calcutta, I was posted to Dum Dum airfield, just north of the city, where I was initially employed in air movements, dealing with freight and mail, and later, in flying control, logging aircraft schedules.

Outside the cantonments, it was a time of growing political turmoil, with the movement for home rule turning to riots. One of spare aircrews' regular duties was to act as guard transporting passengers by lorry from Calcutta to the airfield. Driving in that area was always wild, but on the first of these trips it was little short of frenetic, so that I found myself, and my Sten, thrown from side to side. It was only then that I switched on, and realised that earlier riots had left the streets strewn with bodies that the driver was trying to avoid without slackening speed. I counted over a hundred on the main road alone, with countless others in the side streets.

Six months after my posting, and before the National troubles peaked, however, my demob number came up and I was sent to Bombay, bound for home. I was to travel on the former P&O liner *Mooltan*. This time, though, as a warrant officer, I rated a cabin on my own. So I boarded in high spirits. And was further bucked up by a tannoy message calling for Warrant Officer Cooke: heartening to think they did indeed, know my status! Only to be given the good news. Wartime ranks were being reclassified. Accordingly, I was no longer a warrant officer, but only a sergeant. No more personal cabin. Instead, back to the bilges once again. Although I did rate a personal hammock.

I suppose the miserable trip home helped jaundice me with the war years. Having left the Service I went into a variety of jobs until I settled with the water-supply industry, eventually pursuing a career with Severn Trent Water. It was only much later, when I came into contact with the squadron association, that I began to reflect upon those days.

On occasion I'm asked if I was scared on ops. And I have to think hard. The tension engendered affected people in so many ways. I mentioned John, our wireless operator, staying behind his curtain, notwithstanding which he seemed to breeze through his first tour and was happy enough starting his second. Butch, on the other hand, was deeply affected from the start. Perhaps he was more introspective than most aircrew. But he too carried on. What did upset him after the crash, however, was to be assigned to a section engaged in returning corpses to Japan.

I suppose I would have to say that I was never really scared. Not on ops. In fact, although we did thirty-two all told, the trip that unnerved me most was one when we never left the ground.

It had been back at Fiskerton. At briefing, the Intelligence chap had spent a long time explaining the routing to us. The red line on the target map went far to the north, and even then made a series of dog-legs before turning for the target. Most outbound tracks did this, of course, not only to confuse the defences regarding the actual target, but in order to avoid flak clusters and night-fighter airfields. This red line though, deviated from the straight-line track to an extreme degree: the No. 5 Group planners clearly felt the defences to be so intensive and so alert as to warrant leading the bomber stream well clear.

We duly began to start up. Only to discover a massive mag drop – an ignition fault all too common in piston engines. Jack and Sticky tried to clear it, but had no luck. In the end we had to disembark, and run across to the spare aircraft. Setting this up took time, so that when we taxied out, we were lagging behind everyone else.

Then, a Lancaster turning onto the runway suffered a tyre burst, blocking the taxiway. This meant that the rest had to enter the runway lower down, run up to the stranded Lanc, swing about into wind, and take-off. Initially this looked hopeful, for it slowed the process down, giving us time to tag on the end. Even so, by the time we entered at the intersection and started our own downwind positioning run towards the stalled Lanc, the others had all gone. Jack kept the speed up, but just as he prepared to slow and swing around into wind, we heard him curse, then rap out, 'Bloody brake failure!'

To avoid hitting the stranded – and bombed-up – Lanc, he chopped the port engines, and opened up the starboard ones to swing our equally fuelled and bombed-up aircraft about. Only to run into the metal piping of the FIDO fog clearance installation at the runway's edge, the impact denting the pipes and bringing us to a wretched halt.

***No. 49 Squadron Lancaster at Fiskerton, showing the FIDO pipes***

The groundcrews were onto us like a flash, and soon had us checked over, and facing the right way. Not that we were that interested. We'd tried our darnedest, and the gremlins had bested us. Mentally, we'd geared ourselves up to go. Twice. Only to be twice let down flat. Enough was enough. Except that, just then, one of the Intelligence wallahs drove up and, waving a chart, came over to where the Group Captain was discussing the situation with Jack and the engineering officer.

'Sir,' he opened. 'I've worked it out. If we can get Parkin and crew away now, and they route direct, they'll arrive at the same time as the stream. It'll improve our night's figures.'

And that's when I was really scared. More scared that at any other time. The chairborne clot was actually proposing to send us in a straight line over virtually every hotspot in Europe, merely to improve statistics!

As it was, the Station Master said nothing, only gave him a look. But it was to be many hours before my nerves began to settle. Indeed, how many years has it been now? Yet still the memory sends a shiver up my spine.

Send them direct, indeed!

*Bill with his polka-dotted operational scarf, 2013*

# 10. A Wonderful Life

## Flight Lieutenant Ken A.J. Ellis, DFC, pilot

As the American lads in Georgia had explained, all they needed was a tight-packed formation of scuds of heavy bombers to give interdependant cover from fighter attack. ... Unfortunately, all the German flak crews needed was a tight-packed formation of scuds of heavy bombers ...

*Ken Ellis at Newquay, from group photo, September 1941*

I've enjoyed a wonderful life. A life studded by apparent setbacks which time and again proved godsends.

I was born in Derby on 27 August 1922 and in the course of time won a scholarship to the notable Bemrose School. This took me up to the sixth form, but by then we'd moved to Littleover, outside the town limits, and competing, as I then had to, in the wider, county area, I couldn't get the necessary scholarship: the first of those aforementioned apparent setbacks!

Thinking of it as second best, I obtained a job in the County Education Offices. What this gave me, in fact, was a thorough grounding in business studies. My years there showed me the way to lay out paperwork, and instilled neatness in all my written work – as my flying log books, it is said, bear testimony. Additionally, frequent committee work prepared me well for so many meetings down the years, not least those of the later-life Allotment, and the Bee-Keepers' Associations, the latter taking me to committees from Brussels to Adelaide.

The Second World War, of course, coloured everything for my generation, so having developed a yen for the sea, I went with two other like-minded lads to the Derby recruiting office and applied to become a pilot in the Fleet Air Arm (FAA).

We were all three snapped up and sent to Birmingham for medical and aptitude testing. The other two were cock-a-hoop to pass with first-class eyesight. I, though, was dismayed to find my vision below the standard required for the FAA. I was, however, acceptable to the RAF. That medical hiccup aside, the aptitude tests were satisfactory, so on 13 June 1941 we were all attested, them into the FAA, me into the RAF.

From now on I'll not bother counting each apparent setback, but in the course of time we all completed flying training. The others were posted to the biplane Swordfish torpedo bomber, a antiquated stringbag if there ever was one, and sent to attack capital warships. Neither survived for more than a matter of weeks ...

*Arriving at Lord's Cricket Ground, St John's Wood,*
*Aircrew Reception Centre*

I had to wait until the end of September 1941 before being called forward to the Aircrew Reception Centre at Lord's Cricket Ground. During a ten-day stay here we received our kit and all our jabs, lived in requisitioned flats and ate in London Zoo, after which my group was posted to No. 8 Initial Training Wing at Newquay, in Cornwall. This ushered in some three months of square-bashing – foot and arms drill and physical training – while working through the Pre-Flight Training Syllabus of signals, meteorology, mathematics, engines, armament, navigation, and principles of flight, and the ready recognition of, not only aircraft, but war gases! We passed out in mid January 1942, after which it was up to Manchester, to Heaton Park, where we waited two weeks for a passage to the United States where my batch were to carry out our flying training.

On 2 February 1942, having positioned to Gourock, we boarded the USS *Chateau Thierry* which had just brought some of the first American troops to Britain, the United States having entered the war just two months before. We sailed in convoy, with a destroyer escort, the crossing to Halifax taking twelve days, a voyage that, after three years of wartime austerity, truly took us into a new world. A world of white bread and T-bone steaks, of unlimited chocolate, and cigarettes at a half-crown for 200!

Our initial destination was Royal Canadian Air Force (RCAF) Monckton, New Brunswick, which was No. 31 Personnel Disposal Unit. Two months of lectures there and we moved south on the long train ride down to Georgia in the States.

The United States Army Air Force (USAAF) – until June 1941, the United States Army Air Corps (USAAC) – had got flying training well in hand by that time, so that I shared a four-berth room with three American trainees. The instructors, formerly civilians, but since December inducted into the army, were very experienced and the training proved second to none. One big advantage, of course, was the fine weather, which afforded us the continuity so important in flying training. Even so the whole course took from February until November 1942, months which I found so absorbing that I never had time for the jitters that many pupils suffered from as the severe standards took their toll and many departed north for

RCAF Monkton, either to become bomb aimers or to be returned to the UK for disposal.

True, my logbook records an occasion when a particular instructor commented somewhat harshly on my responses, and my ability to react to stress, an observation that might have temporarily dented my confidence, for I would have been unaware that ever afterwards, whether in flying training, on a squadron, or indeed in post-Service flying, I was never again to be assessed as anything less than 'above the average'. With hindsight, the poor chap might even have been feeling liverish that morning ...

The training followed the normal gamut. Straight and level, circuit flying, stalling and spinning, aerobatics, navigational exercises – those wonderful placenames: Vidalia, Eufaula, and Tallahassee! –, and the all-important flying by reference to instruments and flying at night. Intriguing entries in my log book, I see, record exercises devoted to 'Blackout Landings', and 'Blitz Approaches'. Night landings with lighting restricted to a single line of gooseneck flares, perhaps?

Our initial training was carried out on the Boeing Stearman PT-17 biplane trainer. We then progressed to the monoplane Vultee BT13A, a smaller version of the Harvard – the AT-6A – which we also flew. For experience in twin-engined operation we flew the Beechcraft AT-10 which strongly resembled the British Airspeed Oxford.

We started our training with two weeks' ab initio flying at Turner Field, Albany, Georgia, which had three concrete runways but accommodation that verged on the pre-fabricated. We then settled in for three months' flying training proper at Souther Field, Americus, taking up a syllabus slightly compressed by the USAAF from that previously taught by the civilian school originally assigned to the RAF contract.

A further two months was spent at Cochran Field, Machon, with our training to 'Wings' standard being completed during a two months' stay at Moody Field, Valdosta. After which, with some 130 hours in my log book it was farewell to Georgia – whose friendly folk and kindly weather had made things so pleasant for me – and back up north to RCAF Moncton once again.

Just two weeks here awaiting a passage, after which we boarded the speedy *Queen Elizabeth* which did not bother with laboured and time-consuming zigzags but powered us home with just a single destroyer as escort.

On disembarking we passed into the care of No. 7 Personnel Reception Centre at Harrogate, where we were variously accommodated in hotels. Here, still driven by that yen for the sea, I made known my preference for Coastal Command. I was told, however, that the aforementioned amendment of the syllabus by the USAAF had left me undertrained in navigation. On the other hand I had passed out highly graded, so instead of being posted to Bomber Command with the rest, I was sent off on a series of detachments where my navigational shortcomings might be made good.

This meant initially to No. 11 Pilots' Advanced Flying Unit at Shawbury, and its relief landing ground at Wheaton Aston, where I flew the Airspeed Oxford and became accustomed to UK's temperate weather conditions – which in February and March were hardly temperate in any sense. Then came a stint at No. 1524 Beam Approach Training flight at Newton, near Nottingham, flying various marks of Wellington, before being posted as a staff pilot to No. 4 Radio School at Madley, near Hereford.

The job here was to fly pupil wireless-operators around, singly in twin-seat Proctors, and then in groups, in the biplane De Havilland Dominie – the Dragon Rapide: like me, still driving around in 2013! Effectively this meant my doing all the navigating as the trainees battled with their dits and dohs and tried to get their trailing aerials wound in before we touched down. With most nearly always succeeding ...

There was no opportunity to do any navigational plotting on a chart – the only thing I can think of that the modified USAAF syllabus lacked – but my map reading certainly improved. What was also honed was my ability to fly by reference to instruments alone despite the thickest and most turbulent cloud the UK weather could produce. Of near-equal importance was that my experience in terms of hours flown was steadily increasing.

Though in a training bywater, I never doubted that I was helping to produce good aircrew material for the war that had so far eluded me.

The idyll came to an end in mid December 1943 with a posting to No. 26 Operational Training Unit (OTU) at Wing, near Leighton Buzzard. Not, however, to learn to operate a Coastal Command type, but one of Bomber Command's Stirling bombers. In truth, this came as no real shock to me. I had been keeping an eye on things operational and was well aware that the Battle of the Atlantic against U-boats had been pretty well won. The need now, as it had been for a good year or so, was for bomber crews.

And the bomber scene was another I had been eyeing closely. In the early days of the war the RAF had been confident of its strategy, with Hampden and Wellington bombers setting off for German targets, by day, and quite often, alone: their target a specific factory or group of shipping. Virtual decimation by German fighters had swiftly led to a reversal of such strategies, after which night operations had become the order of things. In the years since, expertise had grown, and now a massed main force would bomb area targets – as opposed to specific ones –, dropping on markers laid by specialist units.

As I had learnt from my room-mates in Georgia, the United States Army Air Force (USAAF) – the formation the Americans would employ in the European Theatre – having watched the RAF's bombing campaign progress, had it sorted. They had a bombsight which could put a bomb in a pickle barrel – whatever that was – from any given altitude. Operating by day to make navigation easier, all they then needed was plenty of defensive machine guns and a tight-packed formation of scuds of heavy bombers to give interdependant cover from fighter attack.

What they'd left out of their equation for success was that all the German anti-aircraft-gun crews needed was a tight-packed formation of scuds of heavy bombers ...

As it was, therefore, by night and by day, bomber crews of both Allied air forces had suffered horrendous losses. Among them, indeed, the lads who had returned from the States when I had, but had been posted directly to Bomber Command ...

My posting, then, was to the Short Stirling. It might well have been the Lancaster, the *class* bomber of the Second World War. But it was the Stirling. On the other hand, as a pilot I found the Stirling a delightful aircraft to fly. Others found the way it reared nose high twenty-three feet above the tarmac daunting, and dreaded the problems of touching down in any cross wind. It just happened to suit me.

I was well aware of its limitations. I knew that Shorts had retained the wing profile proven on their Sunderland flying boat but had been forced by officialdom to make other modifications that robbed the Stirling of performance, and specifically prevented it from making any decent height. When operating with a main force, therefore, we would be stuck at something like 11,000 feet while all the rest, from Wellingtons to Lancasters, would be soaring around at twenty-plus thousand feet, not only free from much of the flak but actually showering us low fliers with their bomb loads ...

A hiccup without a doubt ... But hardly a bad thing. For as a consequence we found ourselves taken off main force operations, and set, first to mining, and then to specialising on attacking oil installations.

First, though, that most vital of all things in flying operations, the crew. The method of coming together in those days was mutual selection. On first arriving at the OTU I had struck lucky in having a wireless operator and a mid-upper gunner approach me as their prospective pilot. The sole survivors of a crew who had crashed en route to the Middle East, they would almost certainly have taken note that my battledress was near threadbare, and my wings well chafed by a seat harness. They might even have known that in contrast to the 300 to 400 hours' experience of the other pilots on offer, I had flown nearly 1,000 hours. As with all my crew, I was so very lucky to get them. But as for names, let me swiftly claim Anno Domini.

In Warrant Officer Bob Parrish, I had a wireless operator/air gunner, and in Flight Sergeant Mac McGarrity, a mid-upper gunner, each of whom proved exemplary in his field. I also gathered to me a bomb aimer, Warrant Officer Colin Frith, who – in the way we operated, with the navigator dropping the ordnance – would more often serve as second pilot; a flight engineer, Flight Sergeant Ken Wilson; and a rear gunner, Flight Sergeant Eddie Bertram. All three names I confess, have had to be recovered from squadron records – by the good offices of Mr Steve Smith of No. 218 (Gold Coast) Squadron Association –, having escaped my increasingly elusive memory. And yet how close we were as crew! Though not that many crews got as close as we did when (later in the war) temporarily operating from a French airfield, Mac, a staunch Roman Catholic, needed to go to confession. Not being able to speak French he had me squeeze into the confessional and translate for him!

Our navigator though, is not to be forgotten. My commission had come through, accordingly I approached a smart-looking sprog navigator in the officers' mess and asked if he would be mine. He coyly refused, being spoken for.

'The chap you need,' he advised, 'is Jock Robertson. In nav school he came top of everything there was to come top of but refused his commission, wanting to stay in the sergeants' mess with his drinking pals. He can afford to be picky, so he's not crewed up yet ...' And so the rest of us came together with Jock.

We finished the OTU in mid March 1944, spent a month at Methwold, in Norfolk, and a spell with No. 1653 Conversion Unit at Chedburgh, in Suffolk, before being posted to No. 218 Squadron, and finally going to war.

No. 218 Squadron was, at that time operating from Woolfox Lodge, immediately adjacent to the A1 in Rutland. After three months, however, it moved first to Methwold, and then to Chedburgh, where it remained for the rest of our time on strength.

Although to all intents and purposes we were a sprog crew, Jock's quality was recognised – another lucky stroke! –, and when the specialised radar gear Gee-H became available we were among the first selected to operate it.

Ordinary Gee was a radar aid to navigation which gave good results from a lattice display. Its sophisticated development Gee-H effectively led us over the target and in telling us when to drop gave an accuracy of seventy yards regardless of weather conditions. This typically meant that we would lead, at the most, a dozen or so bombers who would formate closely on us and drop either when they saw our bombs go, or when they saw our marker flare. For us, in the lead, it meant a quick in, and more importantly to many, a quick out.

Important to many? And to us, of course. But folk vary in their reaction to stress. And I have to claim – having given much thought to the matter –, that I was never consciously aware of being afraid. I would have been well cognizant of the statistics spelt out by the empty seats in the dining hall after an op. Such things could not be ignored: one had only hours since left a sky filled with flak, lit too by the sudden flare of so many stricken bombers. But all that one accepted as merely part of life's pattern ...

Perhaps, in our specialised role, we were less at hazard than many. In fact, I remember just two known close calls. On one occasion flak did find us. Fortunately the half-dozen or so pieces of shrapnel we discovered back at base had struck nothing vital; nothing vital to any of us, or to our technical bits and pieces. Certainly none had touched either our bomb load or our fuel tanks ...

The second occasion was a little later, on Lancs, when the aircraft closest to us suddenly went up in a welter of flame and debris, with streaking tracers to tell us it hadn't been flak! Instantly Mac, from his mid-upper turret had rapped the imperative, 'Corkscrew starboard!'

It was an evasive manoeuvre we had practised until it was near second nature. No finesse. Just stick forward, and over, hard right, and full-booted right rudder. The hope was that the fighter, running in, homing mainly on the glow of exhaust stubs, would find nothing to aim at, and bugger off to bother someone else. Which in this case is just what happened.

Mac had shown great judgement in seeing the apparently-aware fighter and calling the corkscrew, rather than opening fire. Downing the fighter would have covered him in glory. Had he missed, however, his tracer would definitely have given us away. No hesitation, of course, in my reacting to his order to corkscrew – and I use the word 'order' advisedly. Crew co-operation was everything. And how much we owed to it!

Such tense moments were far outweighed by many hours of tedium. Hours of wearing concentration, for flying on instruments is demanding. Droning on, eyes periodically lifting from the dials to sweep the night sky, adhering to Jock's occasionally amended headings, aware with part of your mind that around you might be up to a thousand other bombers, all making for the same initial point – a selected position, ideally one that could be easily identified, some miles short of the target –, each navigating independently, at a slightly different speed, each trying to keep a given altitude, and all in pitch darkness, with radio silence, and unseen. Until flak below backlit the stream, or an aircraft brewed up and momentarily threw the scores of others into frightening focus.

Far more pleasing to the memory, were those trips laying mines. In the Baltic, for example. Holding a massive great machine like the Stirling to the North Sea waves to avoid the enemy radar, lifting up to skim Denmark, down again to hug the Baltic, then pulling up to a safe dropping height as Jock counted down to the release point for the mines. Exhilarating to any pilot at any age!

We carried out our first nine operations in the worthy Stirling. The first of these was on 10 June 1944 – four days after the D-Day invasion – when we sowed mines off Gravenhague – the Hague. Later that month we were mining again, but in Brittany, at Lorient: never a healthy location with so much flak and naval opposition. In between times we bombed targets in Brest, but another early mining operation took us back to Holland, to Ijmuiden, by then *Fortress* Ijmuiden, the heavily protected – and defended – lair of the German fast torpedo boats. With the enemy having made Ijmuiden virtually impervious to air attack, we sought to hinder both its E-Boats and its midget submarines in getting to sea and interfering with the traffic supplying the invasion beaches.

On 31 July 1944, after two months on the Stirling, we converted to Lancasters. But though that suggests a conversion course, in our case it simply meant a two hour twenty minute dual familiarization trip, then getting airborne for another two hour trip solo; 'solo', of course, meaning 'as a crew'. Two days later, on 4 August 1944, we collected a new Lancaster, NF906, did a thirty-five minute night flight, and began what was to be a further twenty-six operations: not reckoning one sortie reluctantly, but necessarily, aborted in the Channel Islands area due to engine trouble – we weren't in the business of throwing common sense out of the window.

Again, due to Jock's expertise, our Lancaster was Gee-H equipped, so even when we flew with main force we were in the lead and ahead of the ruck, arriving (in our own minds at least) before the flak reached its full intensity and the fighters learnt what the main target really was that night and finally came abuzzing in force.

Our German mainland targets included Mannheim – its Opel works at Rüsselheim –, where we dropped one 4,000 pound high-explosive bomb and 110 four-pound incendiaries; Düsseldorf, Duisberg, Essen, and Cologne. We also raided the heavily defended island of Borkhum; similarly Walcheren Island, off Antwerp, in both instances precisely targeting gun positions and at Walcheren specifically aiding the temporarily bogged-down army assault.

Indeed, army support loomed large in our operations, so that we were detailed to neutralise enemy strongholds at Calais, St Malo, Cap Gris Nez, and Le Havre. Again, we gave the ground troops support at Heinsberg, on the Dutch border, acting as marker, so that we did two runs over the target, using four 250 pound target indicators, additionally delivering one 4,000 pounder, six 1,000 pounders, and two 500 pounder high-explosive bombs. Army support targets aside, our regular bomb load was eleven 1,000 pounders and four 500 pounders, the load we delivered on 31 October 1944 when we bombed from 19.000 feet through 10/10s (total) cloud cover. The low cloud prevented our crew from reporting results but another crew, following on, saw fires surging upwards through the overcast.

Our speciality, as I have said, became oil targets, typified by our attack on Homberg's Rheinpreussen synthetic oil plant which we marked with a single target indicator and damaged with one 4,000 pounder and fourteen 500 pound general-purpose bombs.

Not all raids went without a hitch, however. So that when we set out to raid the Fulda rail yards, in Hesse, our Gee-H set broke down. Fortunately Jock had his finger well and truly out and we successfully bombed our secondary target, some 45 miles away, Butzbach rail complex, dropping one 4,000 pounder and thirteen 500 pounders. The three target-indicator flares we had not used at Fulda, however, we brought back with us. We also brought back our passenger, a Flight Lieutenant Hodnett, who – as the custom was – had flown with us as a second dickey preparatory to embarking on ops with his own crew.

At that time a first tour comprised 35 completed operations, our final op of the tour coming in late November 1944 when we raided Cologne, acting in the van of main force as 'Spearhead and Marker'. Since May, we had flown a total of 161 operational hours.

Now tour complete, we were formally asked to forgo our break, and instead to carry out a second, fifteen-op tour as a Pathfinder crew. I was keen to do so. However, two of the crew were newly married, and dead set against carrying on. The crew had become so central to our thinking, certainly to mine, that I didn't give a thought to seeking another group to carry on with, but along with the others, turned down the complimentary offer, and put in my leave pass.

On returning to duty on 17 January 1945 it was back to RAF Wing, near Leighton Buzzard, once again. This time, however, to No. 60 (Signals) Group's Radio-Navigation-Aids Test Flight. For the next eight months I flew a variety of aircraft to check the accuracy of every conceivable sort of radio-navigational aid: 'radio' being wireless and radar. It was a job that took us extensively to the continent, and on occasion as far north as Iceland, to confirm the accuracy of the Loran – long-range navigation – system. The people we worked with were boffin types, the very cream of the signals' world; the IT wizard's of the day. What we were part of, in fact, was the modernization of European aviation.

We'd become used to radio beams in the States, the core of their airways system. Then again, on ops, such aids as Gee and Gee-H had become tools of the trade. However, there remained great yawning gaps in technology. On one occasion, forced to divert when our home station was obscured by fog, we had been obliged to take advantage of FIDO, in which blazing petrol was used to heat the air and locally dispel the fog over the runway. Truly terrifying ...

Then again there was a 'get-you-home' system known as Darky which relied upon the abysmally short range of our contemporary voice wireless sets. A ground operator, knowing that any aircraft he heard calling had to be relatively close, could pass it his own position, which would often suffice to allow the crew to re-start their own navigation. He could even have other stations help direct the lost aircraft towards the nearest airfield. We'd joke, rather cruelly, that our American allies navigated by Darky. We, of course, had Jock.

More futuristically, I'd trained on radio-beam landing approach systems at Newton. Then again wide-area radio control was becoming ever more efficiently exercised, around London, for example. Technically monitoring such developments was our pigeon.

It was a tour which was to bring me many benefits. But one in particular. I sometimes positioned to check out Link Trainer establishments in a Magister, but on this occasion, having carried out a visit I was to be driven back to base by road. Emerging from the building, it was to discover the most attractive WAAF driver awaiting me. For her too, it transpired, a sprightly twenty-two year old came as a surprise when she had been expecting an ancient boffin. However, as I neared her I happened upon a dead mole. 'You'd look wonderful in a fur coat,' I said, dropping it into her lap, 'Here's the first instalment.' Not the most brilliant, or thoughtful, of openings, perhaps, but one that paved the way for over fifty years of happy marriage.

Another chance meeting was very nearly as productive. It would have been August 1945 when I had occasion to call at No. 60 Group's Headquarters at Leighton Buzzard. I wasn't that happy with any of the plans the RAF seemed to have for my future. However, while waiting I fell into conversation with an administrative orderly who mentioned that her fiancée, a navigator, had just been released to the British Overseas Airways Corporation (BOAC). Intrigued by the notion, I promptly sent off a letter myself, received a reply a few days later, and was welcomed by the corporation with open arms. Not in any sense a hiccup, but certainly a case of right time, right place ...

On 20 September 1945 I reported to their central training school at Whitchurch on a four month course during which I obtained my civil pilot's licence. And from 1 February 1946, I began operating with BOAC, being officially released from the RAF on 14 October 1946.

That encounter at Group Headquarters started me on a career that would keep me contently flying until I retired in 1975. It truly was a fulfilling way of life. I started off flying European routes on Dakotas, not least those which took us into and out of Berlin, where up-to-date information about Russian Yak fighter 'exercises' were of paramount importance!

*Ken Ellis in BOAC uniform with the Russian-flight movements board*

Eventually we re-equipped with Constellations and Stratocruisers, on which I graduated to Transatlantic flights to Canada and the States, and to the Caribbean, passing on to world-wide flights on such Boeing jetliners as the 707.

But then I had the best of both worlds. For just as the war ended so Evelyn, my WAAF driver, found herself facing an unwelcome posting to Germany. Hours later she turned up – she'd become a dear and frequent visitor –, and although she did not quite get down on one knee, insisted that, to get her out of the posting, I marry her. Which, of course, I was only too ready to do. And so I became a flying family man, grouping around us as the years went by, four wonderful children.

Wartime flying was not all fun, no matter how one enjoyed certain aspects of it. But I would not have missed it for anything. And yet, although I have extolled the crew, we none of us ever kept in touch. I once tried to contact Jock, but the address I had proved out of date, and I had to let it go ...

Back in April 1945, His Majesty King George the Sixth had invested me with the Distinguished Flying Cross. Taking it from its presentation box after all these years, I see what the *London Gazette* said about the award: in the course of numerous operations against the enemy I had invariably displayed the utmost fortitude, courage, and devotion to duty ... For *I*, of course, read, *his crew* ...

*Ken Ellis with the DFC/DFM postage stamp, September 1990*

*DFC, but no Aircrew Europe Star*

Anyway, after the ceremony I was told that I was one of two recipients the Queen (HM Elizabeth Bowes-Lyon) had invited to dine that evening at nearby Sandringham. I was tremendously excited, but utterly taken aback at the soup stage to be faced with croutons. I was endeavouring to manage them with my fork, when Her Majesty, seated next to me, leant over and said softly, '*Fingers*, Ellis.'

Eleven years later, in 1956, I was called upon to fly the new queen and her husband, Prince Phillip, to Nigeria on a royal visit. Just before the royal couple arrived, the (now) Queen Mother and Princess Margaret came aboard, unannounced, for a private, last-minute leave-taking. Eyeing me, the Queen Mother enquired, 'We've met before, haven't we?'

'Yes, Ma'am. The croutons. *Fingers*, Ellis,' I reminded her.

Crews, however, both RAF and civilian, have big ears, and it was a long time before I lost the nickname ...

An equally gratifying recognition, to be approved by the royal passenger I had carried in 1956, was to be a far longer time in coming. Nearly seventy years. Though lionised by all when needed, once danger passed Bomber

Command fell into opprobrium. It was all political, but it was the lads and their leaders who suffered the cold shoulder. The crack in the wall of aloofness came when the 'Butch' Harris' statue appeared near Trafalgar Square in 1992, followed in 2012 by a memorial to the crews themselves. But only as I undertook this account, on 26 February 2013, was full recognition granted with the award of a Bomber Command Clasp to all those who had flown on bomber operations. Bittersweet recognition. But then what else can come out of any war ...

*Ken Ellis, February 2013*

The performance figures given can only be a rough guide. Indeed, flying any one of a line-up of a given aircraft type will show all such data to be merely representative. Regarding machine-gun armament, British aircraft invariably employed Browning, Lewis, or Vickers 0.303 inch (7.7 mm) calibre guns.

# Allied Machines

### *Airspeed Oxford*

The 1937 twin-engined Airspeed Oxford was a general-purpose trainer which had a basic crew of three but could accommodate other trainee-aircrew. Typically powered by two 375 horsepower Armstrong Siddeley Cheetah Ten radial engines it had a maximum speed of 188 mph (163 knots), a cruising speed of 163 mph (142 knots), a ceiling of 19,000 feet and a range of 700 miles.

### *Armstrong Whitworth Atlas*

This 1931 twin-seat, dual-control dedicated army co-operation machine was the RAF's standard advanced trainer until 1935 when it was replaced by the Hawker Hart. Powered by a 450 horsepower Armstrong Siddeley Jaguar 4C engine, it had a maximum speed of 143 mph (124 knots), a ceiling of 16,800 feet and a range of 480 miles.

### *Avro Anson*

The 1935 Avro Anson began life in the maritime reconnaissance role and remained in RAF service until 1968, serving as general-purpose trainer and communications aircraft.

Two 350 horsepower Armstrong Siddeley Cheetah Nine radial engines gave it a cruising speed of 158 mph (138 knots), a ceiling of 19,000 feet and a range of 800 miles. Its design-role armament was two machine guns; a fixed, forward-firing Vickers, and a single Lewis in a dorsal turret. The nose had a bomb-aimer's station and 360 pounds of bombs could be carried.

### *Avro Lancaster*

The seven-crewed Lancaster, developed from the twin-engined Manchester, first flew in January 1941 and was designed for ease of production and subsequent servicing, 7,737 being built by 1946. Powered by four 1,640

horsepower Rolls-Royce Merlin Mk. 24 in-line engines, its maximum speed was 280 mph (243 knots), it cruised at 210 mph (182 knots) or, on three engines, at 140 mph (122 knots), operating up to 22,000 feet over a range of 2,500 miles. The standard bomb load was 14,000 pounds or, if modified, one 22,000 pounder – in a comparison often made the Flying Fortress's standard load was 6,000 pounds. Armament was eight machine guns; four in the tail, and two each in nose and dorsal turrets.

### Avro Manchester

The 1936 spec Manchester was withdrawn from operations in June 1942 after its twin Rolls-Royce 1,760 horsepower Vulture engines proved unsatisfactory. It had a maximum speed of 265 mph (230 knots), a ceiling of 19,200 feet and a range of 1,630 miles. It had three power-operated turrets with two machine guns in the nose and dorsal turrets and four in the tail. Its maximum bomb load was 10,350 pounds.

### Avro York

A 1942-designed four-engined, long-range transport that carried five crew and up to twenty-four passengers. It cruised at 298 mph (259 knots), had a ceiling of 23,000 feet and a range of 3,000 miles.

## Beechcraft AT-10 Wichita

American two-crewed, twin-engined trainer used to prepare students for multi-engined bombers. Powered by two Lycoming 295 horsepower engines it had a speed of 198 mph (172 knots), a ceiling of 16,900 feet and a range of 770 miles.

## Boeing B-17 Flying Fortress

The upgraded B-17G version of the 1935 design relied for its defence on up to thirteen heavy-calibre – 0.5 inch (12.7 mm) –, Browning machine guns, this fire-power being enhanced by groups of aircraft flying in defensive formations. The standard crew complement was ten, comprising pilot, co-pilot, navigator, bombardier, flight engineer, and radio operator. In combat the flight engineer would man the top turret, and the radio operator a swivel-gun in the roof of his compartment. The remaining four crew were dedicated gunners to man the ball-turret, the left and right waist positions, and the tail turret.

The B-17 was typically powered by four 1,200 horsepower Wright Cyclone R-1820-65 9-cylinder air-cooled engines which, with Hamilton three-bladed, constant-speed, fully-feathering propellers, gave it a cruising speed of 225 mph (196 knots) and a ceiling of 40,000 feet. It had a normal range of 3,000 miles and a standard bomb load of 6,000 pounds, although this could be increased to 12,800 pounds, and over a very short range, to 20,800 pounds. For a comparison often made, the Lancaster's standard bomb load was 14,000 pounds; if modified, however, the Lancaster could carry a 22,000 pound bomb.

### Boeing Stearman, Model 75

The Stearman (Boeing) 75 Series Kaydet biplane trainer was widely used in the USA and Canadian flying schools during the Second World War. Its 220 horsepower Continental R-670-5 engine gave it a maximum speed of 124 mph (108 knots), a ceiling of 11,200 feet and a range of 505 miles.

### Boeing 707

1958 swept-wing long-range four-jet passenger aircraft. Various marks carried 140 to 189 passengers over ranges varying from 2,500 to 5,750 miles at speeds of 550 to 600 mph.

### *Consolidated B-24 Liberator*

This long-range heavy bomber and maritime reconnaissance machine was manned by 8 to 10 crew. Typically powered by four 1,200 horsepower Pratt & Whitney Twin Wasp engines the Liberator had a cruising speed of 220 mph (191 knots), a ceiling of 36,000 feet and a range of 2,500 miles. It was armed with up to fourteen 0.5 inch (12.7 mm) calibre machine guns in four turrets and two waist positions and it could carry 8,000 pounds of bombs.

### *Cessna AT-17 Bobcat*

American five-crewed, twin-engined advanced trainer and passenger aircraft with electrically operated retractable main undercarriage and trailing-edge flaps. Powered by two Jacobs 245 horsepower engines, it had a maximum speed of 169 mph (147 knots), a cruise of 152 mph (132 knots), and a ceiling of 22,000 feet.

### Boeing 377 Stratocruiser

1947 long-range, propeller-driven, pressurized transport with four radial engines. It carried 100 passengers on two deck-levels, cruised at 300 mph (261 knots), at 32,000 feet, over a range of 4,200 miles.

### Bristol Beaufighter

The two-seater Beaufighter night-fighter had interception radar and also served as a long-range strike fighter and torpedo carrier. Two 1,770 horsepower Bristol Hercules radial engines gave a maximum speed of 303 mph (263 knots), a cruise of 249 mph (216 knots) a ceiling of 15,000 feet, and a range of 1,470 miles. Four forward-firing, nose-mounted 20 mm (0.79 inch) calibre Hispano cannon and six forward-firing, wing-mounted Browning machine guns were supplemented by a single Vickers in the rear. Either a 2,127 or a 1,605 pound torpedo could be carried, alternatively, eight 90-pound rockets together with two 250-pound bombs.

## Bristol Beaufort

The four-crewed, twin-engined Beaufort was Coastal Command's standard torpedo bomber from 1940 to 1943. Typically powered by two 1,130 horsepower Bristol Taurus engines, it had a maximum speed of 265 mph (230 knots), cruised at 200 mph (174 knots), had six hours' endurance and a range of up to 1,600 miles. Typically armed with a machine gun in the nose and another in the dorsal turret, it carried 1,500 pounds of bombs or a 1,605-pound, 18- inch torpedo.

## Bristol Blenheim

In 1935 the prototype Blenheim proved faster than any fighter. By 1939, however, it was outclassed by most German types but, although swiftly withdrawn from bombing operations, it served on as a radar-equipped night-fighter, and later, as an advanced crew trainer. Driven by two 905 horsepower Bristol Mercury Fifteen radial engines, a representative

Blenheim had a ceiling of 27,000 feet, a cruising speed of 198 mph (172 knots) and a range of 1,460 miles.

Armed with two machine guns in a power-operated dorsal turret, with two remotely-controlled guns below the nose, and a fifth in the port wing, it could also carry 1,300 pounds of bombs.

### *Consolidated BT-13 Vultee Valiant*

American 1939 tandem, two-seat, fixed undercarriage basic trainer. Powered by a 450 horsepower Pratt and Whitney with a two-position variable pitch propeller it had a maximum speed of 168 mph (146 knots), cruised at 140 mph (122 knots), a touchdown speed of 53 mph (46 knots), a range of 1,560 miles and a ceiling of 20,000 feet.

### *Curtiss AT-9 Jeep*

American two crew, twin-engined advanced trainer powered by two Lycoming R680 295 horsepower engines. It had a maximum speed of 197

mph (172 knots), cruised at 175 mph (152 knots), had a range of 750 miles, and a service ceiling of 19,000 feet.

### De Havilland Dominie (civilian Rapide)

The long-lifed, twin-engined, biplane light transport developed during the 1930s and used by the RAF as an eight- to ten-seater communications machine, and as a five- to six-seater navigation and radio trainer. Rapides were still flying in 2012.

### De Havilland Fox Moth

1931 single crew biplane carrying 3-4 passengers. Powered by a 120 horsepower Gipsy 3 engine it had a maximum speed of 106 mph (92 knots), a cruise of 91 mph (79 knots), a range of 425 miles and a ceiling of 12,700 feet.

## De Havilland Mosquito

The private-venture, two-crewed de Havilland Mosquito, conceived in 1938 as a fast, high-flying bomber, first flew in November 1940. The wooden construction saved on scarce alloys, the 1,620 horsepower Rolls-Royce Merlin 25 in-line engines giving a cruising speed of 325 mph (283 knots), a ceiling of 33,000 feet and a range of 1,650 miles.

It filled many roles: photo-reconnaissance (often unarmed), bomber, intruder, fighter-bomber, night-fighter, and communications-cum-freighter. Armed versions typically carried four 20 mm (0.79 inch) calibre cannon and four machine guns in the nose; a typical bomb load was 2,000 pounds.

## De Havilland DH82A Tiger Moth

The 1934 tandem two-seater biplane de Havilland trainer was used at over eighty wartime elementary flying training schools. A 130 horsepower de Havilland Gipsy Major in-line engine gave it a cruising speed of 93 mph (80 knots), a ceiling of 13,000 feet and a range of 300 miles. To maintain the centre of gravity a solo pilot sat in the rear seat. Although demanding to fly accurately, and invariably giving a freezing-cold ride, the much revered Tiger Moth had no vices.

### De Havilland Vampire

The 1946 twin-boomed de Havilland Vampire, the third of Britain's jet aircraft, was a private de Havilland venture which had a lot in common with the Mosquito, the whole forward zone being predominantly aluminium-skinned wood. Nippy, yet essentially stable and easy to fly, the Vampire proved a useful stop-gap advanced trainer for Flying Training Command. The dedicated twin-seat, side-by-side trainer version, the T.11 ('Tee Eleven'), became available in 1950.

The T.11, with its Goblin 3 centrifugal-flow, turbo-jet engine developing 3,200 pounds of thrust, had a maximum permitted speed of 523 mph (455 knots), a medium-level cruising speed of 265 mph (230 knots), a range of 730 miles, and it was to remain in RAF service until 1966. Although nominally a trainer it could mount two or four 20 mm calibre cannon, and provision was made to carry rocket projectiles or bombs.

### Douglas Dakota (DC-3)

The 1935 Douglas DC-3 Dakota, basically an airliner manned by a crew of three and carrying twenty-one passengers, was still flying commercially in 2012, its roles, however, have been infinite. Two 1,000 horsepower Wright Cyclone radial engines gave a cruising speed of 194 mph (169 knots) and a ceiling of 21,900 feet; the stalling speed was 67 mph (58 knots) and the range 2,125 miles.

### *Gloster Meteor*

The 1943, single-seat, twin-jet Meteor, delivered to the RAF in July 1944, was the only Allied jet aircraft to see service during the Second World War. Early versions were powered by two 1,700 pound thrust Rolls-Royce Welland turbojet engines which gave a top speed of 415 mph (361 knots) and a ceiling of 40,000 feet. It carried four 20 mm calibre cannon and was successfully deployed against the V1 pulse-jet Flying Bombs.

### *Handley Page Halifax*

The 1940 seven-crewed, twin-finned Halifax heavy bomber found favour with its versatility, for besides its design role it was employed in both the transport and maritime fields, also as an ambulance, a glider tug, and as a clandestine and paratroop-delivery vehicle.

Typically, four 1,615 horsepower Bristol Hercules Sixteen radial engines gave it a cruising speed of 215 mph (187 knots) and a ceiling of 24,000 feet. It had a range of 1,030 miles and could carry 13,000 pounds of bombs. It mounted nine machine guns, one in the nose, and four each in dorsal and tail turrets.

An unfortunate characteristic of early Halifaxes was that fully-laden aircraft could enter an inverted, and effectively uncontrollable, spin. A retrospective modification of the tailfin leading-edge shape from triangular to quadrilateral helped overcome this stability defect.

### *Handley Page Hampden*

This 1936 four-crewed bomber was powered by two 1,000 horsepower, 9-cylinder, Bristol Pegasus Mark Eighteen radial engines. A 1942 source gives the cruising speed as 217 mph (189 knots) but users wrote of it being nearer 130 mph (113 knots). The makers gave the ceiling as 15,000 foot and most sources agree that it had a range of 1,885 miles with 2,000 pounds of bombs, reducing to 1,200 miles when the full 4,000 pounds was carried.

The earliest Hampdens carried four 0.303-inch calibre machine guns, two in the nose (one being fixed) and two rear-facing, one firing above and the other below the fuselage. Later, the single guns would be twinned. It showed up poorly against German fighters and just a month into the war was restricted to night operations, to leaflet dropping, and to minelaying.

Pilots found it pleasant to handle, although the crew, isolated from one another in flight, found their positions cramped.

### Hawker Audax

The 1931 Audax was the army co-operation variant of the Hart. The RAF received the Audax in February 1932, using it mainly as an advanced trainer. It was typically powered by a 530 horsepower Rolls-Royce Kestrel engine, had a maximum speed of 170 mph (148 knots), could climb to 10,000 feet in some ten minutes, had a ceiling of 21,000 feet and an endurance of three and half hours. It could carry a bomb load of 230 pounds and was armed with a forward-firing Vickers machine gun and an aft-mounted Lewis.

### Hawker Hart

The RAF's standard light bomber from 1930 to 1935. With two crew and powered by a Rolls-Royce 525 horsepower Kestrel it had a maximum speed of 184 mph (160 knots), a range of 470 miles and a ceiling of 21,320 feet. Armed with two machine guns, a Vickers forward and a Lewis aft, and carrying 500 pounds of bombs, it was superseded by the Hind.

### Hawker Hind

The Hawker Hind biplane day bomber was a refined version of the Hart, its fully-supercharged, 640-horsepower Rolls-Royce Kestrel engine giving it a maximum speed of 186 mph (162 knots). It had a range of 430 miles, a ceiling of 26,400 feet, could carry 500 pounds of bombs, and was armed with two machine guns; a Lewis to the rear and a forward-facing Vickers.

### Hawker Hurricane

Conceived in 1933 this celebrated monoplane fighter first flew in October 1937 and was only withdrawn from service in 1947. Typically, a 1,280 horsepower Rolls-Royce Merlin Twenty in-line engine gave the Hurricane a maximum speed of 342 mph (297 knots), enabled it to cruise at 296 mph (257 knots), to climb at an initial rate of 2,700 feet a minute, and ultimately, to attain 36,500 feet. It had a range of 480 miles, although this could be extended to 985 miles by the use of external fuel tanks. As armament the fighter/bomber version carried twelve forward-firing, wing-mounted 0.303 inch calibre machine-guns, together with a 500 pound bomb load.

### Lockheed Constellation

1943 four-engined, propeller-driven, long-range transport. It carried 62 to 95 passengers at a cruising speed of 340 mph (295 knots) over a range of 5,400 miles at up to 24,000 feet.

### Martin B-26 Marauder

This 1940 support bomber was powered by two 2,000 horsepower Pratt and Whitney Double Wasp engines which gave a maximum speed of 346 mph (300 knots), a cruise of 250 mph (217 knots), a range of over 3,000 miles, and a ceiling of 24,500 feet. It was armed with twelve 0.5 inch calibre machine guns, two in the nose, lateral, and mid-upper, four in the fuselage and one in the tail. Bomb load was 2,400 pounds.

## Miles Magister

The Service version of the 1936 tandem-seated, low-winged, metal-skinned Miles Hawk elementary trainer. Powered by a 130 horsepower de Havilland Gipsy Major One in-line engine, it had a cruising speed of 123 mph (107 knots), ceiling of 18,000 feet, and a range of 380 miles. It boasted wheelbrakes, power-operated flaps, and a tailwheel – as opposed to a skid –, and could be flown solo from either seat, although the front seat was preferred.

## Miles Martinet

Two-seater target tug derived from the Miles Master. It carried five drogues which were retracted using a powered winch. A single Bristol Mercury 870 horsepower radial engine gave a maximum speed of 240 mph (209 knots), a cruise of 199 mph (173 knots). Its range was 694 miles.

## *Miles Master Marks.1 and 3*

Development of the 1935 Miles Kestrel which aimed to give an easier transition between the Tiger Moth and first-line fighters. The Master Mk.1's 715 horsepower Kestrel Mk.30 in-line engine gave a maximum speed of 226 mph (196 knots), an initial climb rate of nearly 1,500 feet a minute, a ceiling of 28,000 feet, and a range of 500 miles.

The 1940 Master Mk.3 had an 825 horsepower Pratt & Whitney Wasp Junior radial engine which gave it a maximum speed of 232 mph (202 knots) and a cruising speed of 170 mph (148 knots) while retaining the 85 mph (74 knots) landing speed of the Mk.1s and Mk.2s. Additionally it had a ceiling of 27,300 feet, and at a maximum take-off weight of some 5,500 pounds, a range of 320 miles.

## *North American Harvard*

American 1935 advanced trainer used by the RAF from 1939 until 1955. A typical engine fit was a 550/600 horsepower, 9-cylinder Pratt and Whitney Wasp, air-cooled, and driving a Hamilton two-bladed, two-position controllable-pitch propeller. Together these produced a top speed of 206 mph (179 knots) and a cruising speed of 180 mph (156 knots). The landing speed was 63 mph (55 knots) with an initial climb rate of 1,350 feet a minute. The ceiling was 23,000 feet and the range 730 miles. Although popular, the Harvard was a demanding machine, and therefore, a good advanced trainer.

### *North American B-25 Mitchell*

American twin-engined, twin-fin-and-rudder, medium bomber. Powered by two Wright 1700 horsepower engines it had a maximum speed of 272 mph (236 knots), cruised at 230 mph (200 knots), a range of 1,350 miles and a ceiling of 24,200 feet. As armament it had 12-18 0.5 inch calibre machine guns (12.7 mm) and a bomb load of 3,000 pounds. The crew of six comprised: pilot, co-pilot, navigator/bombardier, turret gunner/engineer, radioman/beam gunner, and tail gunner.

### *North American P-51 Mustang*

After December 1943 the Rolls-Royce Merlin-engined, long-range-escort Mustang arrived in Europe and provided fighter support throughout entire missions.

Typical performance figures based upon the 1,520 horsepower Packard Rolls-Royce Merlin V-1650-3 liquid-cooled engine driving a Curtiss electric constant-speed propeller, give a maximum speed of 425 mph (369 knots), a ceiling of over 40,000 feet and a range of over a thousand miles. Armament was six or eight 0.5 inch (12.7 mm) calibre machine guns, or four 20 mm (0.79 inch) calibre cannon, with 1,000 pounds of bombs mounted underwing.

### *Percival Proctor*

A 1939 single-engined, three- to four-seater monoplane used for communications and radio training.

### *Short Stirling*

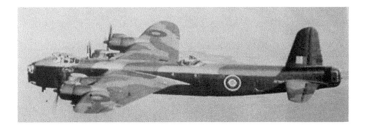

With its cockpit rearing a lofty 22 feet 9 inches above the tarmac the Stirling was the first of the RAF's heavy bombers. Shorts re-used their successful Sunderland-wing profile but Ministry requirements limited the span to 100 feet (not, 'to fit into RAF hangars': these were 125 feet wide). Such modifications detracted from the design performance to give the Stirling a ceiling of only 17,000 feet.

It was very manoeuvrable, however, and powered by four 1,650 horsepower Bristol Hercules Sixteen radial engines, had a maximum speed of 270 mph (235 knots), a cruise of 200 mph (174 knots), and a range of up to 2,000 miles dependent upon bomb load, itself a maximum of 14,000 pounds. It had eight machine guns; four in a tail turret, and two each in nose and dorsal turrets.

Though popular with its 7-8 man crews its bomb bay could not be adapted as bigger bombs were developed and it ceased bomber operations in September 1941. It was then very successfully employed in the glider-tug, transport, and clandestine-operations roles. There was also a transport variant.

### *Short Sunderland*

A 13-crew, long-range general reconnaissance and anti-submarine patrol flying boat. Four 1,200 Pratt & Whitney Twin Wasp engines gave a maximum speed of 213 mph (185 knots) and a ceiling of 17,900 feet; endurance was 13.5 hours and range, 2,980 miles. Crews loved its luxury.

### *Supermarine Spitfire*

The 1936 Spitfire metamorphosed through over a score of variant Marks. Representative performance figures for early versions with the 1,030 horsepower Rolls-Royce Merlin Mark Two in-line engine, driving a two-bladed, wooden, fixed-pitch propeller, give a maximum speed of 350 mph (304 knots), a cruising speed of 265 mph (230 knots) and a ceiling of 30,500 feet. Range was 630 miles and armament eight wing-mounted machine guns.

The later 2,050 horsepower, supercharged Griffon engine, gave a maximum speed of 448 mph (389 knots), time to 20,000 feet of seven minutes, ceiling of 44,500 feet, and range, with an external tank, of 850 miles. A regular armament fit of two 20 mm (0.79 inch) cannon and four machine guns was upgraded when the latter were replaced by two guns of 0.5 inch (12.7 mm) calibre.

## Vickers Wellington

In designing the 1937 Wellington, the celebrated Barnes Wallis used repeated junctions of Meccano-like alloy members to form a cocoon of great strength. This 'geodetic' – parts of a circle – structure was then covered with doped fabric. The operational crew of four comprised a pilot, a navigator/bomb aimer, a wireless operator/air gunner, and a rear gunner.

A typical power fit was two 1,500 horsepower Bristol Hercules Eleven radial engines which gave a ceiling of 19,000 feet and a maximum speed of 235 mph (204 knots).

Quoted cruising speeds vary with source, ranging from 232 mph (202 knots) to 166 mph (144 knots). A former Wellington pilot suggested 173 mph (150 knots), with a normal bombing altitude of 12,000 feet.

The armament comprised eight machine guns; four in the tail turret, two in the beam, and two in the nose. The bomb load was 4,500 pounds.

### *Westland Lysander*

The 1936 Lysander was a purpose-designed, two-seater, army co-operation machine delivered to the RAF in 1938. After heavy losses it was withdrawn from first-line service but continued to serve as a target tug and in the air-defence-co-operation and air-sea rescue roles. Its short-field performance made it an ideal clandestine delivery machine for the Special Operations Executive (SOE).

With its cockpit standing fourteen-and-a-half feet above the ground the Lysander was typically powered by an 870 horsepower Bristol Mercury Twenty or Thirty radial engine which gave it a maximum speed of 212 mph (184 knots) and a ceiling of 21,500 feet. It had a range of 600 miles.

# Enemy machines

### *Focke-Wulf Fw190*

This 1941 fighter evolved through forty variants but is typified by a maximum speed of 408 mph (355 knots), a time to 29,000 feet of twenty minutes, a ceiling of 37,000 feet, a range of 500 miles, and a combat endurance of one hour. Many carried four 7.92 mm (0.31 inch) calibre machine guns and two 20 mm (0.79 inch) calibre cannon; later versions employed 30 mm (1.18 inch) cannon and a wide range of underslung rockets. A comparison flight with a relatively early mark of Spitfire showed the FW190 to be superior in all respects except for turning capability.

### *Messerschmitt Bf109*

The 1935-designed, much modified Messerschmitt Bf109 was typically powered by a 1,475 Daimler-Benz twelve-cylinder, liquid-cooled engine which gave it a maximum speed of 386 mph (335 knots), an initial rate of climb of 3,346 feet a minute, a ceiling of 41,000 feet and an endurance of about an hour. It had a range of 620 miles and commonly carried two 7.9 mm (0.31 inch) machine guns and a 20 mm (0.79 inch) cannon; later, a 30 mm (1.18 inch) cannon.

Trials found the Spitfire and the Bf109 to be evenly matched between 12,000 and 17,000 feet with the Bf109 performing better above 20,000 feet.

### *Messerschmitt Bf110.*

Powered by two Daimler-Benz 1,475 horsepower engines, the 1936-designed, twin-engined, 2-3-crewed Messerschmitt Bf110 had a maximum speed of

352 mph (306 knots), a ceiling of 26,000 feet, time to 20,000 feet of nine minutes and a range of 745 miles.

Typical armament was two nose-mounted 20 mm (0.79 inch) calibre cannon and four 7.9 mm (0.31 inch) machine guns, plus another in the rear cockpit. There was also provision for two more forward-firing 20 mm cannon in an underbelly tray. Night-fighter variants carried a 30 mm (1.18 inch) cannon, and could be fitted with the twin *Scräge Musik* upward-firing 30 mm cannon.

### *Messerschmitt Me262*

This single-seater twin-jet fighter was powered by two Junkers Jumo 0004B engines each giving 1,984 pounds thrust to produce a maximum speed of 540 mph (470 knots), a rate of climb of 4,000 feet a minute, a ceiling of 37,730 feet and a range of 650 miles. Its standard armament fit was four 30 mm (1.18 inch) calibre cannons but later versions carried rockets.

### *V-1 (Vergeltungswaffe) Flying Bomb [popularly Doodlebug, or Buzz-bomb]*

The German *Fern Ziel Geraet* (effectively: Long-range Aiming Apparatus), their *Vergeltungswaffe 1* (Reprisal Weapon Number One), was a pilotless flying bomb which carried a ton of amatol high-explosive. It might be politic to emphasise that the V-1 – nowadays so-often termed 'V-1 *rocket*' – was a pulse-jet aircraft.

### *V-2 Vergeltungswaffe 2 (Reprisal Weapon) A-4 ground to ground rocket:*

Essentially, fuelled with water and alcohol activated by liquid oxygen, the rocket carried a 1,000 kg (2,000 pound) warhead up to 200 miles but had a circle of error of 11 miles.

### *V-3 Vergeltungswaffe 3 (Reprisal Weapon).*

The barrel of this 150 mm (5.9 inch) calibre super-cannon was 150 metres long and rocket-boosted along its length to give the 150 kg shell greater impetus and a range of 550 miles. The guns intended for bombarding London were constructed in caves in the Pas de Calais but were bombed before completion.

# Glossary

***Ab initio***: from the beginning. This referred to aspiring flyers who had passed aptitude selection but were yet to be tested for suitability in the air.

**Ack-Ack**: see Flak

**Aircrew**: on 19 January 1939, airmen aircrew (observers and gunners) were accorded the status of sergeants, although the situation was not regularised until early 1940 when heavy bombers appeared. World War Two aircrew categories comprised: pilot; navigator [observer, pre 1942]; wireless operator/air gunner; air gunner; flight engineer [post 1941]; bomb aimer [post 1942]; air signaller [post 1943]. There was also the observer radio (radar) of 1941, the navigator/wireless operator category, and similar combinations involving navigators.

**Aircrew Europe Star**: a well-regarded award for air operations carried out over Europe from Britain between 3 September 1939 and 5 June 1944 inclusively. The qualifying time was two months during that period, a stipulation which meant that many aircrew operating after D-Day did not receive the award. Although they received the France and Germany Star, this did not reflect their aircrew status.

**Arriving, Arrival chit**: when reporting on posting, 'arriving' personnel would check in, on signature, at every section on the station relevant to them (clothing stores, accounts) so that they were known to be on strength for issues and services. Similarly, personnel would 'clear' with their 'clearance chits' on being posted away.

**Astrodome**: a perspex hemisphere set on the top of the fuselage, designed for taking sextant readings, but also used as a viewing station and, often, as an emergency hatch.

**ATS** (Auxiliary Territorial Service): the women's army; became the WRAC (Women's Royal Army Corps) in 1949.

**Battledress**: the RAF began to adopt the blouse-style jacket for aircrew in 1940, and generally from 1943.

**Beam Approach**: see Standard Beam Approach, below.

**BOAC**: the British Overseas Airways Corporation, the state's long-haul airline until 1974, when it became British Airways.

**Bombs**: in general, these become armed only when a time-delay mechanism has operated.

**Bullseye**: a sortie designed to simulate an operation. It might involve photographing a UK target or approaching an enemy coast as a diversion.

**Caterpillar Club**: after Lieutenant Harold R. Hams, escaped by parachute from his disabled aircraft in America on 20 October 1922, a club was formed for those who were forced to make an emergency descent. The Caterpillar symbol was chosen because early parachutes were made of silk, and in order to survive the insect had to leave its cocoon.

**Central Flying School (CFS)**: established in 1912 (at Upavon), to train RAF pilot instructors.

**Chiefy**: familiar form of address for flight sergeant.

**Circuits**: A 'circuit' – circuits and landings – involves taking off into wind and climbing to (in the period) 1,000 feet, turning downwind parallel to the runway, flying past the airfield, then turning back, descending, touching down, and rolling to a stop before clearing the runway. A 'roller' (circuits and bumps), on the other hand, requires the pilot to touch down but, without coming to a halt, to put on full power, reconfigure the aircraft for flight, and take off again.

**Cook's tour**: flights laid on after VE Day, often to show non-aircrew personnel the former target areas. Derived from the 1841 travel firm, Thomas Cook, of Melbourne, Derbyshire.

**Corkscrew**: a spiralling, tight-turning descent designed to throw off fighters. A starboard corkscrew was initiated by 'stick forward, and over, hard right, and full-booted right rudder'.

**Crossbow**: an anti-V-weapon sortie (V-1 and V-2).

**Crown**: flight sergeants displayed a brass crown above sergeant's stripes.

**D-Day**: 6 June 1944. The invasion of Europe in the Cherbourg-Peninsular area. All Allied aircraft were painted with white and black stripes on wings and fuselage for instant recognition.

**Dicey**: dangerous (also, dicing with death).

**Dorsal**: as with a turret, on the back, or the upper surface of the fuselage. (Ventral, the belly).

**EFTS** (Elementary Flying Training School): basic flying was taught, but the unit could also be used as a Grading School, where aspirant pilots were allowed some fifteen hours' flying (it varied) during which their suitability for further training would be assessed.

**Empire, or Commonwealth, Air Training Scheme**: set up in 1939 to take advantage of the favourable flying conditions in various Commonwealth countries: discontinued in late 1944.

**Feather**: to electrically or hydraulically turn the blades of a propeller edge-on to the airflow to cut down the drag: as with an oar in rowing. The propeller of a failed engine left blade-on to the airflow, and therefore, said to be 'windmilling', creates an inordinate amount of drag.

**FIDO** (Fog, Investigation and Dispersal Operation): a poor-visibility landing aid in which burning petrol was used to locally heat the air along the runway and temporarily disperse the fog. It took twenty minutes to become effective.

**Flak**: Enemy anti-aircraft gunfire, from *flugabwehrkanone* (aircraft defence cannon). The Allied equivalent was ack-ack, after the then-current phonetic for AA (anti-aircraft). The 'modern' term anti-aircraft-artillery (AAA) was, in fact, contemporary to the period, though rarely used.

**Forty Millimetre Mercury Test**: A medical endurance test, introduced by researcher Martin William Flack in 1920 and highly rated by aviation medics. It required the candidate to sustain a 40 mm column of mercury in a U-shaped manometer for as long as possible with a single expiration. Pulse-reading variations showed the patient's response to the stress of the effort and to discomfort (breathlessness) generally.

**Gardening**: codeword for mine-laying operations.

**Gazetted**: *The London Gazette (Published by Authority)* promulgates awards.

**Gee** (Ground Electronic Equipment): a radar aid by which master and slave ground-station signals were plotted on a lattice chart to give a very accurate fix. Gee's range was 350 to 400 miles.

**Gee-H**: a development of the Gee radar-navigational equipment which owed much to the Oboe bombing aid. Using Oboe, an aircraft (effectively) flew down a beam until a ground signal advised that it was time to drop its bombs. Whereas only one aircraft at a time could use Oboe, Gee-H could accommodate 80 to 100. Aircraft equipped with Gee-H had yellow stripes painted on their fins: other aircraft could then formate on them to ensure an accurate drop.

**Gen**: information, genuine, or Pukka; as opposed to Duff, or inaccurate.

**Gharri**: (Gharry) Indian horse-drawn cart, hence lorry, or transport.

**Gremlins**: manikins whose *raison d'être* was to harass aircrew by creating technical problems. They appeared in 1940, got into print in the *RAF Journal* in 1942, indoctrinated fighter pilot Roald Dahl a little later and subsequently Walt Disney: Known to be 'green, gamboge and gold; male, female and neuter; and both young and old', yet there were fliers who thought them fictitious.

**Harris**: Marshal of the Royal Air Force Sir Arthur Harris, Baronet, GCB, OBE, AFC, LLD (1892–1984), Air Officer Commanding-in-Chief, Bomber Command, 1942-1945.

**H2S**: map-presentation radar. Originally, BN: Blind Navigation. Until a scientist observed, 'the whole thing is stinking through not having been done years ago.' Hence, H2S, the hydrogen-sulphide smell of bad eggs.

**ITW** (Initial Training Wing): the training unit teaching drill and elementary air-related subjects.

**Kriegie**: *kriegsgefangener*, prisoner of war, POW.

**Link Trainer**: a flight simulator originally designed in 1929 by Ed Link, an American organ maker.

**LMF** (Lack of moral fibre): the term the RAF used during the Second World War for combat fatigue or post-traumatic stress disorder. Since the 1700s also known as Nostalgia, Melancholia, Hysteria, Wavering, Shellshock, and Flying Sickness D (debility).

**'Lootenant'**: American usage of lieutenant, which for the British services remains 'leftenant'.

**Mag Drop**: ignition in piston aero engines is supplied by a pair of electrical generators known as magnetos. Before getting airborne each of these is earthed in turn to ensure that the other is serviceable. The falling-off to be expected in engine revolutions during this test – one magneto producing slightly less electrical power than two together – must not exceed a stated value.

**Mandrel, Shiver, and Carpet**: airborne radio transmitters used to jam and swamp German long-range ground radars such as Freya.

**Mention (in Despatches)**: recognition of a job well done, but not meriting higher award. Denoted throughout the period by a bronze oak leaf (since 1993, by a silver one).

**Missions**: see Operations – ops.

**Monica**: a rearward-looking radar for detecting attacking fighters whose use was discontinued because German fighters could home onto it.

**Nickel**: a propaganda-leaflet drop.

**Oboe**: a blind bombing aid employing two ground stations. In essence, one provided a beam to lead the aircraft over the target, the other told it the bomb-release point. Using stations at Dover and Cromer, it was first employed against a Ruhr target on 21 December 1942 with an accuracy of some 80 yards. After the invasion 24 mobile stations were placed on the continent.

**Operations – Ops**: throughout the Second World War, offensive sorties by the RAF against the enemy were termed operational flights, or ops. The equivalent term employed by the United States Army Air Force was missions. While there were variations in the rules by which RAF operations were reckoned, even within Bomber Command, the standard operational tour required may be taken as thirty: statistics suggested that this would give crews a reasonable chance of survival. It is noteworthy that in 2014 modern usage has the RAF flying missions (that similarly, wounded personnel are injured, and stations are bases).

**OTU (Operational Training Unit)**: the unit at which aircrew were made familiar with the machines and the techniques of the commands they were to join.

**Pooh-Bah**: a character in Gilbert and Sullivan's *The Mikado* who is 'First Lord of the Treasury, Lord Chief Justice, Commander-in-Chief, Lord High Admiral ... Archbishop of Titipu, and Lord Mayor'.

**Port/starboard**: left and right, viewed looking forwards.

**Prang**: a crash. But in that context, very strictly Second World War slang. Also to carry out a successful bombing raid.

**POW**: prisoner of war.

**Psycho device**: this encoded plain language into five-symbol groups for transmission by morse.

**Q-Code**: a three-letter brevity code, basically civilian, for often-used messages in morse. Some still linger in R/T usage: notably QNH, and QFE, in altimetry. (There was also an X code, and a military Z code).

**QDM**: the brevity code for the magnetic heading to be steered.

**Reserved occupation**: the 1938 Schedule of Reserved Occupations was aimed at avoiding a blanket conscription stripping key industries of workers (as happened in the First World War). The time came, however, when those volunteering for aircrew or for service in submarines could be released.

**Retrospective recognition (awards):** in 2005 the Malaysian Government awarded the *Pinjat Jasa Malaysia* to all Commonwealth participants in the Malayan Emergency (1948–1960). Though Her Majesty, the Queen, accepted it at that time, Authority only approved its wearing by UK recipients in late 2011. In 2008, Authority recognized the services of the Women's Land Army (1939–1950) with a commemorative badge. Hard upon this, in 2009, similar awards were made to the code-breakers of Bletchley Park, to the Bevin Boys, and to the Air Transport Auxiliary. In 2013 the Arctic Star and a Bomber Command Clasp (to be worn on the 1939/45 Star) were authorised. It is just possible, then, that aircrew status will someday be recognized for all operational fliers of the Second World War.

**R/T** (radio telephony): voice.

**Schräge Musik**: upward-firing cannon. *Schräg* from slanted; colloquially, *'Jazz Music'*. Widely used by Luftwaffe aircraft which positioned below a bomber. The guns characteristically employed a mix of 30 mm calibre rounds whose tracers left only a vestigial trail.

**Service ceiling**: effectively the highest altitude achievable by a given aircraft. Essentially, the density altitude at which the rate of climb falls to 100 feet a minute

**Sprog**: inexperienced.

**Standard Beam Approach (SBA)**: a radar landing aid which transmitted a 30 mile long, very narrow radio beam down the extended centre-line of the runway. This told a pilot receiving the aural 'on-the-beam' signal that he was somewhere along the projected centre-line of the runway. To furnish an exact location *along* the beam, an 'Outer Marker' radio beacon was sited at a known distance from touchdown. This sent a coded signal vertically upwards to tell an inbound pilot that he should commence descending on his final approach. SBA developed to become the Blind Approach Beacon System (BABS) and was, therefore, the forerunner of the Instrument Landing System (ILS).

**Sten gun**: a British 9 mm calibre sub-machine gun hurriedly produced when invasion threatened and the supply of Thompson machine guns dried up. Utilitarian and cheap, it had a 32-round magazine. The name is an acronym contrived from the surnames of the designers, **S**heperd and **T**urpin, and **En**field.

**Stick** (control column): despite some contemporary objection, 'stick' has always been the preferred term; 'pole' is equally acceptable but somewhat informal, 'joystick' antediluvially archaic, and 'control column' too pedantic even for Central Flying School. So stick it is, even where the aircraft in question has a wheel, or a yoke.

**Trailing aerial**: when operating with stations using high frequencies, a wire fixed from fuselage to tailfin gave the standard RAF wireless equipment a satisfactory range. Getting a reasonable range on medium frequencies required a wire to be streamed beneath the aircraft.

**U-boat**: *Unterseeboot*, submarine.

**United States Army Air Force** (USAAF). The military aviation arm of the US Army during the Second World War. It succeeded the United States Army Air Corps in June 1941 and became the US Air Force in 1947.

**Upward-firing cannon**: see *Schläge Musik* above.

**V-1**: *Vergeltungswaffe* 1 (Reprisal Weapon) unmanned Fiesler 103 pulse-jet flying bomb. (*Not* a rocket!) Popularly, Doodlebug.

**V-2**: *Vergeltungswaffe* 2 (Reprisal Weapon) A-4 ground-to-ground rocket.

**V-3**: *Vergeltungswaffe* 3 (Reprisal Weapon) rocket-boosted, long-range gun.

**VE Day**: 8 May 1945. Victory in Europe, end of hostilities in Europe.

**Ventral**: as with a turret, below the fuselage, or belly. (Dorsal, the back) Note 'tin' usage, in text.

**VHF**: very high frequency.

**VJ Day**: in UK, 15 August 1945. Victory over Japan, end of Second World War. (August 14 in the Pacific/Americas area due to time-zone difference; also September 2, 1945, when the surrender was actually signed. Written too as V-J, and V-P [Pacific]).

**Windmilling**: see Feather.

**Window**: air-dropped strips of paper-backed aluminium foil cut to some correlation with the wavelength of the enemy's air-defence radars and designed to confuse their controllers.

**Woodbridge** (Suffolk): along with Manston (Kent), and Carnaby (Yorkshire): dedicated emergency airfields, 3,000 yards long, 250 yards wide, in three strips, with extensive grassed under- and over-shoot areas.

**Z-Code**: similar to the Q brevity code (see above) but for military communications, and therefore restricted.

## Selective References

Air Ministry (1937) *Royal Air Force Pocket Book, AP1081.* London: HMSO

Air Ministry (1943) *Elementary Flying Training, AP1979A.* London: HMSO

Bennett, D.C.T. (1936) *The Complete Air Navigator.* London: Pitman

Cathcart, Ted; Ward, John. (2007) *Ted the Lad.* Belper: JoTe Publications

Fellowes, P.F.M. (1942) *Britain's Wonderful Air Force.* London: Odhams

Ferguson, G.W. (1935) *How To Find Your Way In The Air.* London: Pitman

HMSO (1944) *Target: Germany.* London: Air Ministry

Monday, David (1982) *British Aircraft of World War II.* London: Chancellor Press

Saville-Sneath, R.A. (1945) *Aircraft of the United States.* Harmondsworth: Penguin

Stewart, Oliver. (1941) *The Royal Air Force in Pictures.* London: Country Life

Terraine, John (1985) *The Right of the Line.* London: Hodder and Stoughton

Thetford, Owen (1958) *Aircraft of the Royal Air Force 1918-1958.* London: Putnam

White, Graham (2006) *Night Fighter over Germany.* Barnsley: Pen & Sword